For All the Saints

FOR ALL THE SAINTS

Evangelical Theology and Christian Spirituality

edited by
Timothy George and Alister McGrath

Westminster John Knox Press
LOUISVILLE • LONDON

Unless otherwise indicated, Scripture quotations are from *The Holy Bible, New International Version.* Copyright © 1973, 1978, 1984 International Bible Society. Used by permission of Zondervan Bible Publishers.

Scripture quotations marked JB are from *The Jerusalem Bible,* Copyright © 1966, 1967, 1968 by Darton, Longman & Todd, Ltd., and Doubleday & Co., Inc. Used by permission of the publishers.

See Acknowledgments, pp. ix–xi, for additional permission information.

Book design by Sharon Adams
Cover design by Eric Walljasper, Minneapolis, MN
Cover illustration: Dome Mural in Beeson Divinity School's Andrew Gerow Hodges Chapel on the campus of Samford University, painted by Romanian artist Petru Botezatu.

First edition
Published by Westminster John Knox Press
Louisville, Kentucky

This book is printed on acid-free paper that meets the American National Standards Institute Z39.48 standard. ♾

PRINTED IN THE UNITED STATES OF AMERICA

03 04 05 06 07 08 09 10 11 12 — 10 9 8 7 6 5 4 3 2 1

Library of Congress Cataloging-in-Publication Data

For all the saints : evangelical theology and Christian spirituality / edited by
    Timothy George and Alister McGrath.
        p. cm.
    Includes bibliographical references and index.
    ISBN 0-664-22665-5 (alk. paper)
        1. Evangelicalism—Congresses. 2. Spirituality—Congresses. I. George, Timothy. II. McGrath, Alister E., 1953-

    BR1640.A2F67 2003
    248.4'804—dc21

                                                                2003041169

For

John R. W. Stott

with gratitude
for his wisdom, encouragement, and
friendship in Christ

Contents

Acknowledgments

Grateful acknowledgment is made to the following for permission to quote from copyrighted material:

The C. S. Lewis Company. Excerpts from *God in the Dock* by C. S. Lewis, copyright © C. S. Lewis Pte. Ltd. 1970. Excerpts from *Letters to Malcolm* by C. S. Lewis, copyright © C. S. Lewis Pte. Ltd. 1963. Excerpts from *Screwtape Proposes a Toast* by C. S. Lewis, copyright © C. S. Lewis Pte. Ltd. 1959. Excerpts from *Surprised by Joy* by C. S. Lewis, copyright © C. S. Lewis Pte. Ltd. 1955. Excerpts from *The Weight of Glory* by C. S. Lewis, copyright © C. S. Lewis Pte. Ltd. 1970. Excerpts from *The World's Last Night* by C. S. Lewis, copyright © C. S. Lewis Pte. Ltd. 1960. Extracts reprinted by permission.

Harcourt, Inc. Excerpts from *Letters to Malcolm: Chiefly on Prayer*, copyright © 1964, 1963 by C. S. Lewis Pte. Ltd. and renewed 1992, 1991 by Arthur Owen Barfield, reprinted by permission of Harcourt, Inc. Excerpts from *Surprised by Joy: The Shape of My Early Life* by C. S. Lewis, copyright © 1956 by C. S. Lewis, and renewed 1984 by Arthur Owen Barfield, reprinted by permission of Harcourt, Inc. Excerpts from "The Efficacy of Prayer" from *The World's Last Night and Other Essays*, copyright © 1958 by C. S. Lewis and renewed 1986 by Arthur Owen Barfield, reprinted by permission of Harcourt, Inc.

Harvard College. Excerpts from Aristotle: Vol. XIX: *Nicomachean Ethics*, Loeb Classical Library Volume 73, translated by H. Rackham, Cambridge, Mass.: Harvard University Press, 1926. The Loeb Classical Library ® is a registered trademark of the President and Fellows of Harvard College.

Classical Library Volume 75, translated by Richard M. Gummere, Cambridge, Mass.: Harvard University Press, 1917. The Loeb Classical Library ® is a registered trademark of the President and Fellows of Harvard College. Excerpts from Virgil: Vol. I: *Eclogues. Georgics. Aeneid Books 1–6*, Loeb Classical Library Volume 63, translated by H. Rushton Fairclough, Cambridge, Mass.: Harvard University Press, 1916. The Loeb Classical Library ® is a registered trademark of the President and Fellows of Harvard College. Excerpts from Virgil: Vol. II: *Aeneid Books 7–12, Appendix, Vergiliana*, Loeb Classical Library Volume 64, translated by H. Rushton Fairclough, Cambridge, Mass.: Harvard University Press, 1918. The Loeb Classical Library ® is a registered trademark of the President and Fellows of Harvard College. Excerpts from Xenophon: Vol. IV: *Memorabilia and Oeconomicus*, Loeb Classical Library Volume 168, translated by E. C. Marchant, Cambridge, Mass.: Harvard University Press, 1923. The Loeb Classical Library ® is a registered trademark of the President and Fellows of Harvard College. Excerpts from Xenophon: Vol. V: *Cyropaedia*, Loeb Classical Library Volume 51, translated by Walter Miller, Cambridge, Mass.: Harvard University Press, 1914. The Loeb Classical Library ® is a registered trademark of the President and Fellows of Harvard College.

Smyth & Helwys Publishing. Excerpts from *C. S. Lewis: Life at the Center* by Perry Bramlett (Macon, Ga.: Peake Road, 1996). Extracts reprinted by permission.

Wm. B. Eerdmans Publishing Co. Excerpts from C. S. Lewis, *Christian Reflections*, copyright © 1967 C. S. Lewis Pte. Ltd. Extracts reprinted by permission.

Introduction

Timothy George

Timothy George is the founding dean of Beeson Divinity School of Samford University and an executive editor of *Christianity Today*. He holds degrees from the University of Tennessee at Chattanooga (B.A.) and Harvard Divinity School (M.Div., Th.D.). A noted historian and theologian, George has written and edited numerous books including *Theology of the Reformers, Baptist Theologians, John Calvin and the Church*, the New American Commentary on Galatians, and, most recently, *Is the Father of Jesus the God of Muhammad?* George is a member of the editorial boards of *Books and Culture, First Things*, and *Harvard Theological Review*. He also chairs the Theological Education Commission of the Baptist World Alliance and is a widely sought-after speaker on matters of Christian higher education, theological and biblical issues, and cultural trends.

In this introductory chapter George provides an overview for the essays that follow in this book. He explains what he and coeditor Alister McGrath meant by "the coinherence of evangelical theology and Christian spirituality." He also identifies seven themes that recur throughout the volume.

✧✧✧ ✧✧✧ ✧✧✧

During the past two decades the rise of spirituality among evangelical Christians has been one of the most notable features of a growing, worldwide movement better known for its doctrinal disputes, evangelistic fervor, and activist temperament. Like many others, evangelicals have adopted the buzzword *spirituality*, but there has been little reflection on how this theme relates to basic theological commitments and other distinctives of Christian life and work.

This book seeks to answer the question: How do evangelicals express the coinherence of intellect and piety? How do they bring together head, heart, and hands in a way that honors the best instincts of their own heritage while appropriating the spiritual treasures of the wider Christian tradition? And what are the implications of an evangelical spiritual theology for ethics and worship as well as for the teaching and preaching mission of the church?

With one or two exceptions, the essays presented here are not technical studies of this theme but rather personal and pastoral reflections from some of the leading shapers of evangelical theology today. The Puritan divine William Ames once defined theology as "the teaching of living to God."[1] These essays all grapple with the implications of that definition, with the element of "both . . . and," with how both the theological wisdom and the spiritual vitality of the Christian faith can be expressed in the evangelical idiom. Several of the essays offer practical suggestions and helpful examples both for cultivating a life of disciplined devotion and for gathering prayerful, thoughtful, and meditative communities of faith. We have brought some of these suggestions together in a concluding chapter.

We have divided the essays into five major sections, although there is considerable overlap in theme and perspective. The first three chapters deal with foundational *concerns* and set forth a rationale for the coinherence of evangelical theology and Christian spirituality. The two following chapters examine some of the biblical and classical *sources* that evangelicals share with all other Christians. The next section picks up on specific theological concerns, including a *critique* of how evangelicals have often appropriated the rhetoric of spirituality in uncritical and simplistic ways. The section on *applications* deals with how true spirituality influences ethical concerns and responses to issues such as stewardship of the earth and racial reconciliation. The final section of the book looks at some of the spiritual *disciplines*, their use and abuse among evangelical believers.

These essays were first presented at a conference, "For All the Saints: Evangelical Theology and Christian Spirituality." This conference was jointly sponsored by two theological institutions: Wycliffe Hall, an evangelical Anglican school affiliated with Oxford University, and Beeson Divinity School, an evangelical interdenominational school affiliated with Samford University, a Baptist-related university in Alabama. Both the conference participants and the speakers whose talks are published here represent the trans-denominational and international, not to say interracial and multicultural, shape of the evangelical church in its quest for an authentic spirituality. Some of the essays here reflect the spoken character of the presentations as originally delivered.

While Alister McGrath and I did not seek to impose any single definition of spirituality on the contributors, we did circulate a letter in which we expressed our own concern about an evangelical theology divorced from the life of faith, on the one hand, and a trendy spirituality unrooted in the rich soil of historic orthodox teaching, on the other. As several of the contributors note, we were interested in overcoming this dichotomy through the coinherence of sound evangelical theology and genuine Christian spirituality. This is what we meant by "coinherence": the full and mutual sharing of one thing in the complete reality of the other. We wanted to encourage the development of what John Calvin called "a firm and certain knowledge of God's benevolence towards us founded upon the truth of the freely given promise in Christ, both *revealed to our minds and sealed upon our hearts*" (*Institutes* 3.2.7).

One of the great metaphors of the spiritual quest, and of the Christian life, is that of a journey. It is a theme that recurs throughout this volume. Indeed, it is a theme deeply woven into the fabric of the biblical narrative—from the exodus to the exile, from the long trek of the Magi to see the Christ child in Bethlehem to the great missionary journeys of the apostle Paul. *Peregrinatio*, pilgrimage, was one of Augustine's favorite words for the Christian life. His *Confessions* is the story of his own journey from the fleeting pleasures of youth toward his true *patria*, his eternal and abiding homeland, which he defined as nothing less than God. Thus he opened the *Confessions* with these famous words: "You have made us for yourself, O Lord, and our hearts are restless until they find their rest in You."

For evangelicals, the classic retelling of the Christian life as a journey is John Bunyan's famous allegory *The Pilgrim's Progress*. It is the story of a man named Christian who leaves his family and friends and sets out on a long and dangerous journey toward the Celestial City. Along the way he encounters many hazards and hardships. He struggles with dragons and demons of the dark. He is tempted, allured, betrayed by untrustworthy friends. But on he goes, supported by a few faithful fellow pilgrims until at last he reaches his goal. Along with a Bible and John Foxe's *Book of Martyrs*, Bunyan's *The Pilgrim's Progress* was one of the three books generations of Protestant pioneers brought with them when they came from the Old World to the New. Foxe told the Christian story in terms of a great battle, conflict, struggle, suffering. Bunyan, in good Augustinian fashion, emphasized life as movement—as either a moving forward in grace and truth or a slip-sliding away into shadowy byways and dangerous detours.

Evangelicals are well known for their emphasis on conversion, for calling on their hearers to make a "decision for Christ." David Bebbington has identified this emphasis on conversion as one of four defining characteristics of the evangelical movement—the other three are biblicism, activism, and a cross-centered theology of the atonement.[2] For evangelicals, biblical conversion always involves disorientation. It involves a yes and a no, repentance and faith; a taking leave and a moving forward. It involves what Martin Luther called *Gelassenheit*—a word he adapted from the medieval mystics—meaning to let go, to turn loose, to abandon completely.

Yet this "letting go" is not something we can accomplish on our own apart from God's interposing grace. Just here, the doctrine of justification by faith alone becomes so crucial for evangelical spirituality. In the monastery, Martin Luther was trying to let go, trying to strip away all those excrescences that had kept him from knowing a lasting peace with God. The truth of justification by faith came to Luther as a word of liberation and deliverance; for he discovered that what he could never do on his own, God, in Jesus Christ, had already accomplished, once and for all.

Evangelicals claim the theological heritage of the Reformation when they understand that the journey of faith is itself a gift. Dallas Willard makes an important distinction between earning and effort. We can never earn God's favor and goodwill toward us—that is what is so amazing about grace! And yet the journey is no less a journey because it is a gift. God's grace does not save us from, but rather delivers us in the midst of, temptations, struggles, hardships, doubts. But evangelical piety turns upside down the medieval paradigm of a pathway to God. There the journey of faith began with purgation, moved on to illumination, and, finally, ended in unification, that is, union with God. In the evangelical understanding, we begin with union with Christ (the new birth) and move on through Word and Spirit to illumination and the process of sanctification until, at last, in heaven we see Christ face to face.

The deadly divorce between theology and spirituality, noted by several of our contributors, has arisen in part because these two realities, justification by faith alone and union with Christ, have not been seen as indissolubly bound together—as two distinct but inseparable aspects of the same saving event. In one sense, then, this volume is a contribution to an evangelical *réssourcement*— the retrieval of a more holistic spiritual theology, one that seeks the renewal of the church through the renewal of the Christian life.

The essays in this book explore the shape of evangelical spirituality in various ways. Together they present a mosaic of the lived experience of Christian faith. They draw various maps of the spiritual journey, with appropriate warnings and signposts noted along the way. Among others, these seven themes occur throughout the book.

1. *Spirituality is about the whole person.* Spirituality is not about the mind alone, nor the emotions alone; it is about the whole person. Therefore it must involve every aspect of our being, our feelings, our affective life, our intellectual life, our volitional life. Historically, much evangelical theology has focused on apologetic concerns and a tough-minded defense of the faith

against liberalism and secularism. These essays call for a recovery of the evangelical soul. They believe that a one-sided emphasis on rationalist and evidentialist methods has too frequently obscured a more basic concern for the life of prayer, devotion, and the habits of "knowing God," to quote the title of J. I. Packer's classic study.[3] But there is surely a danger on the other side as well—the danger of a subjectivism run riot and a spiritual narcissism that causes us to lose sight of the objectivity of "the God who is there" (Francis Schaeffer).[4] For this reason we must be reminded of God's revealed Word in Holy Scripture and God's presence among God's people in the history of the church. Spirituality is about being all of who God has made us to be.

2. *Spiritual theology is about the Trinitarian God of love and grace.* Why is the Trinity so important? The Trinity is not a mathematical problem of how one can be three and still be one. Nor is it a metaphysical puzzle of how the essence of God relates to contingency and time and space. The Trinity is about relationship, community, and love. The doctrine of the Trinity is the necessary theological framework for understanding the story of Jesus as the story of God. It tells us that God is love. It tells us that God invites us into his innermost heart and life. The God who has forever known himself as the Father, the Son, and the Holy Spirit is the God whose innermost being is marked by giving and receiving, by the kind of mutuality and reciprocity that is at the heart of generosity. Faith in the three-personed God of Holy Scripture is both the basis and the goal of true evangelical spirituality.

3. *We are sustained in the journey of faith by the means of grace.* Although it might sound foreign to some evangelicals today, both John Calvin and John Wesley used the term *means of grace* to describe the holy mysteries that draw us into the heart of God. We need these "traveling mercies" precisely because we are still pilgrims, wayfarers, still on the road. Nor are we disembodied spirits on the road; we are frail, finite creatures who carry about an infinitely precious treasure in the unadorned clay pots of our ordinary lives, as Paul says (2 Cor. 4:7). Chief among the means of grace are the Bible, understood not only as a deposit of divine revelation but also as the meeting place of the believer and the living Christ; the sacraments (some evangelicals prefer the term *ordinances*) of baptism and the Lord's Supper, understood not as "mere" symbols devoid of real spiritual power but rather as the enacted Word of God that effectually conveys the promise and presence of Christ by faith; the life of prayer, both private and communal; and the act of preaching, through which the living voice of the gospel is conveyed to the gathered congregation.

4. *The spiritual life is the journey from achievement to rest.* Evangelical spirituality is challenged to recover a place for contemplation within the frenetic pace of our daily lives and the activism that emphasizes "doing" and "going" over

"being" and "listening." Authentic spirituality enjoins us to find time to be with God, to seek the face of God. This theme is prominent in the Psalms:

> One thing I ask of the LORD,
> this is what I seek:
> that I may dwell in the house of the LORD
> all the days of my life,
> to gaze upon the beauty of the LORD
> . . .
> My heart says of you, "Seek his face."
> Your face, LORD, I will seek.
> Do not hide your face from me.
>   (Ps. 27:4, 8–9)

5. *Spirituality is about obedience.* Several years ago there was a major row among North American evangelicals concerning the Lordship of Christ. Some held that it was possible to receive Jesus as Savior but not as Lord. They wanted to stress that salvation was based on grace alone, not on human striving or effort. But in doing so, they obscured one of the basic themes of Jesus' own teaching: discipleship. We cannot separate conversion and discipleship any more than we can divorce justification by faith from union with Christ. At its best, evangelical piety has always been concerned with the mission of the church, with following Christ in his concern for the poor, the marginalized, the neglected. As a popular evangelical hymn puts it, we must "trust and obey for there is no other way to be happy in Jesus but to trust and obey."[5]

6. *The cauldron of an enduring spirituality is suffering and conflict.* The great evangelical preacher Charles Haddon Spurgeon once wrote: "All the way to heaven we shall get there only by the skin of our teeth. We shall not go to heaven sailing along with sails swelling to the breeze like seabirds with their fair white wings, but we shall proceed full often with sails rent to the ribbons, with masts creaking and the ship's pumps at work both by night and day. We shall reach the City at the shutting of the gate but not an hour before."[6] A spirituality that endures is born in the cauldron of suffering, trouble, and even despair. In this volume, that perspective is most poignantly represented by Dr. Robert Smith, who draws from the genre of spirituals in the African American tradition to show how the context of deprivation and oppression gives depth and meaning to the "comfortable" words of Christian hope.

7. *We are not alone on the journey.* There is no such thing as a table for one at the banquet of the Lord. This is a wonderful, encouraging thought. We travel with a company of God's pilgrim people, with all the saints. We are surrounded by "a great cloud of witnesses," those who have come before us, weathered the storms, and emerged triumphant into the presence of the Lord. From their better vantage point they say to us, and to all pilgrims who travel

with us: "Fear not the depths or the storms or the streams. Trust boldly that vessel and that faithful Pilot. We trusted him and none of us have miscarried. All of us here have landed safe." Who would not follow such a multitude of excellent persons?

A final word about the title of this book is in order. "For All the Saints" carries at least two meanings for us. First, this term recognizes that all followers of Jesus are saints in the New Testament sense of this word. We have been set apart and called to live a life of holiness and devotion to Christ. Evangelicals, with all Protestants generally, have emphasized the priesthood of all believers to show that we are all redeemed by God's grace and that none of us can claim any special favors on the basis of ordination or office. But doesn't this same theology impel us to declare "the sainthood of all believers"? We are called to live lives that reflect the character of Christ in a world that knows all too little of God's love and grace. Evangelical spirituality is "for all the saints," that is, for all who know Jesus Christ and wish to make him known to others, even if we acknowledge with Martin Luther that we are saints and sinners at the same time (*simul iustus et peccator*) and thus ever in need of God's mercy and forgiveness.

"For All the Saints" has a wider connotation as well. Jesus prayed to the heavenly Father that his disciples would be one so that the world might believe (John 17:21–23). The renaissance of spiritual theology among evangelicals has fostered the spirit of Christian unity because we have been able to recognize and claim as our own so many spiritual treasures from the wider Christian heritage. The goal of true ecumenism must surely be for the whole church to take the whole gospel to the whole world. The mutual recognition of one another's saints, of all the saints, is an important step in this process. The essays in this book show that it is a process well under way.

PART 1

Foundations

1

Loving God with Heart and Mind: The Theological Foundations of Spirituality

Alister McGrath

A native of Belfast, Northern Ireland, Alister McGrath came to the study of theology from a background in the natural sciences, especially biochemistry. An ordained minister in the Church of England, he was appointed lecturer in Christian Doctrine and Ethics at Wycliffe Hall, Oxford, in 1983. Since 1995, he has served as principal of Wycliffe Hall. He also holds a personal chair at Oxford University, and in 2001 he was awarded an Oxford doctorate of divinity for his research on historical and systematic theology. A prolific author, he has written numerous books including *Iustitia Dei: A History of the Christian Doctrine of Justification*, *The Genesis of Doctrine*, *Christian Spirituality: An Introduction*, and *The Journey: A Pilgrim in the Lands of the Spirit*.

In this opening chapter, McGrath weaves together reflections on the development of his own spiritual life with a critique of spirituality based on an "arid evangelical rationalism." McGrath draws lessons from the lives and thought of Thomas à Kempis and J. I. Packer, showing how the riches of Scripture and Christian theology should nourish our hearts as well as our minds. This theme is further explored through encounter with a hymn by Isaac Watts and a sermon by Jonathan Edwards.

࿊࿊࿊ ࿊࿊࿊ ࿊࿊࿊

I recall a conversation some years ago with Donald Coggan, formerly archbishop of Canterbury. We were discussing some of the challenges to theological education and had ended by sharing our concerns over folk who left theological education knowing more about God but seemingly caring less for God. Coggan turned to me sadly and remarked: "The journey from head to heart is one of the longest and most difficult that we know." I have often reflected on that comment, which I suspect reflects his lifelong interest in theological education and the considerable frustrations it generated—not to mention his experiences of burned-out clergy, who seemed to have exhausted their often slender resources of spiritual energy and ended up becoming a burden instead of a gift to the people of God.

As the title of this chapter makes clear, I have no hesitation in affirming that theology is of central importance to Christian life and thought. I have little time for the various efforts to dumb down the preaching and teaching of our churches or simply to focus on the development of new and better techniques for the care of souls and the growth of the churches. But I am an honest person, and I admit from the outset that focusing simply on doctrinal affirmations is seriously deficient. Theological correctness alone is no balm for the wounds of our frail and sinful humanity. We cannot nourish the mind while neglecting the heart. Like its political counterpart, an obsession with theological correctness can simply engender the kind of harsh, judgmental personality that is eager to seek out and expose alleged doctrinal errors and cares little for the fostering of Christ-imaging relationships.

THE IMPORTANCE OF SPIRITUALITY

In my first period as a Christian, I found my attention focusing on *understanding* my faith. I continue to regard this as being of the utmost importance. There is a marvelous coherence to Christian doctrine, and wrestling with the great truths of our faith provided me with both spiritual encouragement and intellectual challenge. Yet it seemed to me that my "knowledge" of the Christian faith was rather dry and cerebral.

Part of the difficulty was that I was, like most people of my generation, deeply influenced by the Enlightenment. Christianity was all about *ideas*—and it was important to get those ideas right. As a result, theological correctness had become something of an obsession with me. I had failed to realize that the gospel affects every level of our existence—not just the way we think but the way we *feel* and *live*. The Enlightenment had championed the role of reason and vetoed any engagement with emotions or imagination. Yet I knew that writers such as Jonathan Edwards and C. S. Lewis had emphasized the importance of precisely these latter aspects of our lives. I gradually came to the realization that my faith was far too academic.[1]

My realization of the importance of spirituality began around 1989 but really blossomed from around 1992. I was invited to lead a regular summer school course in Oxford on "medieval and Reformation spirituality." This allowed me to engage with some of the great texts of Christian spirituality, including many from the period of the Reformation. As my students and I wrestled with these texts, we found ourselves challenged to deepen the quality of our Christian faith through being more open to God. I found that the quality of my Christian life deepened considerably as a result.

As I mentioned earlier, my basic understanding of Christian doctrine has not changed over the last ten years. I remain deeply committed to the fundamentals of Christian orthodoxy. What has happened is that these ideas have taken on a new depth, both as I appreciated more their implications and as I realized that my grasp of the totality of the Christian gospel had been shallow.

Traditional theology makes a distinction between two senses of the word *faith*. On the one hand, there is the "faith that believes"—that is, the personal quality of trust and commitment in God. On the other, there is the "faith that is believed"—that is, the body of Christian doctrine. Using this way of speaking, I could say that, in my case, the "faith that is believed" remained unaltered. What developed, matured, and deepened was the "faith that believes." The New Testament often compares the kingdom of God to a growing plant or a seed taking root. What happened to me was that a plant that had grown to some extent underwent a new spurt of growth, leading to increased strength and vitality.

My guess is that many readers will be able to identify with my earlier and rather academic approach to faith and are fed up being told by their doubtless well-meaning friends that they just need to know more *facts* about their faith. My experience is that we need to *go deeper* rather than just *know more*. Perhaps we all have to discover that we have simply scratched the surface of the immense riches of the gospel. Beneath the surface lies so much more, which we are meant to discover and enjoy. The greater our appreciation of the wonder, excitement, and sheer delight of the Christian faith, the more effective our witness to our friends and the greater our enjoyment of the Christian faith.

The growing interest in spirituality within evangelicalism is highly significant, a sure and telling sign that all is not well with the rather cerebral approaches to Christianity that have dominated the academic evangelical community.[2] Spirituality is all about the way in which we encounter and experience God, and the transformation of our consciousness and our lives as a result of that encounter and experience. It is most emphatically not the exclusive preserve of some spiritual elite, preoccupied with unhealthy perfectionist tendencies. It is the common duty and joy of all Christian believers, as they long to enter into the deeper fellowship with the living God that is promised in the Scriptures.

We can think of spirituality in terms of the *internalization of our faith*. It means allowing our faith to saturate every aspect of our lives, infecting and affecting our thinking, feeling, and living. Nobody can doubt how much we need to deepen the quality of our Christian lives and experience, with God's gracious assistance, and live more authentic lives in which we experience to the full the wonder of the love and grace of God. It is about ways in which we can foster and sustain our personal relationship with Christ. Christian spirituality may be thus understood as the way in which Christian individuals or groups aim to deepen their experience of God, or to "practise the presence of God," to use a phrase especially associated with Brother Lawrence (ca. 1614–91).[3]

Any definition of spirituality is likely to make reference to the following themes:

> knowing God, not just knowing about God;
>
> experiencing God to the full;
>
> transformation of existence on the basis of the Christian faith;
>
> attaining Christian authenticity in life and thought.

Spirituality aims to ensure that we both *know about* God and *know* God. It seeks to apply God to our hearts as well as our minds. It deals with the deepening of our personal knowledge of God. Yet this immediately indicates that spirituality is grounded in good theology. Spirituality is about the personal appropriation of what theology signposts and promises. Theology thus provides us with a secure foundation for Christian living.

Many evangelicals belonging to an older generation feel uneasy about the term *spirituality*. It is not, as has often been pointed out, a biblical term. Evangelicals, with their emphasis on the supreme authority and sufficiency of Scripture, are understandably concerned over the use of nonbiblical terms, and this concern deserves respect and understanding. However, it is important to note that evangelicals are perfectly prepared to use nonbiblical terms in other contexts. For example, works have appeared with the phrase "evangelical theology" in their titles. The word *theology* is nonbiblical, yet is widely used by evangelicals because it designates a recognized area of importance. Other words we happily use include *Christology*, *apologetics*, and *homiletics*. Each of these is unquestionably based on both biblical terminology and biblical ideas, even if the precise form of words chosen lacks an exact biblical equivalent. Yet we use them, believing them to be useful for the tasks we face as an evangelical community of reflection and application. I suspect that much the same thing is happening in relation to spirituality. Older words—such as *piety*—are gradually being displaced, even within evangelical circles, by the term *spirituality*.

My impression is that evangelicals have now widely accepted the word *spirituality*, despite the protests of some, and that it is here to stay. If this is so, our task is to ensure that we understand this term in a biblical manner, by insisting that any attempts to deepen the quality of the Christian experience of God are faithful to Scripture and rest on an orthodox theology. There is no inconsistency in speaking of "evangelical spirituality," as the history of the evangelical movement, especially in Great Britain, makes abundantly clear. It is entirely possible that some modern evangelicals have lost sight of their historical roots and resources and thus failed to appreciate how much nourishment we may receive from the past, as we seek to articulate and shape evangelical approaches to spirituality.[4] Yet even the most cursory survey of evangelical writings over the last ten years will show how much has been written on this topic by leading evangelicals, such as Marva Dawn, Eugene Peterson, and Dallas Willard.

In what follows, I consider two major issues. First, I point out that good theology is not enough. Let me make it clear that theology is *important*; this I both affirm and celebrate. Theology excites, informs, and challenges the mind, inviting us to discover the full riches of the Christian revelation, of which we so often have grasped so little. My point is that we must build on the foundations that theology offers, rather than leaving these structures bereft of the superstructures for which they were designed and which are meant to be built on the secure base. There is a serious danger of the emergence of an arid evangelical rationalism, which will erode the God-given appeal of the gospel to our hearts, imaginations, and emotions by demanding that we limit our knowledge of God to the mind. We have been down this spiritual dead end before;[5] it came close to destroying the vital power of faith through its arbitrary and deeply unbiblical demand that the gospel be allowed to impact on only one of our God-given faculties.

Second, I explore ways in which we can retain a sound theological basis yet go beyond the limitations attached to any approach to Christianity that treats the gospel simply as an idea—something that relates to our understanding while leaving the remainder of our human nature unaffected. I begin with what is perhaps the easier of these two tasks—considering the limitations placed on theology.

GOOD THEOLOGY IS NOT ENOUGH!

Christian theology has often taken the form of explicitly academic reflection on the content of the Christian faith. In its evangelical forms, this is linked with a rigorous insistence that such reflection shall be based on and governed by Scripture at every point. Theology is thus understood to concern knowledge, reflection, and speculation. Particularly in the modern Western academic context, this can lead to theology becoming so concerned with intellectual intricacies that it loses sight of the relational aspects of the Christian faith.

This point was made particularly clearly during the fifteenth century by Thomas à Kempis (ca. 1380–1471). During the Middle Ages, the theology of the Trinity became the subject of considerable speculation, occasionally leading to the Trinity being seen as little more than a mathematical puzzle or logical riddle. Thomas vigorously opposed this trend, seeing the proper role of theology as leading to love for God, contrition, and a changed life. In his *Imitation of Christ*, Thomas sets out a strongly antispeculative approach to the Christian faith, which rests firmly on the need to obey Christ rather than indulge in flights of intellectual fancy. Speculation concerning the Trinity is singled out as a case of such speculation, which he urges his readers to avoid.

> What good does it do you if you dispute loftily about the Trinity, but lack humility and therefore displease the Trinity? It is not lofty words that make you righteous or holy or dear to God, but a virtuous life. I would much rather experience contrition than be able to give a definition of it. If you knew the whole of the Bible by heart, along with all the definitions of the philosophers, what good would this be without grace and love? "Vanity of vanities, and all is vanity" (Ecclesiastes 1:2)—except, that is, loving God and serving him alone. . . . Naturally, everyone wants knowledge. But what use is that knowledge without the fear of God? A humble peasant who serves God is much more pleasing to him than an arrogant academic who neglects his own soul to consider the course of the stars.[6]

Notice the manner in which Thomas stresses the limits on knowledge and its benefits. Knowledge is not necessarily a good thing; it can be a distraction from God and a temptation to become arrogant.

A recognition of the importance of theology is not in conflict with placing an emphasis on spirituality. Let me illustrate this from the well-known evangelical theologian James I. Packer. Packer found his own spirituality to be informed and enriched by wrestling with the Puritan tradition—always an important resource for evangelicalism. Writers such as Richard Baxter enabled Packer to learn the usefulness of "regular discursive meditation," in which the individual preaches to himself or herself, applying biblical truth from within as if a talented preacher were doing so from outside.[7]

Packer also notes the importance of the Puritan understanding of the Christian life as a "gymnasium and dressing room where we are prepared for heaven."[8] This classic Christian emphasis on the transitoriness of life has, to a large extent, been lost in modern evangelicalism, which has tended to invest heavily in its commitment to the world. For Packer, there is a need to regain an awareness that a "readiness to die" is the "first step in learning to live."

FEEL GOD
KNOW GOD
OBEY GOD

Modern Western evangelicals, cosseted by the comforts of modern medicine, household appliances, and social security, have been insulated from many of the life pressures that were very real to the Puritans. In their physical discomfort, they kept their eyes focused on heaven as their only true comfort. "Reckoning with death brought appreciation of each day's continued life."

And finally—and for many of Packer's readers, most important—the Puritans taught him that "all theology is also spirituality."[9] The Puritans knew the importance of putting doctrine to use. Spirituality has its origins in the application of theology—and the application of bad theology will simply lead to bad spirituality. "If our theology does not quicken the conscience and soften the heart, it actually hardens both." This insight underlies the approach found in Packer's classic work, *Knowing God*.[10] Yet it can be found throughout his writings. A particularly luminous example is provided in his inaugural lecture as the first Sangwoo Youtong Chee Professor of Theology at Regent College, Vancouver, on December 11, 1989. The title Packer chose for this inaugural lecture is telling: "An Introduction to Systematic Spirituality." In that lecture, Packer explored the importance of spirituality to all concerned with the preaching and ministry of the gospel, and the intimate and unbreakable links that exist—and are *meant* to exist—between theology and spirituality.

> We cannot function well as counselors, spiritual directors, and guides to birth, growth and maturity in Christ, unless we are clear as to what constitutes spiritual well-being as opposed to spiritual lassitude or exhaustion, and to stunted and deformed spiritual development. It thus appears that the study of spirituality is just as necessary for us who hope to minister in the gospel as is the study of physiology for the medical trainee. It is something that we cannot really manage without.[11]

Why have I concentrated on Packer at this point? Well, I suppose the honest answer is that, having researched him over the last ten years, I have come to understand him—and it makes sense to write about something that you know about. But there are two deeper reasons for doing so.

First, Packer recognizes the importance of spirituality and of ensuring that both head and heart are nourished. We can learn from that. To emphasize the importance of spirituality is *not* to devalue the place of theology in the Christian life. It is to make sure that head and heart connect.

Second, Packer also illustrates a general approach to spirituality that I commend. You will have noted Packer's regular appeal to the Puritan tradition. In this, he found a mature approach to spirituality that he found to contrast with the somewhat superficial approach that he believed lay behind at least some expressions of twentieth-century evangelicalism. I believe he is right to identify Puritanism in this way. Others have also shown us how much we can learn at the feet of Puritan thinkers. Another helpful study is John Piper's excellent work *God's Passion for His Glory: Living the Vision of Jonathan Edwards* (Crossway, 1998).

But evangelicalism has been nourished by other movements, whose flowing waters may prove to be the answer to our sense of spiritual aridity. Let me mention another example, to which I invite to you add others. The Pietist tradition has been enormously influential in both European and American evangelicalism and continues to be an important resource. Its characteristic emphasis on the need for personal conversion, and its concern to nurture a personal living relationship with Jesus, remains important to us. The Wesleyan tradition—represented by writers such as Thomas C. Oden and institutions such as Asbury Theological Seminary—continues to nourish us. There are certainly differences between the theologies of Puritanism and Pietism, which could easily be allowed to overshadow their common concern to promote Christian integrity and maturity. John Wesley's theological Arminianism placed him at some distance from the more Reformed approach of writers such as John Owen; yet he was sufficiently impressed by the spiritual qualities of the Puritans to include many of their writings in his influential *Christian Library*.[12] And many know the story of Wesley and George Whitefield, whose Calvinism was at times the cause of some friction between the two. Wesley was once, we are told, asked whether "we should see Mr. Whitefield in heaven." Wesley's response ran along these lines: "I rather fear that we shall not. For he shall be so closer to the throne than we that I fear we shall not catch sight of him."

Having argued for the importance of relating heart and mind, a rather more difficult task now awaits me. I must do it myself, to avoid the entirely justifiable criticism that I have simply pointed out a need, rather than doing anything to meet it. In what follows, I explore some ways in which we can begin to do so.

LINKING HEAD AND HEART:
THE APPLICATION OF THEOLOGY

Western Christianity has been deeply affected by a particular way of thinking—a way of thinking that has seriously limited our grasp of our faith and apprehension of its wonder. Many call it the Enlightenment—the period in Western culture that began about 1750 and placed enormous emphasis on the power of human reason. It was inevitable that Christians would be affected by this way of thinking. Its basic demand is this: Understand better! Advancement in the Christian life takes place though a deepened understanding of the basics of Christian teachings and a deeper knowledge of the biblical works. This demand to read, learn, and understand has undoubtedly been helpful in many ways. For a start, it leads to better-informed Christians, with a much better grasp of the basic Christian beliefs.

Yet in another way, it had led to spiritual impoverishment. Its emphasis on reason has been at the expense of our *imaginations* and *emotions*—two God-given faculties that are meant to be fully involved in our Christian life. Spirituality is about linking thought, imagination, and feeling, as we appreciate the full richness and depth of our faith. *The gospel does not just affect the way we think; it changes the way we experience the world.*

Early in my Christian life, I thought that Christian development was all about thinking harder about things I already knew. It brought some useful results. For example, I realized how important it was to explain key Christian ideas faithfully and effectively, and I developed several ways of doing this that have proved very helpful to others. But it soon became obvious that this had its limits. I stalled. It was as if my faith was affecting only a tiny part of my life.

It was then I began to realize the importance of letting biblical ideas impact on my imagination and experience. I read some words of a medieval writer, Geert Zerbolt van Zutphen (1367–1400), who emphasized the importance of meditating on Scripture; *not understanding, but meditating*. Here is what he had to say:

> Meditation is the process in which you diligently turn over in your heart whatever you have read or heard, earnestly reflecting upon it and thus enkindling your affections in some particular manner, or enlightening your understanding.[13]

The same idea can be illustrated from virtually any period of Protestant spirituality, which emphasizes the importance of letting the biblical text impact on every aspect of our life and thought. For example, it is found in the writings of the Baptist preacher Charles Haddon Spurgeon (1834–92), widely regarded as one of the finest preachers of the nineteenth century. For Spurgeon, the danger of an excessively technical approach to reading the Bible could be met by an emphasis on meditation.

> The Spirit has taught us in meditation to ponder its message, to put aside, if we will, the responsibility of preparing the message we've got to give. Just trust God for that. But first, meditate on it, quietly ponder it, let it sink deep into our souls. Have you not often been surprised and overcome with delight as Holy Scripture is opened up as if the gates of the Golden City have been set back for you to enter? . . . A few minutes silent openness of soul before the Lord has brought us more treasure of truth than hours of learned research.[14]

Words like these brought new light and life to my reading of the Bible. I had thought that meditation was some kind of Buddhist practice, off-limits for Christians. Yet I had failed to notice how often Old Testament writers spoke of meditating on God's law. Meditation was about letting the biblical text impact on me, "enkindling the emotions"—what a wonderful phrase—and "enlightening the understanding." And my heart, as well as my mind, was to be involved. The worlds of understanding and emotion were brought together, opening the door to a far more authentic and satisfying way of living out the Christian life.

So how do we ensure that the riches of Scripture and Christian theology nourish our hearts as well as our minds? In what follows, I explore three ways in which this can happen:

1. By bringing about an enhanced appreciation of the profundity of Christian doctrines.
2. By engaging with our emotions, allowing theological formulations to move us, for example, to tears of sorrow or joy.
3. By enabling us to behave in ways that reflect a deepened personal appropriation of the truth of the gospel.

Let me make it clear that there are other manners in which such an interaction may take place; my concern here is to illustrate, rather than exhaust, possibilities.

Enhancing Our Appreciation

First, let us consider how we may go about gaining an enhanced appreciation of Christian doctrines. I explore this point with reference to one of the more difficult aspects of Christian theology—the doctrine of the Trinity.

The doctrine of the Trinity gathers together the richness of the complex Christian understanding of God, to yield a vision of God to which the only appropriate response is adoration and devotion. The doctrine knits together into a coherent whole the Christian doctrines of creation, redemption, and sanctification. By doing so, it sets before us a vision of a God who created the world and whose glory can be seen reflected in the wonders of the natural order; a God who redeemed the world, whose love can be seen in the tender face of Christ; and a God who is present now in the lives of believers. In this sense, the doctrine can be said to "preserve the mystery" of God, in the sense of ensuring that the Christian understanding of God is not impoverished through reductionism or rationalism. The Brazilian liberation theologian Leonardo Boff makes the following point.

> Seeing mystery in this perspective enables us to understand how it provokes reverence, the only possible attitude to what is supreme and final in our lives. Instead of strangling reason, it invites expansion of the mind and heart. It is not a mystery that leaves us dumb and terrified, but one that leaves us happy, singing and giving thanks. It is not a wall placed in front of us, but a doorway through which we go to the infinity of God. Mystery is like a cliff: we may not be able to scale it, but we can stand at the foot of it, touch it, praise its beauty. So it is with the mystery of the Trinity.[15]

"Your God is too small!" There is a serious danger that theology may have precisely the reverse effect of that which is intended. At its best, theology is intended to deepen our appreciation and understanding of the richness of the Christian revelation, offering us fresh perspectives on its contents and inner dynamics. In this sense, a Trinitarian theology challenges us to expand our vision of God by reflecting on the person and works of the God who has called us and redeemed us. Yet that same theology can also *limit* our vision, if we define theology as the mere repetition of formulas without engagement with the realities that lie behind them.

Let me cite from a classic Reformed catechism, which sets modern evangelicalism an exciting and challenging agenda. "What," asked the Westminster Shorter Catechism, "is the chief end of man?" The answer given is rightly celebrated as a jewel in evangelicalism's theological crown: "to glorify God and enjoy him for ever." This brief statement sets us on a journey of theological exploration—to gain a fresh apprehension of the glory of God, so that we might return that glory to God and have our spiritual lives enriched by the knowledge of such a God. To catch such a glimpse of the full splendor of God is also a powerful stimulus to evangelism. Was it not by catching a glimpse of the glory of God in the Temple that Isaiah responded to the divine call to go forth in service? There is a need for us to allow our minds, imaginations, and emotions to be stimulated and informed by theology. Rightly grasped, it will force us to our knees in adoration and praise, as we catch a glimpse of the immensity of this God who loves us and has called us to be God's own.

Engaging Our Emotions

It is often suggested that the British male is characterized by a "stiff upper lip"—meaning that he refuses to show any emotions, regarding this as unmanly, demeaning, humiliating, or a worrying sign of immaturity. I am no psychologist and cannot comment on whether this is wise or healthy. But as the reaction to the death of Princess Diana in 1997 makes clear, the British seem perfectly capable of emotional release when the occasion is seen to demand it. So why, I find myself wondering, do so many evangelicals seem to believe that any form of emotional engagement is a worrying sign of spiritual immaturity?

I do not suggest that public displays of emotion are to be encouraged as a matter of principle. Yet surely it is not just impossible but unthinkable to read the accounts of the suffering and death of Jesus Christ without being moved— perhaps moved to tears? Isaac Watts (1674–1748) was convinced that much of the Christianity of his day was superficial. He longed to go deeper and learn more. His advice to his readers reflects this concern: "Do not hover always on the surface of things, nor take up suddenly, with mere appearances; but penetrate into the depth of matters, as far as your time and circumstances allow."[16] We see this concern to "penetrate into the depth of matters" in his devotional hymns, which stimulate personal devotion through active engagement with their themes.

His best-loved hymn takes the form of a meditation on the cross, intended to evoke a sense of sorrow, wonder, and commitment on the part of its audience. In "When I Survey the Wondrous Cross," Watts offers a reflection on the cross designed to allow its audience to see the attractions of the world in their proper perspective. In addition to painting a vivid word-picture of the cross, Watts emphasizes that all else pales into insignificance in its light. By building up a verbal picture of the sufferings of Christ for his audience, Watts hopes to move them deeply—to repentance, sorrow, and an increased commitment to their Savior.

> When I survey the wondrous cross
> On which the Prince of Glory died,
> My richest gain I count but loss,
> And pour contempt on all my pride.
>
> Forbid it, Lord, that I should boast
> Save in the Cross of Christ my God!
> All the vain things that charm me most,
> I sacrifice them to his blood.
>
> See from his head, his hands, his feet,
> Sorrow and love flow mingled down!
> Did e'er such love and sorrow meet,
> Or thorns compose so rich a crown!
>
> Were the whole realm of nature mine,
> That were an offering far too small;
> Love so amazing, so divine,
> Demands my soul, my life, my all.[17]

Notice how Watts leads his readers to meditate on the cross. The hymn builds up a verbal picture of the cross, focusing attention on the pain experienced by the dying Christ and the fact that this is the means by which the redemption of the world has been accomplished. Watts reminds us of the physical suffering of the Son of God that underlines any theology of forgiveness. "Forgiveness" is a simple idea to understand. Yet we *need to experience the reality to which that word points.* It is fatally easy to think that we have understood the word, without entering into the real world of experience and life to which it refers. Forgiveness is what restores a relationship that really matters, when you have messed it up. It is about the restoration of something that means everything to you and that you thought you lost forever on account of your foolishness.

If you have ever been through that situation, the word *forgiveness* will mean the transformation of your life, evoking powerful emotions and calling to mind the situation that made it necessary. Someone who has never needed to be forgiven will never know the full richness, wonder, and joy of that simple word *forgiveness*. This point is made powerfully by J. Randall Nichols, who wrote of an experience he had while visiting the Greek island of Corfu. "Some of the most beautiful music I ever heard was the chanting of Greek peasant women, tears streaming down their lined and hardened faces, in a church on Corfu one Good Friday. I asked someone why they were weeping. 'Because,' he said, 'their Christ is dead.' I have often thought that I will never understand what resurrection means until I can weep like that."[18] Nichols's point is that we can never appreciate the joy and hope of the resurrection, unless we have been plunged into the sense of hopelessness and helplessness which pervaded that first Good Friday. What is true of the resurrection is also true of forgiveness. Christian spirituality is grounded in an awareness of being a condemned sinner—an experience that is utterly transformed by divine forgiveness. We can never understand what forgiveness really means until we have wept the tears of condemnation.

Now, suggesting that we allow our theology to impact on our emotions in no way detracts from its intellectual integrity. It simply helps us identify a legitimate emotional component to our theology. Music (for example, J. S. Bach's passion chorales) and art (for example, Matthias Grünewald's depiction of the crucifixion) can help us in this quest for a proper emotional engagement with our theology. Some evangelicals are critical of any tendency to allow music and art to have any role in the life of faith, echoing similar concerns expressed in the patristic and Reformation periods.[19] Yet I believe that these can be seen as means of grace that, rightly used, have potential for helping us focus on the person and work of Christ, and thus deepening the quality of our faith.

Enabling Us to Behave

Theology affects the way in which we live and behave. An excellent example is provided by the Christian vision of the new Jerusalem, which is meant to encourage us to lift our eyes upward and focus them on where Christ has gone before us. Paul makes this point as follows in his letter to the Colossians:

> Since, then, you have been raised with Christ, set your hearts on things above, where Christ is seated at the right hand of God. Set your minds on things above, not on earthly things. For you died, and your life is now hidden with Christ in God. (Col. 3:1–3)

Our belief concerning the new Jerusalem ought to encourage us to behave as people who are looking forward to finally being with Christ, and to view the world accordingly. This point is made, in different ways, by Jonathan Edwards and John Stott. Each makes points of importance to our theme.

One of Edwards's most compelling works is a sermon titled "The Christian Pilgrim." In this sermon, Edwards is concerned to help us orientate ourselves correctly as we travel along the road of faith. As we pass through the world, what should be our attitude toward it? Because it is God's creation, we cannot reject it as evil. Yet because it is not God, it falls short of the true glory of the ultimate goal of our journey. Edwards reminds us that our final goal is God, and that nothing has the power to satisfy or right to be adored other than that same God.

Edwards thus declares that "God is the highest good of the reasonable creature; and the enjoyment of him is the only happiness with which our souls can be satisfied." We may therefore pass through the world and enjoy all that it has to offer, while realizing that the final delight of being with God will totally overwhelm whatever joy and delights this world may offer. Edwards sets out this approach in his famous sermon:

> We ought not to rest in the world and its enjoyments, but should desire heaven. . . . We ought above all things to desire a heavenly happiness; to be with God; and well with Jesus Christ. Though surrounded with outward enjoyments, and settled in families with desirable friends and relations; though we have companions whose society is delightful, and children in whom we see many promising qualifications; though we live by good neighbors and are generally beloved where known; yet we ought not to take our rest in these things as our portion. . . . We ought to possess, enjoy and use them, with no other view but readily to quit them, whenever we are called to it, and to change them willingly and cheerfully for heaven.[20]

Edwards thus offers us a new perspective on our journey. As we travel, we are not being asked to ignore the beauties of the world through which we are passing. We may appreciate it and see it as a foretaste of the beauty of God, whom one day we shall see in all God's radiance. Nor are we being asked to withdraw from the company and love of other people. Rather, we are asked to value and appreciate this, seeing it as an anticipation of being in the presence and love of God. One day we shall have to relinquish that which is good for that which is the best. But in the meantime, we may begin to anticipate how wonderful that entry into the presence of God will be and allow that thought to encourage and excite us as we travel on our journey.

A related point made by John Stott brings out clearly how the hope of future glory illuminates and transforms the present. In a series of addresses given to the InterVarsity Mission Convention at Urbana, Illinois, in 1976, Stott developed the importance of the hope of glory for theology, spirituality, and especially evangelism. His addresses issued a clarion call for the recovery of this leading theme of the Christian faith and its application to every aspect of our present Christian lives.

> Lift up your eyes! You are certainly a creature of time, but you are also a child of eternity. You are a citizen of heaven, and an alien and exile on earth, a pilgrim travelling to the celestial city.
>
> I read some years ago of a young man who found a five-dollar bill on the street and who "from that time on never lifted his eyes when walking. In the course of years he accumulated 29,516 buttons, 54,172 pins, 12 cents, a bent back and a miserly disposition." But think what he lost. He couldn't see the radiance of the sunlight, and sheen of the stars, the smile on the face of his friends, or the blossoms of springtime, for his eyes were in the gutter. There are too many Christians like that. We have important duties on earth, but we must never allow them to preoccupy us in such a way that we forget who we are or where we are going.[21]

Stott encourages us to renew our acquaintance with the glory that awaits us and to begin to anticipate its wonder—and allow that to impact on us *now*.

CONCLUSION

My concern in this chapter has been to offer some preliminary reflections on the importance of relating our minds and hearts and some brief thoughts on how we might go about doing this. Happily, others have developed such insights in much greater detail. Theology offers us a firm foundation on which we may build, ensuring that the great riches and truths of the gospel stimulate and nourish our minds, emotions, and imaginations. Yet we cannot abandon the building once the foundation has been laid; the superstructure must be erected and inhabited. Paul wrote these words: "I consider everything a loss compared to the surpassing greatness of knowing Christ Jesus my Lord" (Phil. 3:8). I pray that we may know the full reality of that "surpassing greatness," and that it may inspire us and encourage us as we journey on the road to the new Jerusalem.

2

Christian Spirituality: A Contextual Perspective

James M. Houston

Perhaps more than anyone else in North America, James M. Houston has pioneered the serious study and practice of spirituality among evangelical theologians and scholars. Born in Edinburgh, Scotland, in 1922, Houston received his D.Phil. in the field of historical geography. In this discipline he has had a lifelong interest in the history of ideas. He was a lecturer and tutor at Oxford for twenty-three years.

Houston's interest in the history of Christian spirituality grew out of his own deep personal faith in Christ, rooted in the tradition of the Brethren but enriched by many ecumenical contacts. At Oxford, he enjoyed a personal friendship with C. S. Lewis and Malcolm Muggeridge. In 1970, Houston moved to Vancouver, British Columbia, to become the founding principal of Regent College. Since 1978 he has served as professor of spiritual theology in this school. He has written several books on spirituality including *In Search of Happiness*, *The Heart's Desire*, *The Transforming Power of Prayer*, and, most recently, *The Mentored Life*.

In this chapter, Houston examines the theological and historical contexts for appropriating themes of Christian spirituality. He draws on the wisdom of the past as well as more recent theologians such as Dietrich Bonhoeffer, Gustavo Gutierrez, and Hans urs von Balthasar to present a richly textured discussion of the challenge of Christian spirituality today. The theme of context is further explored by Houston's discussion of what it means to live biblically "in place." He defines spirituality as a transformative process in which we uncover our inner lives and attain a "depth" not available in the shallowness of modern life, dislodged from its spiritual roots.

୧୬ ୧୬ ୧୬

It is apparent that we are living in an age of transition that challenges us with alternatives to traditional wisdom. Already at the end of the nineteenth century Friedrich Nietzsche (1844–1900) had a sense of the fragility of the philosophical systems of his age: "The ice that still supports people today has become very thin; the wind that brings the thaw is blowing; we ourselves who are homeless constitute a force that breaks open ice and other all too thin realities."[1] Recently, Harold Bloom has surveyed the literature of the Western world as having changed from the theocratic, through the aristocratic and then the democratic, to what is now the chaotic age.[2] Others see that the human rebellion of modernity to jettison the synthesis of God-cosmology-humanity with a wholly secular mind-set ends up with mere fragments of reality, as Louis Dupré has argued in his book *Passage to Modernity*.[3] Different as these writers are, they all point to the profound sense of loss of metaphysical foundations that we are now facing in our Western culture.

CONTEMPORARY POPULAR USAGE OF "SPIRITUALITY"

The popular usage of the word *spirituality* since the 1970s may thus be interpreted as diverse efforts to create a new synthesis out of the fragments left today of metaphysics. It seeks "depth" in a secular existence that now ignores God. Indeed, its usage is a subversive protest against the various forms of reductionism, including rationalism, that cannot contain the human spirit. Indeed, "spirituality" in this vague cultural protest of our times is analogous to the protest of Romanticism in the early nineteenth century. The literary criticism of F. R. Leavis and the school associated with him in the periodical *Scrutiny* (1932–53) is seen as a protest for the self-understanding of the individual in a technological society, where the utilitarianism of Jeremy Bentham (1748–1832) prevailed; this takes the idea of the greatest happiness for the greatest number as the guiding principle of ethics. No, protested Leavis, the "nature" of human nature is "the need of significance," which he overtly uses as the equivalent of "spiritual." So he states, "My own recourse to the word 'spiritual' is determined by the contemplation of a world in which the technologico-Benthamite ethos has triumphed at the expense of the human spirit—that is, of human life. There is an intrinsic human nature with needs that don't exist for the technologist and the Benthamite as such; there is a need for significance, for that which is lived significantly—something that can't be discussed or taken into account of in terms of what can be measured or averaged or defined, although rationality and intelligence (whether they know it or not) are thwarted when it fails."[4]

Another movement equally potent in latent spirituality is psychoanalysis. D. W. Harding, a social psychologist and also a founder-contributor to

MEANING   SIGNIFICANT

FUNCTION   URGENT

Scrutiny, interpreted psychoanalysis as not so much self-discovery as the discovery of others, to liberate relationships in bondage within the culture and the self. Melanie Klein and her pupils, such as D. W. Winnicott and W. R. Bion, have had immense repercussions on our society by the retrieval of the psychic structures of infancy and interpreting their significance in the adult. Then David Cooper and Ronald D. Laing brought psychoanalysis into the realms of politics and spirituality in a major convocation in London in 1967.[5] Such voices of protest against bland conformity led to the broader countercultural movements of the 1970s—to protest against the loss of the American "soul" in Vietnam, against the racial segregation in the South, over women's issues, and so forth. From these broadly humanistic perspectives, our society is viewed as sick indeed, even while Christians have seemed often to embrace and adopt its ways much less critically. In this definition, secular critics have been more "spiritual" than Christian conformists.

Within Christianity, the same period saw the advent of the Charismatic movement. In some regards it was a social movement comparable to the Oxford Group movement that had preceded it, for both sought deeper experiences and expressions of a serious Christian life as a shared, communal faith. Its openness to the presence and work of the Holy Spirit engendered the expectation of "spiritual waves" that anticipated new "happenings" in the life of the church, vague and ambiguous as they continued to be in such further movements as the "Toronto blessing." Originally a development within the Vineyard Fellowship, the Toronto Blessing is a charismatic movement known for bizarre spiritual manifestations, such as uncontrollable laughter, and animal noises, such as barking like a dog. Its influence has spread beyond Canada to other communities within the Christian world. In 1967, shortly after Vatican Council II had sought renewal in the Roman Catholic Church, the Charismatic movement affected a group of Catholics in Dusquesne University, then at Notre Dame and Ann Arbor, and eventually spread to many parish prayer groups both in the United States and overseas. All these movements are expressive of an intense desire to experience the presence of the Holy Spirit, to seek emotional healing and reconciliation, to experience renewal, to have "openness" in one's experiences, and to experience ecstasy, outside of the realm of conventional living. Personal, lived experiences, more than prescribed general explanations, have engendered such religious interest in spirituality.

This popular interest in spirituality has created a publisher's dream, a vastly extending market for books of all kinds that focus on the word *spiritual*. It has helped to open the Eastern world to the West and has generated particular attention to "meditation," as the offspring of "depth psychology." Thus, focus on the "therapeutic" and on self-meditation have engendered new interest in human consciousness, at both neurological and popular levels.

INTELLIGENCE NOW INTERPRETED
AS MULTIDIMENSIONAL

Within the last decade, popular books have been published on the distinction between the cognitive and emotional processes of the brain. The evidence of brain damage has been studied to map out distinctive spheres and functions. This led Antonio Damasio to write his popular summary of such findings in his book *Descartes' Error: Emotion, Reason, and the Human Brain*.[6] This, in turn, led a science journalist, Daniel Goleman, to write *Emotional Intelligence: Why It Can Matter More than IQ*.[7] Goleman speaks of how our modern world has tended to hijack our emotions or to suppress them, so that many of our social woes can be attributed to the lack of empathy, attentiveness, and, indeed, the lack of emotional wisdom.

The results, too, of depth psychology have encouraged some psychiatrists such as Robert Langs[8] and Andrew G. Hodges to argue we only use our brains as the tip of the iceberg. So we are urged to "discover the untapped potential of your subconscious mind."[9] However, if we can measure our intelligence with both an IQ and an EQ, or emotional intelligence quotient, it is now also possible to talk of a "spiritual" intelligence quotient. In fact, this is now claimed by Danah Zohar and Ian Marshall in their recent book *Spiritual Intelligence: The Ultimate Intelligence*. The study of epilepsy has suggested there is actually an identifiable deep area in the brain that may be called a "God spot," where spiritual experiences can be triggered. The authors are careful, however, to distinguish "spiritual intelligence" as expressive of the whole person from merely the brain's receptivity to having "spiritual experiences."[10]

However speculative some of this thinking may be, it all points to the growing awareness that human consciousness is far more complex than the traditionally assumed views of being "rational" or, indeed, of having "common sense." Half a century ago, Michael Polanyi gave us, in his profound study of "personal knowledge," awareness of how significant the role of the "tacit dimension" of learning is, even in the sphere of science.[11] Theologians soon began to appreciate how significant "tacit knowledge" must be in Christian discipleship, although much remains to explore in this direction.[12] Two philosophers who were "passionate thinkers," Søren Kierkegaard (1813–55) and Ludwig Wittgenstein (1889–1951), have both been influential in shaping a more robust expression of Christian faith. Certainly, Paul L. Holmer indicates his indebtedness to them. His book *The Grammar of Faith* expresses the need to "make sense" of our faith, not only cognitively but emotionally, morally, and volitionally as well.[13] Such writers seek to have more "depth" in Christian expressions of faith.[14]

Since religion has ceased to integrate society and culture in the West as it once did, it has become increasingly a matter of individual decision. But the prevailing spiritual emptiness of the secular culture spills over into the inner lives of Christians too; hence the greater desire to have personal "experiences," to liberate one from one's own inner silence, and perhaps to look back and to benefit from the richer spiritual lives the past saints of the history of the church seem to have exemplified. So reading their classics of faith and devotion, it is assumed, will inspire us today to possess similar depth.

Clearly, then, by "spirituality" we now mean a more multidimensional approach to living than the shallowness of modern life tends to give us. For factors that keep us in the shallows are those that are impersonal, such as the "crowd" mentality; perspectivalism, which rejects any truth claim based on direct experience of reality; and positivism, which rejects any truth claim not subject to scientific method. All these would reject personal spirituality out of hand. In doing so, they tend to overlook motive, as when we ask, "Did I have the right spirit?" Or again, I may ask, "What spirit do I have?" suggesting my spirit may not be strong enough to persist and carry on. Or I may probe even further: "Do I have contact with God's Spirit, in my desire to be transformed, seeking God's will and Spirit, not my own?"

So spirituality is essentially a transformative process in which we uncover our inner lives, to seek emancipation from our narcissism. Essentially, then, there is a deepening receptivity to whatever spiritual realities help us let go of our self-centered identities and their preoccupation with control, power, status, and allow us to live more openly, freely, and unpossessively. Thus the growth of spirituality moves from the question "What ought I to know?" to "what ought I to do?" to "what ought I to be?"

What is confusing for the Christian is that all the above features can be tested by nonbelievers who want simply to be both emotionally and spiritually wise in their own growth and in relations with others. So, when such encounter Christians who are less emotionally or spiritually mature than themselves, they might see little or nothing that would commend the Christian faith as communicated by such people.

Thus being "spiritual" may simply mean seeking "openness" to one's life, instead of the self-closure that characterized previous generations. We can read this in people's faces, especially those of our grandparents who have not yet disclosed the personal horrors they went through in World War II. We see today also the consequences of therapeutic narcissism. The emotional well-being now claimed has its converse of mental health in the new attentiveness demanded, to be "listened to" and to have one's feelings more understood. So those contrasted faces that shine out with love for others, with hearts warmly turned to others in need, direct our attention to their hidden sources of spirituality. Yet there are always degrees of openness, so depth psychology and a century of psychoanalysis are exposing layers of differing forms of closedness.

These are not only pride and self-centeredness but self-humiliation, shame, and other hidden paralyzing or wounded forces as well.[15]

Spirituality also probes the kind of spirit we have, with regard to issues of motive, attitude, and personal freedom. For we cannot take each other at face value only. Indeed, we cannot even assume we know ourselves well enough. "Tunnel vision" can be as much inwardly toward ourselves as to external objects, and most of all toward God. If, then, openness is expressive of spirituality as a new disposition of our times, we can begin to recognize how readily this can also tempt us to become eclectic, ecumenical, ecological, indeed global in our sentiment and thought. Such openness can become excessive, seeing everything as broken up into individual perspectives or points of view that become wholly subjective as mere opinions. The caution given by G. K. Chesterton, then, becomes relevant: that if you open your mouth wide, make sure you close it again on something nutritious and substantial.[16] The climate of such spirituality can be conducive to many false forms of syncreticism.

Thus our cultural attention to spirituality is complex in origin and may have apparently little religion about it. It may be a protest against the self-inflating closure of subjectivism on the one hand or the external closure of objectivism on the other.[17] Just as there was a strong cultural reaction in Western Europe in the eighteenth century toward "enthusiasm," for fear of religious fanaticism, so our own society has become "open" in reaction to whatever we find stifling and restrictive of the human spirit. To balance this, another aspect of spirituality is recognized to be "connectedness." Mountaineers, even those who have given their lives to climb Mount Everest, have spoken of the mystical experience of being "connected" to the mountain. Somehow they feel a bond, a link, with a transcendent reality beyond themselves. So, too, the religious person can speak of seeking "God's presence," of the great angst of uniting and communing with God. Thus, Bernard Lonergan can seek to understand the intellectual and spiritual processes that move us in faith toward "spiritual integration" as a dialectical habit of soul that unites "head" and "heart" in deeper integrity of Christian faith and life.[18]

Yet it was not so long ago that the word *spirituality* was used as somehow needing to be "disconnected," in order to ascend a higher plane of being. In his private journal in 1958, Thomas Merton recalled that as a young monk he had almost decided to give up writing in order to go "upward" into a "higher spirituality."[19] As a negative term, it was first used in the seventeenth century, as somehow connected with asceticism and spiritual elitism, and so disconnected with ordinary life. Like the word *mysticism*, which Michel de Certeau has researched, both terms were coined in the same period to describe esoteric experiences.[20] Both are reversed to refer to those elements that enrich and give more "thickness" to the ordinary lives we live.

OBJECTIVE SUBJECTIVE or SUBJECTIVE OBJECTIVE ?

RIGHT DOCTRINE BROADLY SHARED ASSUMPTIONS or PERSONALLY LIVED FAITH

THE CHALLENGE OF
CHRISTIAN SPIRITUALITY TODAY

The emphasis now in Christian spirituality is no longer merely on accuracy of communication, as "right doctrine," but on the wholeness of the experience of what is being communicated, as a "lived faith." Kierkegaard, in his *Concluding Unscientific Postscript*, says something similar: "Christianity is not a doctrine, but an existential communication."[21] But instead of broadly shared assumptions of faith within the whole body of Christ, we now seek it personally with greater intensity perhaps than before. So we may instead speak of "Christian spiritualities" as the diverse ways in which each of us is shaped by the common teachings of the Word of God. While we live before a "great cloud of witnesses" (Heb. 12:1), we do so more consciously, as "persons" having our own unique identity.

The liberation theologian Gustavo Gutierrez has developed a three-stage schema of how the formation of a tradition of Christian spirituality occurs:[22]

1. Remarkable individuals have had powerful experiences, perhaps of conversion or of later shattering events in their lives, that have broken the paradigm previously lived in conventionally, to give them new perceptions and new ways of interpreting and experiencing the Spirit of God in their lives.
2. They, in turn, have affected others around them, or later, to follow in the same way, to found new communities of faith, such as we may describe in the Cistercians following on Bernard of Clairvaux, of the Franciscans following on Francis of Assisi, or indeed of the Puritans and Pietists following on writers such as William Perkins and Johann Arndt.
3. These do not end historically at a given movement of history but are sustained and live on in later generations, as their writings and teachings continue to be reread and repeated in their practices.

Indeed, this has been the whole history of Christianity: first, a way of life, whose existential quality is the basis; second, for reflection and teaching, a formal theological system. Then, third, this has been the further basis for the ongoing ecclesial tradition of the church and of further theological reflection.

Thus Christian spirituality would remind us that there is a long historical series of traditions behind us, in the interpretation and shaping of the Christian life. But it also rebukes us if we think Christian faith is merely imparted to us in various pedagogical ways. Jesus does not merely say we should follow his teaching but that we live in his way. So Christian spirituality is really about Christian discipleship. As Dietrich Bonhoeffer has stated in his classic book, *The Cost of Discipleship*: "Discipleship means adherence to Christ, and, because Christ is the object of that adherence, it must take the form of discipleship. . . . Christianity without discipleship is always Christianity without Christ."[23] This must mean, then, that Christian spirituality cannot be an individualistic therapy, some private appropriation suited to one's own personality. Rather, it is a missionary call to go into all the world with the gospel of the triune God of grace, whose initiative it is to transform human beings into God's image and likeness. But it is also a call to communicate the faith appropriately, as a "lived and experienced faith," not merely a discursive faith.

LIVING BIBLICALLY "IN PLACE"

I have been privileged to be the first holder among evangelicals of a chair in Spiritual Theology. When our nominating committee at Regent College offered me the choice of a professorship in Spirituality or in Spiritual Theology in 1977, I saw the choice as being essentially confessional, not one of merely being countercultural. Since then, there has been ample evidence of how the willfulness of the human spirit can use spirituality counterculturally, to become a further instrument of subversion, for good or evil. It indeed glorifies the human quest for freedom, whether it be against bureaucratic management, the stifling culture of modernity in its postmodern protest, or, indeed, against God. Its quest of "openness" can entice our youth into the drug culture. It is precisely because of the plethora of spiritualities that there is increasing potential for chaos and confusion to reign today in religious life; for conventionality has been superceded by spirituality.

In my previous profession as a geographer, one of my colleagues was always quoting against his colleagues who studied faraway places and were not challenged to concentrate on their immediate environs: "The eyes of the fool are upon the ends of the earth." But he did not quote the full context: "A discerning man keeps wisdom in view, but a fool's eyes wander to the ends of the earth" (Prov. 17:24). Nor did he realize that this "wandering" was not just of the "eyes," in curiosity, but of the spirit of disloyalty to the covenanted life of Israel. Thus it expressed disobedience, indeed, rebellion against God.

When, then, in John's Gospel, Jesus is depicted as bearing the yoke of divine filiation, the promise he gives is pregnant with meaning: "Do not let your hearts be troubled. Trust in God; trust also in me. . . . I am going there to prepare a place for you. And if I go and prepare a place for you, I will come back and take you to be with me that you also may be where I am"—that is, the Father's eternal bosom of divine love (John 14:1, 2b–3). So the "beloved disciple" in John's Gospel is perhaps the archetype of how Jesus wants all his disciples to live for him, "in place," uniquely so, because of his love for each of his own.

SPIRITUAL THEOLOGY – CONFESSIONAL
SPIRITUALITY – COUNTER CULTURAL

"Being placed" in Christ's sonship implies one is never "spaced out" by all the events and vicissitudes of life. For "place" is specific, contextual, wholly one's own, while "space" can be without boundaries, general, even boundless. Jesus Christ has what the early church fathers called unique *hypostasis*, as "the One and Only," yet is also "one with the Father," each in perichoretic union, one mutually and reciprocatingly in, for, and by the other. So, too, the identity of the Christian is likewise safeguarded "in Christ." One is then never confused about gender issues, nor personal identity, nor one's calling and moral obligations to others. Nor need one feel confused about denominational issues, which have become increasingly more politically motivated, especially over power struggles. Nor, indeed, should one seek to become a "Christian leader," as if no worthwhile Christian can be anything less than a leader in American society today.

Rather, the call to be an "ordinary Christian" is increasingly needed, the more performance, profession, and programs are being exalted as the mark of becoming a "successful Christian." Richard Baxter (1615–91), who coined the phrase a "mere Christian" in the seventeenth century, did so after the events of the English civil war, waged in the cause of religion. C. S. Lewis (1898–1963) used the phrase to explain why an academic don of English literature transgressed across professional disciplines to be a popular religious broadcaster, when he was not "ordained" or "trained professionally" to act in this way. Perhaps, likewise, the "mere Christian" now is the ascetic who does not aspire to a position of leadership or of being successful but seeks rather to be like the prophet Micah, "filled with power, with the Spirit of the Lord," "to act justly and to love mercy and to walk humbly with your God."[24]

What, then, is "out of place" in Christian spirituality today is to confuse it with the general cultural interest in spirituality; for the latter is further expressive of the intensely individualistic and, indeed, narcissistic spirit of our times. It has become the mandate of permissiveness, to foster an experimental way of life, of novelty, faddishness, and subjectivism. It is expressive of a new gnosticism, having no awareness of sin but interpreting curiosity as a virtue, whereas for medieval saints it was condemned as a vice. Indeed, it is the exaltation of the self, to seek and to find salvation within the depths of one's own being, as being closer to the divine. This is also expressive of an ethic of authenticity that believes inwardness is closer to the truth. It lives also in alliance with a therapeutic culture, whose "right to happiness" is assumed to be as unquestioned as the American Constitution.

What is also "out of place" is the competitive spirit, even among Christians, to compare and contrast evangelical spirituality with Catholic traditions of spirituality. This attitude arises from the awareness that traditions of Catholic spirituality have a long history, whereas evangelicals have seized on this interest only in the last two decades. There is always the natural desire to "catch up," to be "with it," and so to claim a place for "evangelical spirituality" also. To the "mere" Christian, these are not issues of any substance, but the more institutional and professional one's ambitions become, the more they do matter.

But Christian spirituality is a "subversive" influence, since it is deeply concerned with motive and attitude, as we have already seen. Other than the name of Jesus, it is not tempted into name-dropping, nor are other Christians to be damned by association, as the party spirit tends to do. For such reasons, Christian spirituality is revisionist and can be an instrument of radical reinterpretation. It helps to keep a prophetic stance of detachment from the corrupting influences of our culture, and to discern with spiritual clarity and in faithfulness to God's Word.

CHRISTIAN SPIRITUALITY MUST BE UNDERSTOOD HISTORICALLY AND THEOLOGICALLY

However, modern Christians are frequently blind because they lack a historical as well as a theological perspective. Modernism is fascinated by its own Cartesian spirit of instrumental reason, assuming that the mentality of "how to do things" is the only knowledge worth having. This ahistorical consciousness explains the strongly pragmatic spirit of much Christian activism today that distorts the ministry of the gospel, as if it were all about "programs." It is also undiscerning, then, of the quality of the "lived presence" of Christ and of the need of his indwelling Spirit. The history of traditions of Christian spirituality is thus an antidote to this "death of the past," as J. H. Plumb has delineated this modern retreat from historical consciousness.[25]

Newton Flew once made the comment: "The *Theologia Dogmatica* of the future may be built on the *Spiritualis Theologia* of the past."[26] This means tracing spirituality that purports to be Christian back to its apostolic roots, and then to the councils and teachings of the Fathers of the church. For Christian spirituality is not a new emphasis, nor merely an aspect of the Christian life, but it is the Christian life in response to the Spirit of God. The Latin noun *spiritualitas* first appears in a letter of the fifth century once ascribed to Jerome, exhorting his reader to advance "proficient in spirituality."[27] The context is Pauline, just as the apostle in writing to the Corinthians distinguishes those who live as the *pneumatikos* (1 Cor. 2:10–15f.), having faith in the Lord and in the Spirit (1 Cor. 6:17).

It was not until the twelfth century that a new breed of scholars arose who, using a rational and dialectical approach, began to study a new science called theology. Until then, the contemplation of God had been known as "divinity." Such was effort of the Aristotelian logician Abelard (ca. 1079–1142), twice condemned as a heretic.[28] But Bernard of Clairvaux (1096–1153) feared that such arguing and reasoning about the Christian faith, instead of living it out reverently in daily experience of meditation and the practice of the liturgy, might then explain it away altogether. Moreover, it became only too clear with Abelard's behavior that such a rational explanation does not require scholars to become saints.

Whereas, following the dictum of Evagrius of Ponticus, "to be a theologian is to pray," Bernard of Clairvaux insisted that it is also to live daily in the experience of God's presence in God's Word. The direct experience of the living Word was Bernard's central conviction of being engaged with the Divinity.[29] This is why constant meditation on the Song of Songs was the key biblical focus for Bernard and the contemplatives of the next three centuries. This was the life of the contemplation of the love of Christ, and it was assumed this was possible only in the cloistered life. This alone was truly spiritual. Thus, from the rise of scholasticism in the twelfth century onward, terms such as *ascetic*, *monastic*, and *mystical theology* arose, to distinguish such a lived, contemplative faith from rational speculation about it.

In the Protestant world after the Reformation, new terminology was adopted, such as *piety, godliness, holiness,* each with its own theological context and historical movement. By the eighteenth century, the term *spiritualities* had so wholly lost its meaning that it was defined in the first edition of the *Encyclopaedia Britannica*, in 1771, as "the profits of a bishop, and not as a baron of parliament . . . the income of his jurisdiction."[30] Meanwhile, in Roman Catholic circles, it had become a pejorative term for excessive devotion, and only in the nineteenth century was it recovered to focus attention on the diverse traditions of spirituality in differing monastic and other movements. From the end of the nineteenth century, a renewed interest in mysticism, shared by Catholics, Anglo-Catholics, and even Quakers, promoted a recovery of historical sources of the lives of the saints. In 1922 this led to Pierre Pourrat's three-volume survey on *Christian Spirituality*, defining it as "that part of theology which deals with Christian perfection and the ways that lead to it,"[31] both in terms of ascetic practices and of mystical experiences. There followed Louis Bouyer's *History of Christian Spirituality* in 1960,[32] and a great flood of publications since then. Several dictionaries have also been issued, especially the ongoing, authoritative *Dictionnaire de spiritualité*, which commenced in 1932.

Meanwhile, the divorce between theology and spirituality has become much more apparent, leading to what Hans urs von Balthasar has condemned as "the disappearance of the 'complete' theologian . . . the theologian who is

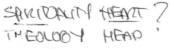

SPIRITUALITY HEART ?
THEOLOGY HEAD

also a saint."[33] But it is with the recovery of Trinitarian theology in the past two decades that the divine and relational life of God has become more challenging, as the life God intends the Christian to share with him. Christian doctrine cannot be taught abstractly, for God is not abstract in nature. Thus the mystery of the Trinity is about the intrinsically relational nature of God and God's desire to create fellowship and community with us, that we also may share our lives with each other. The new focus now in the relationship between theology and spirituality is how to overcome the divide between the experience of faith and intellectual reflection on it.[34]

Likewise, if spirituality is challenging us to reconsider the presentation of theology, it is also asking questions of the meaning, interpretation, and method of historical inquiry. We must take the past seriously on its own terms, sympathetic to the attitudes and nature of its own periods of changing consciousness, including self-understanding. Then we must continue to revise our own heritage in the light of past influences and contributions to our own times. Also, we need to be more aware of the greater versatility of the human condition than we tend to restrict it in our own mind-set. So even a study of medieval society has the potential to expand our own consciousness, if we refrain from interpreting it as restrictive. Indeed, because it was more "religious" than our spiritually starved secular environment, it may actually enlarge our vision of the Christian life. Even our basic notions of what we mean by sanctity, devotion, prayer, Bible reading, love of God and of neighbor, may be enlarged and deepened.

Meanwhile, these new understandings may cause significant revision of our traditional historical interpretations of past religious movements and of people. For now we see more clearly there has always been an underside to history, kept hidden by the oppression of powerful interests. The writing or ignoring of past events is still a selective choice often made by those in authority, whereas the nature of the body of Christ should be one of recognition of all the people of God, the marginalized as well as those given prominence.[35] When we read the spiritual classics, we are also exposed to the strangeness of previous expressions of faith, which challenge us rather than confirm us in our restrictive, even biased, readings and perspectives.

From all we have surveyed, it is evident the challenge of Christian spirituality is a major event in our times. Could it be that instead of Bloom's contemporary phase of "cultural chaos," which we noted early in the chapter, we may be entering instead new possibilities for a relational reformation, through the endorsement of Christian spirituality?

3

Spiritual Formation in Christ Is for the Whole Life and the Whole Person

Dallas Willard

Dallas Willard is a professor of philosophy at the University of Southern California in Los Angeles, where he has taught since 1965. He holds degrees from Tennessee Temple College, Baylor University, and the University of Wisconsin (Ph.D.). An expert in the philosophy of Edmund Husserl, Willard has emerged as one of the most prolific and influential voices calling for the renewal for spiritual theology among evangelical Christians. Among his most popular books in this area are *The Spirit of the Disciplines* (1988), *The Divine Conspiracy* (1998), *Hearing God* (1999), and *Renovation of the Heart* (2002).

Willard writes with warmth, clarity, and a sense of urgency, all of which are evident in this essay. He examines here the coinherence of theological integrity and spiritual vitality by focusing on the theme of discipleship and obedience to Christ. Spiritual formation is interpreted as "shaping our spirit toward union and action with a triune God." Working from both biblical and theological materials, Willard addresses eight issues related to the emergence of spiritual formation as a major concern for evangelicals.

∽✧∾ ∽✧∾ ∽✧∾

When the letter of invitation from Dean George and Professor McGrath came, I was happy to see that the conference was supposed "to emphasize the coinherence of theological integrity and spiritual vitality."

That is a lovely term: *coinherence*. The idea it conveys is that theological integrity and spiritual vitality are to be properties of the same thing, the individual life. That's what coinherence means. When you have a lump of sugar to drop into your coffee (if you do that sort of thing), square, white, and sweet are properties that "coinhere" in the same thing, the lump of sugar.

In the case of theological integrity and spiritual vitality, I think the idea is that you really can't have the one without the other. Anyone who has the one must have the other. Can we accept that meaning? If we do, then we are in real trouble with our current practices. For today the most common circumstance is that we find them, or what is claimed to be them, in separation from each other.

I try to address some of the issues that I think are most important here, and I have eight points to cover.

Jesus said, "I will show you what he is like who comes to me and hears my words and puts them into practice. He is like a man building a house, who dug down deep and laid the foundation on rock. When a flood came, the torrent struck that house but could not shake it, because it was well built" (Luke 6:47–48). And Jesus said, "Why do you call me, 'Lord, Lord,' and do not do what I say?" (Luke 6:46). Again he said, "All authority in heaven and on earth has been given to me. Therefore go and make disciples of all nations, baptizing them in the name of the Father and of the Son and of the Holy Spirit" (Matt. 28:18–19). I hope you will agree with me that he didn't just mean getting them thoroughly wet as we say the words "over them," but rather that "baptizing them in the name" refers to surrounding them, immersing them in the reality of the Trinitarian community. And then we are to "teach them to do everything that I have commanded you." That would be a natural next step, completing the process Jesus assigned to his people. "Everyone who hears these words of mine and puts them into practice is like a wise man who built his house on the rock. The rain came down, the streams rose, and the winds blew and beat against that house; yet it did not fall, because it had its foundation on the rock" (Matt 7:24–25).

Would a person be excused if they took these words to mean that Jesus intends *obedience* for us? The missing note in evangelical life today is not in the first instance *spirituality* but rather *obedience*. We have generated a variety of religion to which obedience is not regarded as essential.

I do not understand how anyone can look ingenuously at the contents of the Scripture and say that Jesus intends anything else for us but obedience. So my first point is simply, "Life in Christ has to do with obedience to his teaching." If we do not start there, forget about any distinctively *Christian* spirituality. Such obedience is expressed in the great words as well as the small words—the great words, "Love the Lord your God with all your heart and with all your soul and with all your strength and with all your mind" and "Love your neighbor as yourself" (Luke 10:27); the little words, "Bless those that curse you," "Go the second mile," and so forth.

Now, you may think you will not explicitly encounter the big words in ordinary life, and they are a bit more elusive. But you certainly will run into the small words. Even if you only do such a thing as drive an automobile in our society, you will find people who curse you, and you will be given the challenge of blessing them. "And if anyone gives even a cup of cold water to one of these little ones because he is my disciple, I tell you the truth, he will certainly not lose his reward" (Matt. 10:42)—and so forth. These are some of the "small" words of Christ.

Being alive in Christ is a spiritual matter (see John 3). So life in Christ essentially involves spirituality. When you survey the scene on the Internet, you almost want to run from what shows up when you put "spirituality" after the "www." It's unbelievable! And of course, with "Christian spirituality," so called, one also finds there, and in life generally, a weird, weird world. But we have to remember that, all this notwithstanding, God *is* spirit, and God is looking for those who will worship God *in spirit* and in truth. I believe that means people who, in the core of their being, beyond all "appearance" in the physical world by means of their body, want to stand clear and right before God. They are people who wholly devote their innermost being—the heart, will, or human spirit—to doing so.

God is looking for such people. Occasionally, God might find someone who was not perfectly guided doctrinally or practically but *was* looking for God and trying to worship God in spirit and truth. God might just communicate with such a person and enliven his or her spirit with God's Spirit. God might lead them onward toward himself, whereas there isn't much hope for one who is not seeking to worship God in spirit and in truth. Paul says in Philippians 3:3, "For it is we who are the circumcision, we who worship by the Spirit of God, who glory in Christ Jesus, and who put no confidence in the flesh." That means we put confidence in the spiritual: our spirit together with God's Spirit (Romans 8 and 2 Corinthians 4 and 5).

"The flesh" most often shows up in the Scripture not in association with cigarettes and whiskey and wild, wild women but with religious activities. When Paul in Philippians 3:4 says, "I have more [reasons to put confidence in the flesh]," he proceeds to give us a list of *religious credentials* that is quite overwhelming. When, to the Corinthians, Paul talks about *carnal* Christians, he is referring to people who are disputing about who is the best speaker and leader in the church. This is a sobering thought when you consider what is routinely done among us today. The flesh stands, basically, for the natural—the spiritually unassisted—abilities of human beings. It is possible in our religious activities to depend entirely on the flesh in this sense.

I beg you to study Romans 8:1 carefully: "Therefore, there is now no condemnation for those who are in Christ Jesus, [who do not live according to the sinful nature but according to the Spirit,] because through Christ Jesus the law of the Spirit of life set me free from the law of sin and death." I say to you very soberly that this is *not* a passage about *the forgiveness of sins*. Indeed, I should just state at this point that we have a serious problem within our usual evangelical hermeneutic of reading passages that are *not* about forgiveness of sins as if they were, when they are really about *new life* (that is, foundational "spirituality") in Christ.

One of the most famous of these passages is John 3. This is not a forgiveness passage. It is about life from above. It is about spiritual life. It is about life in the Spirit and about those who are born of the Spirit. When you come to the end of that great passage in Romans 8:1–14 you find "those who are led by the Spirit of God are sons of God." As you study that passage you will realize, I think, that Paul is referring to a power that enters our life, a spiritual power that comes with regeneration. This power is, of course, God, and all the instrumentalities at God's disposal, from the Holy Spirit, to the resurrected Christ in his kingdom, to the power of the written Word, to the angelic ambassadors, to other individuals who are heirs of salvation, and to the spiritual life and treasures that are in the body of Christ, visible as well as triumphant.

What then is *spirit*? Spirit is *unbodily, personal reality and power*. In the way you might expect from someone who spends most of his time in philosophy, I'm going to try to use words very carefully, and one of the things I find most distressing in the current scene is that many of us have no concept of *spirit* at all. As a result, God becomes, for many Christians, little more than an oblong blur. We have people today in "Christian" settings who believe in Jesus but not in God. They do not have a clear enough idea of God to form a belief about him. And much of their problem derives from their lack of understanding of the spiritual type of being.

Biblically, God is, paradigmatically, unbodily personal power. Everything that is bodily—the physical universe, in whole and in part—comes from God and depends on God. Spirit can enter into and be with body (as is the case with the human spirit), but it is not *from* body, even in the human case. It does not derive from the physical.

Spirit is *personal*, not impersonal. None of that "the force be with you" stuff is relevant here. This is one of the major things we have to understand in today's context. Of course, the *personal* nature of spirit is seen at its highest and clearest in the Trinitarian nature of God. The Puritans saw God as a sweet society. What personality is, is finally understandable only in the light of the Trinitarian nature of God. God is Spirit. God is personal reality and power— the power that works by thought and choice and evaluation—not a blind force that can be manipulated if you can only find the correct technique.

What you see when the veil is drawn back on the many "spiritualities" of our day is that they are so many versions of *idolatry*. They are nothing but human attempts to use human means to achieve identity and power for the individual. Idolatry is marked by the will to use God for our purposes. So many of our "spiritualities" today, including many that go under the name of "Chris tian," are really forms of idolatry.

I was leading a retreat at a Catholic retreat center some time ago, and one of the staff came around to make an announcement that included the line "Father so-and-so will be holding sessions on Zen spirituality at such-and-such a time. Father so-and-so is famous for *reintroducing* Buddhist meditation into Catholic theology." Reintroducing? Many people today in the broad fields of "spirituality" actually think that Zen spirituality was seen in Jesus and, unfortunately, lost until recently, when some have "reintroduced" it. Zen spirituality is one form of idolatry of the human self.

Spirituality as now generally understood usually refers to *a human dimension*, not to the power of God. Sometimes it even refers to the power of demons and the power of the devil, because he, too, is a spiritual being, as explained above.

"A spirituality," as that term has now come to be used, simply refers to *a way of conducting religious life*. A spirituality may, then, be no more than an exercise of human abilities. So now we have Quaker spirituality, Franciscan spirituality, Benedictine spirituality, and even Baptist spirituality.

It is true that there are different ways of "doing" religion. There is a way Catholics do it, Baptists do it, Hindus do it, and so forth. A few years ago, I got on the plane in Chicago to go to Louisville and everyone on that plane looked like a Baptist to me. There is an outward form of being Baptist. Now, I can't actually state how Baptists look—I can't say what it is. But I can recognize it because I've been in the middle of it all my life.

That is why I find a special thrill in standing under the picture of Lottie Moon in the dome of Beeson Divinity Chapel. She has been a part of my life since I was a child: the yearly missions offering, teaching about Lottie Moon's life, and so on. I'm so glad to see her standing up there by all these other guys. She's great. It's a thrill to be a part of what she's part of. All of this relates to the fact that, as Paul says to the Corinthians, "We have this treasure in jars of clay" (2 Cor. 4:7). You cannot avoid having a vessel or jar of clay. You have a Baptist vessel, and you have a Benedictine vessel, and a Quaker vessel, and so forth.

The problem comes when we mistake the vessel for the treasure, for *the treasure is the life and power of Jesus Christ*. We have to have a form of life, a vessel, a "spirituality" if you wish. None of us is given to be an entirely spiritual being now. Being body, and therefore social, is a part of us. I will eternally be the son of my parents. I will always be the son of Albert and Mamie Willard.

And I will always be the person who was brought up in the First Baptist Church of Buffalo, Missouri, and the First Baptist Church of Willow Springs, Missouri, and Shiloh Baptist Church in Rover, Missouri. I thank God for all that. But to make that "spirituality" my life—that's the point at which I may begin to think that being a good Baptist is more important than being a good Christian, than being obedient with my whole person to Jesus Christ. At that point I am back in flesh and have become spiritually off-balance.

Substitute for "Baptist" anything you want. It doesn't make much difference. It is all the same if "a spirituality" is just a way of conducting the religious life. The problem is that conducting the religious life can become an entirely cultural kind of thing, and we can idolize our religious culture. There are many, many ways of doing this. It is so important for us to remember that a culture can capture us and shut off our access to the supernatural spirituality of the kingdom of God explained in John 3 and Romans 8, for example.

I'm sorry to say this, but too much of what we call Christian is *not* a manifestation of the supernatural life of God in our souls. Too much of what we call Christian is really just human. The church of Jesus Christ is not necessarily present when there is a correct administration of the sacrament and faithful preaching of the Word of God. The church of God is present where people gather together in the power of the resurrected life of Jesus Christ. It is possible to have the administration of the sacraments and the preaching of the Word of God and have it simply be a human exercise. The misunderstanding of the church in this respect is one of the things that creates a primary problem for the integration of theology and spirituality. A bad theology will kill any prospects of a spirituality that comes from life in Christ.

The first of my eight points was that life in Christ, and therefore *biblical* spirituality, has to do with obedience to Christ. My second point was that life in Christ is a matter of the "spirit." My third point was that spiritual life is a matter of living our lives *from* the reality of God. My fourth point is that Christian spirituality is supernatural *because* obedience to Christ is supernatural and cannot be accomplished except in the power of a "life from above."

The will to obey is the engine that pulls the train of spirituality in Christ. But "spirituality" in many Christian circles has simply become another dimension of Christian consumerism. We have generated a body of people who consume Christian services and think that that is Christian faith. Consumption of Christian services replaces obedience to Christ. And spirituality is one more thing to consume. I go to many, many conferences and talk about these things, and so often I see these people who are just consuming more Christian services.

But we must talk about spirituality, and this naturally leads us to talk also about *spiritual disciplines*. Spiritual disciplines are activities in our power in which we engage to enable us to do what we cannot do by direct effort. The singing of hymns, for example, is a major spiritual discipline. I refer not just to singing them in church but to singing them throughout our daily life. Now, we need to say, under this fourth point—that Christian spirituality is supernatural and focused on obedience to Christ—that when we come to sing our hymns, we must keep our mind and will alive to what we are singing. Only so will the outcome be supernatural.

I love that old hymn "Draw Me Nearer, Nearer, Nearer Precious Lord, to the Cross Where Thou Hast Died." But what does that mean, to be drawn nearer to the cross of Jesus? What does that mean in practice? Does that just mean a warmer heart now and then, or does it mean *living* in step with the Jesus of the cross and resurrection? I think it means the latter. I think it means union in action. *Union in action with the triune God is Christian spirituality*. That is where the life is drawing its substance from God. Draw me nearer! Or "Grow in grace." What does that mean? It does not mean get more forgiveness. I return to that point in a moment.

The fifth point concerns *spiritual formation*. "Spiritual formation" refers to the *process* of shaping our spirit and giving it a definite character. It means the formation of our spirit in conformity with the Spirit of Christ. Of course it involves the Holy Spirit in action, but the focus of spiritual formation is the formation of *our* spirit. (Forgive me if I am wrong, but I equate spirit, will, and heart in the human being.) Spiritual formation in Christ is the *process* whereby the inmost being of the individual (the heart, will, or spirit) takes on the quality or character of Jesus himself. That's what spiritual formation is, and we need to say something about why there has been such a buzz around this terminology in recent years.

Spiritual formation is not a new topic in the church at large, but it is a new topic in evangelical circles. I think the reason is that we have come into a time of obvious need for something new and deeper. *Discipleship* is a term that has pretty well lost its meaning because of the way it has been misused. Discipleship on the theological right has come to mean preparation for soul winning, under the direction of parachurch efforts that had "discipleship" farmed out to them because the local church really wasn't doing it. On the left, discipleship has come to mean some form of social activity or social service: from serving in soup lines, to political protest, to whatever. The term *discipleship* has currently been ruined so far as any solid biblical content is concerned.

Another thing that has led to the interest in spiritual formation is the breakdown of the significance of denominational differences. It is rare that you find anyone today who thinks that his or her denominational identity ensures very much in the way of Christian substance. Some might still believe it does, but those will be pretty narrow circles. Sociologically, we have lost the significance of denominational membership. Most people who are confessing Christians, evangelicals or not, drift from one kind of church to another and simply look to the local congregation and its leadership as a basis of choosing their church, not to denomination—or certainly not to it alone. Most younger people, especially, have no idea of what the differences in denominations amount to. Recently the daughter of an acquaintance asked him, "Which chain do we belong to?"

I would be quite interested to know, for example, how many Baptist churches now, as they did in my youth, insist, when you take membership in them, that you move your membership to another *Baptist* church when you move to another location.

With the breakdown of the denominational language and association, in any case, there is a need for a new language, and "spiritual formation" has stepped into that void to express the essence and depth of our commitment to Christ. It is, indeed, an interdenominational or nondenominational language. But the main thing that it tries to do is refer us to the need for *inward* transformation, and it is now statistically and anecdotally common to find that Christians generally do not differ significantly from non-Christians in our culture. Now, some Christians do. If you survey correctly, you will find that there is a group of Christians who do differ radically from non-Christians; but that kind of commitment is, even among Christians themselves, understood to be a kind of spiritual option or luxury. So my fifth point is: spiritual formation is the process whereby the inmost being of the individual takes on the quality or character of Jesus himself.

Now, my sixth point is that such a process is not a matter of the human spirit or heart *only*. We must be careful how we talk about the person and its several parts. Rather, spiritual formation is a whole life process dealing with change in every essential part of the person. We don't work just on our spirit but on everything that makes up our personality.

Spiritual formation does not aim at controlling action. This is an absolutely crucial point, and one that distinguishes spiritual formation in Christ from what is done in most twelve-step groups. If, in spiritual formation, you focus on action alone, you will fall into the deadliest of legalisms and you will kill other souls and die yourself. You will get a social conformity. That has happened over and over again in the past, and it is where the various "spiritualities" past and present begin to exact a dreadful price—focusing on the outward activities and the actions, not on the inward person, not on "the spirit." God is looking for those who worship God in truth and in spirit. We cannot fake before God. We should remember that God looks on the heart, humans look on the outward appearance. To focus on action alone is to fall into Pharisaism of the worst kind and to kill the soul.

So spiritual formation is a holistic process, and to help us grasp this point I am going to suggest you create your own visual aid. If you would draw a circle about the size of a half dollar on a piece of paper, and write in it the words *spirit*, *heart*, and *will*. And then around that another circle, and label it "mind," including thought and feeling. The third circle is "body." The fourth circle is "social relations." Your final circle is your soul. So you have spirit (will), mind (thoughts and feelings), body, social relations, and soul.

If you want to divide the whole person up in other ways, be my guest. The point I need to make is: *spiritual formation is a matter of all aspects of the self.* It is not a matter of just the spirit or heart, or even of the soul. Now, the spirit, heart, or will is the executive center of the self. It is where action ultimately comes from, and it is very important. But it does not operate in isolation from the mind, from the body, from the social relationships, and from the soul. It operates in dependence on them. If we are going to do spiritual formation, we have to work on *all* those aspects.

One of the greatest temptations that we face as evangelicals, including the "charismatic" stream of the church, is the idea that the personality and the heart are going to be transformed by some sort of lightning strike of the Spirit. You can call it revival or whatever you want. There is going to be this great boom, and then suddenly you will be transformed in every aspect of your being. No need for a process; it will all be accomplished passively and immediately.

But now consider. When the people of Israel came into the promised land, the first city they approached was Jericho, and the walls of Jericho, we know, fell down flat. Tell me, how many more walls of cities fell down flat in the conquest of the promised land? What did the Israelites have to do with the rest of those cities? They had to *take* them, didn't they? And we are today lulled into a false passivity by our basic teachings about the nature of salvation and the work of God in our souls. We like to quote verses like "Apart from me you can do nothing" (John 15:5), which is absolutely true. But we forget that *if you do nothing, it will be without God.* And this, while not a Scripture verse, is also absolutely true.

We today are very uneasy about human activity, and we have words such as *synergism*, which in some theological circles is a dirty word. But when we go that route, we will be at a loss before the call of discipleship, or the call, in Paul's language, to put off the old person and put on the new. What we must understand is that spiritual formation is a process that involves the transformation of the whole person, and that the whole person must be *active with Christ* in the work of spiritual formation. Spiritual transformation into Christlikeness is not going to happen to us unless we act. I'll return to that in just a moment as I conclude with my eighth point, which tries to deal with a few troublesome issues.

Now, my seventh point consists in illustrating how the transformation of these various aspects of the human self affects our powers at large. Think a moment about thought. Thought is a subdimension of the mind. Now, if we are going to be spiritually transformed, we have to have transformation of our thought life. Remember that Paul said in Romans 1:28: "They did not think it worthwhile to retain the knowledge of God." Frankly, what that means is they could not stand to think about God and about who God is. If *you* are on the throne of your life, you won't want to think about God, because God is, after all, *God*, and there will not be room for God and anybody else on the throne of your life. And when human beings put God out of their knowledge, as Paul said, God gave them up to themselves.

God is not pushy—for now, in any case. God is not going to overwhelm you if you don't want God. God gives you the power to put the divine self out of your mind. And even if you want God, you have to seek God. I realize that there is a sense in which God is already seeking you, and I am not trying to dispose of that; but we misunderstand what is our part and what is God's part. God is ready to act. God is acting. We are not waiting on God, and, if it doesn't hurt your theology too badly, God is waiting on us to respond. And you know we have a problem here. As I often point out, today we are not only saved by grace; we are *paralyzed* by it. We will preach to you for an hour that you can do nothing to be saved, and then sing to you for forty-five minutes trying to get you to do something to be saved. We really have a problem with activity and passivity in our theology.

We have to think about *working with* God on the contents of our minds. David says in Psalm 16, "I have set the Lord always before me." What do we say to David? Synergism! Works! "I have set the Lord always before me. Because he is at my right hand, I will not be shaken" (Ps. 16:8). Here is *our* action right at the heart of that great messianic psalm.

How, then, shall we set the Lord always before us? *Bible memorization* is absolutely fundamental to spiritual formation. If I had to—and of course, I don't have to—choose among all the disciplines of the spiritual life and take only one, I would choose Bible memorization. I would not be a pastor of a church that did not have a program of Bible memorization in it, because Bible memorization is a fundamental way of filling our minds with what they need. "Do not let this Book of the Law depart from your mouth" (Josh. 1:8). That is where we need it! In our mouths. How did it get in your mouth? Memorization. I often point out to people how much trouble they would have stayed out of if they had been muttering Scripture. You meditate in it day and night. What does that mean? Keep it, and therefore God, before our minds all the time. Can anyone really imagine that he or she has anything better to keep before the mind? "That you may be careful to do everything written in it. Then you will be prosperous and successful" (Josh. 1:8).

I often tell people I can give them one verse that is worth more than any college education, and it is Joshua 1:8. It will guarantee them the life they only dimly dream to be possible. How does it work? Well, I often use phrases from the Twenty-third Psalm, for example. On a given day I will renew constantly in my mind the words "He guides me in paths of righteousness for his name's sake." Or on a particularly difficult day I may use "You prepare a table before me in the presence of my enemies."

Much more could be said about the effects of transforming the arena of our thought life, but the transformation of our feelings is also important. Many people live their lives filled with anxiety or anger or contempt. They fill their lives with resentment. They willingly fill their lives with lust. Our culture constantly excites us to lust. Not just for sex, but of course sex remains one of the most powerful strings to pull to get attention and action, and we constantly have solicitation going on in this arena.

But you have to change all that in spiritual formation. After all, it is not the law of gravity. You have to change your feelings. (Of course, with God's help.) If Joseph had filled his mind with thoughts of romance or sexual indulgence with Mrs. Potiphar, she would have got *him* and not just his coat.

When you hear another story about a man or woman who has, as we say, "fallen," I hope you will realize that the sad thing is not just that the person fell but what has been in the person's mind all along—possibly for many years or even all of his or her life. That is where the work must be done for spiritual formation. It is not just "action control." That is the error of the Pharisee.

But think for a moment of spiritual formation in the arena of social relationships. Think of the person who has, by the grace of God, cultivated in his or her relationships to others *the life of the servant*. Everywhere that person is, and all he or she does, that person performs as a servant.

Remember that Jesus said, "I am among you as one who serves" (Luke 22:27). And he also said, "The one that is greatest among you is the one who is servant of all." By the way, it is dreadful to see this recommended as only another *technique* for succeeding in leadership. Jesus was not giving techniques for successful leadership. He was telling us *who the great person is*. He or she is the one who is servant of all. Being a servant shifts one's relationship to everyone. What do you think that would do to sexual temptation, if you think of yourself as a servant? What do you think that would do to covetousness? What do you think that would do to the feeling of resentment because you haven't got what you think you deserve? I'll tell you. It will lift the burden.

How many of our own personal efforts, as well as our ministerial and teaching efforts, are directed toward spiritual transformation in this holistic sense?

To drive the point home, I often put this challenge: I do not know of a denomination or local church in existence that has as its goal to teach its people to do everything Jesus said. I'm not talking about a whim or a wish, but a *plan*. I ask you sincerely, is this on *your* agenda? To teach disciples surrounded in the triune reality to do everything Jesus said? If that is your goal, you will certainly find a way to bring theological integrity and spiritual vitality together. But as you do so, you will find both your theology and your spirituality refreshingly and strongly modified.

Now, my eighth and final point is just *some issues that always come up*. And the first is *grace and works*. Isn't this "spiritual formation" stuff really just another term for "works"? Aren't we just talking about works? Yes, we're talking about works, if you mean "Am I going to have to do something?" You cannot be a pew potato and simultaneously engage in spiritual formation in Christ's likeness. You have to take your whole life into discipleship to Jesus Christ, if that's what you mean by works. But, in contrast, nothing works like genuine faith or trust in God.

Much of our problem is *not*, as is often said, that we have failed to get what is in our head down in our heart. Much of what hinders us is that we have had a lot of mistaken theology in our head, and it *has* got down into our heart. It is controlling our inner dynamics so that they cannot, without the aid of the Word and the Spirit, pull one another straight.

May I just give you this word? "Grace is not opposed to effort, it is opposed to earning." Earning is an attitude. Effort is an action. Grace, you know, does not just have to do with forgiveness of sins alone. Many people *don't* know this, and that is one major result of the cutting down of the gospel to a theory of justification that has happened in our time. I have heard leading evangelical spokesmen say that grace has only to do with guilt. Many people today understand justification as the only essential result of the gospel, and the gospel they preach is—and you will hear this said over and over by the leading presenters of evangelical faith—that your sins can be forgiven. That's it!

By contrast, I make bold to say, the gospel of the entire New Testament is that you can have new life now in the kingdom of God if you will trust Jesus Christ. Not just something he did, or something he said, but trust the whole person of Christ in everything he touches—which is, everything. "There is one God and one mediator between God and men, the man Christ Jesus" (1 Tim. 2:5). And if you would really like to be into consuming grace, just lead a holy life. The true saint burns grace like a 747 burns fuel on take-off. Become the kind of person who routinely does what Jesus did and said. You will consume much more grace by leading a holy life than you will by sinning, because every holy act you do will have to be upheld by the grace of God. And that "upholding" is totally the unmerited favor of God in action.

It is the life of regeneration and resurrection—*and* justification, which is absolutely vital, for our sins have to be forgiven. But justification is not something *separable* from regeneration, which naturally moves into sanctification and glorification.

If you preach a gospel that has only to do with the forgiveness of sins, however, you will be as we are today: stuck in a position where you have faith over here and obedience and abundance over there, and no way to get from here to there, because the necessary bridge is discipleship. If there is anything we should know by now, it is that a gospel of justification alone does not generate disciples. Discipleship is a life of learning from Jesus Christ how to live in the kingdom of God now as he did. If you want to be a person of grace, then live a holy life of discipleship, because the only way you can do that is on a steady diet of grace. Works of the kingdom live from grace.

The second issue is *perfectionism*. People quickly become worried about this when you get really serious about spiritual formation, and with some good reason, no doubt. But most of us would not have to worry about perfection for a few months, at least. Still, I know many people in evangelical circles who are more stirred up over perfectionism than they are about people continuing in sin. Now, just for the record, as far as I know, we are all going to have room for improvement as long as we live.

I love this quote from St. Augustine:

> If anyone supposes that with man, living, as he still does in this mortal life, it may be possible for him to dispel and clear off every obscurity induced by corporeal and carnal fancies, and to obtain to the serenest light of immutable truth, and to cleave constantly and unswervingly to this with a mind wholly estranged from the course of this present life, that man understands neither what he asks nor who he is that is putting such a supposition . . . If ever the soul is helped to reach beyond the cloud by which all of the earth is covered (cf. Ecclus. Xxiv, 6), that is to say, beyond this carnal darkness with which the whole terrestrial life is covered, it is simply as if he were touched with a swift coruscation, only to sink back into his natural infirmity, the desire surviving by which he may again be raised to the heights, but his purity being insufficient to establish him there. The more, however, anyone can do this, the greater is he, while the less he can do so the less is he.[1]

No matter how far we progress, there will always be in us a subdued, glowing coal of possibility that, if blown by the right wind, will burst into a flame of iniquity. But that doesn't have to happen. And as for people who plead for continuing in sin, I must ask them: "Are you planning on it?" Sometimes it sounds like they are.

So my third issue is, *we cannot have a gospel dealing only with sin*. We have to have a gospel that leads us to new life in Christ, and then spirituality can be presented as a natural development of such new life. But if we divide between justification and regeneration in such a way that the gospel is *only* "Believe Jesus died for your sins and you will go to heaven when you die," we are stuck with a theology that is inherently resistant to a vital spirituality. Now, please don't misunderstand me; that statement is strictly true. But we have come to accept "Believe Jesus died for your sins" in such a way that does not involve "Believe Jesus in everything." The gospel is new life through faith in Jesus Christ. And if you don't preach that, then there will be no possibility of a spirituality that is theologically sound or a theology that is spiritually vital.

Finally, let us remember *the inescapability of serious process over time*. We cannot continue to hope that lightning is going to strike us, and out of this we will come glowing with spirituality. This approach is common among "charismatic" writers. I don't like that language, for I don't really think there is such a thing as a noncharismatic Christian—but that's a different story. Some have critiqued the Charismatic movement as neither very ill nor very well. And, if I may say so, that is true of the Evangelical movement generally. The prescription offered for this malady is new spiritual fire. This renewed fire, we are told, will transform the individual, the church, and the society.

It is the essence of futility to talk this way. And you can translate these words out of the Charismatic movement and into the Evangelical. Generally expressed, baptism in the Spirit, spiritual experiences, high acts of worship, and other experiences of worship *do not transform character*. They just don't do it. I am one who has had glorious experiences, and who owes much to them. They have a special role in the spiritual life. I don't talk about the ones I have had, because I think they are between me and the Lord, and in any case they are to be known by their effects. They have meant a lot to me, but *they* have not transformed my character.

Now, you or others must be the judges of how far my transformed character goes, if that is of any interest at all; but from my own point of view, I can tell you that the transformation of character comes through learning how to act in concert with Jesus Christ. Character is formed through action, and it is transformed through action, including carefully planned and grace-sustained disciplines. And to enter the path of obedience to Jesus Christ—intending to obey him, and intending to learn whatever I have to learn in order to obey him—is the true path of spiritual formation or transformation.

We should expect many profound, key moments. I don't want to miss a one of them. I love them, and sometimes when I get to the end of the Lord's Prayer, having had a wonderful session in it—you can spend hours in it and submerge yourself in it—I don't want to say, "Amen," I want to say,

"Whoopee!" Thanks be to God! Thine is the kingdom! Thine is the power! Thine is the glory! Forever! "Amen" is just a little too mild.

I hope your life is full of "Whoopee!" moments. We should all have them, but they will not transform us. What transforms us is the will to obey Jesus Christ from a life that is one with his resurrected reality day by day, learning obedience by inward transformation.

Paul understood this well. We close with his words to the Colossians: "Since, then, you have been raised with Christ, set your hearts on things above, where Christ is seated at the right hand of God. Set your minds on things above, not on earthly things. For you died, and your life is now hidden with Christ in God. When Christ, who is your life, appears, then you also will appear with him in glory" (Col. 3:1–4).

What's the next move? Does anyone know? It is "Put to death, therefore, whatever belongs to your earthly nature: sexual immorality, impurity, lust, evil desires and greed, which is idolatry. Because of these, the wrath of God is coming. You used to walk in these ways, in the life you once lived. But now you must rid yourselves of all such things as these: anger, rage, malice, slander, and filthy language from your lips. Do not lie to each other, since you have taken off your old self with its practices and have put on the new self, which is being renewed in knowledge in the image of its Creator" (Col. 3:5–10).

What an incredible, sweeping change of mind is this, in which "there is no Greek or Jew, circumcised or uncircumcised, barbarian, Scythian [the Scythian was the utter bottom of the human barrel in Paul's world], slave or free, but Christ is all, and is in all. Therefore, as God's chosen people, holy and dearly loved, ["put on bowels"—guts, hearts, "innards" (as we say in Missouri)—of] "compassion, kindness, humility, gentleness and patience . . . and over all these virtues put on love [agape], which binds them all together in perfect unity. Let the peace of Christ rule in your hearts, since as members of one body you were called to peace. And be thankful. Let the word of Christ dwell in you richly as you teach and admonish one another with all wisdom, and as you sing psalms, hymns and spiritual songs with gratitude in your hearts to God" (Col. 3:11–16). And then comes that great seventeenth verse—which solidly drives home the point of our talk, the whole-life nature of our spiritual formation in Christ—"Whatever you do, whether in word or deed, do it all in the name of the Lord Jesus, giving thanks to God the Father through him."

PART 2

Sources

4

Humility and Prayer: The Lukan Jesus and Classical Tradition

Catherine Wright

Catherine J. Wright is assistant professor of New Testament at Bethel College. She is a graduate of Vanguard University (B.A., M.A.) and Baylor University (Ph.D.) After completing graduate studies at Baylor University, she served as an instructor of religion at both Baylor and Texas Christian University. For seven years she served as the minister to youth at Lake Shore Baptist Church in Waco.

This chapter looks at the themes of prayer and humility as set forth in Luke's portrait of Jesus. Wright finds many parallels between the spirituality of Jesus in Luke and the literary culture of the first-century Mediterranean world. She juxtaposes the Gospel narratives with quotations from Plato, Plutarch, Virgil, Xenophon, Seneca, and others. This chapter shows that Christian spirituality did not develop in a vacuum but was resonant with ethical and religious sensibilities present already in other traditions. Recognition of this fact enabled the early Christians to appropriate those aspects of the classical heritage that they found to be consonant with biblical faith. While Wright does not spell out all the implications of this study, it raises important questions about how Christians today can draw on diverse spiritual traditions in formulating a spirituality that is at once meaningful in contemporary culture and faithful to the biblical and apostolic faith.

∽◌∾ ∽◌∾ ∽◌∾

The spirituality of the New Testament is seldom discussed in the academic field of religious studies. It is a shame that so many biblical scholars have such esoteric interests in the text, especially when one considers the question of how first-century readers would have approached the New Testament. First-century readers would have had an intensely practical interest in the text. They would have come to the text in order to learn how to live righteous lifestyles, how to strengthen their faith, or how to grow closer to God. In moving so far away from the practical nature of the text, much of modern biblical scholarship is involved in hermeneutics that are foreign to the nature of the text itself.

We know that first-century Greco-Roman readers would have approached biblical texts for practical reasons because we know that they approached discussions of spirituality with an interest in their own growth and maturity. There was much discussion in the first century regarding a virtuous lifestyle and nourishing a relationship with the gods. By definition, these discussions were practical in nature. The goal of the sage or philosopher was not the ability to assert the worth of virtue but the ability to attain it. Seneca accordingly says that philosophy "is not devised for show. It is not pursued in order that the day may yield some amusement."[1] Philosophy rather "moulds and constructs the soul; it orders our life, guides our conduct, shows us what we should do."[2] Some of these discussions about matters of virtue and spirituality find strong parallels in the writings of the New Testament. Luke's Gospel, in particular, contains strong parallels to the ways in which prayer and humility are treated in the philosophical writings that were known in the first century C.E.[3]

Luke's readers, who participated in the literary culture of the first-century Mediterranean world, would have expected that their heroes be spiritual leaders. Several ancient biographies reflect the cultural assumptions of the first century regarding the importance of prayer and humility in the lives of their heroes.[4] Since Luke portrays Jesus as exhibiting these virtues, and since there are such strong parallels in the ways in which these spiritual disciplines are treated in Luke and in other first-century literary works, Luke's readers are thus led to an important conclusion about Jesus.

Luke's Jesus looks like the most exemplary heroes in first-century Mediterranean culture. He teaches about the issues of prayer and humility in ways that are often similar to the philosophical dialogues known in the first and second centuries. However, not only does he teach about these virtues, he also models them through his own lifestyle. In a society that judged the worthiness of their leaders based on their ability to practice what they taught, Jesus would truly have been seen as the most ideal kind of hero.

The parallels between the portraits of spirituality among ancient Mediterranean heroes and Luke's portrayal of Jesus' spirituality are strong. Ideal leaders in Luke's literary world and Luke's hero, Jesus, are people who pray on similar occasions, for similar purposes, and witness the same kinds of divine responses to prayer. Ideal leaders and the Lukan Jesus also have similar instructions against pride, while upholding their teaching through their own humble attitudes.

PRAYER

Luke's contemporaries considered prayer to be one of the key virtues of ideal leaders. Because Luke emphasizes that Jesus is a person of prayer, Luke's readers would have been encouraged to see Jesus, too, as an ideal leader.

The Occasions for Prayer

Luke clearly demonstrates that Jesus was a person of prayer. Luke not only includes more about Jesus' teaching and habits of prayer than any other Gospel but transforms many narratives about Jesus into stories about Jesus at prayer. Against the diverse backdrop of prayer among the ancient leaders in Luke's milieu, Jesus' prayer life seems to reflect the motivations for prayer that legendary spiritual heroes such as Numa, Cyrus, or Socrates demonstrated.

Continual prayer

Luke's portrait of Jesus' prayer life ranks among the best ancient portraits of spiritual leadership. While many leaders can be seen as people of prayer, some, as Jesus does in Luke, pray continually. Like Jesus, these individuals seem to regard prayer as the lifeblood for sustaining their unique connection with God. For instance, Plutarch comments that Numa, "inclined to the practice of every virtue," "devoted his hours of privacy and leisure, not to enjoyments and money-making, but to the service of the gods, and the rational contemplation of their nature and power."[5] In fact, Numa "passed most of his time, performing sacred functions, or teaching the priests, or engaged in the quiet contemplation of divine things."[6] Xenophon's Socrates also has a habit of continual prayer. Xenophon has Critobulus tell Socrates, "Well, Socrates, I think you are right when you bid me try to begin every undertaking with the gods' help."[7] Xenophon notes that Socrates "offered sacrifices constantly, and made no secret of it, now in his home, now at the altars of the state temples, and he made use of divination with as little secrecy." He notes, "Indeed it had become notorious that Socrates claimed to be guided by 'the deity.'"[8] Luke's portrait of Jesus' prayer life therefore recalls the prayer lives of some of the most exemplary ancient Mediterranean heroes.

Prayer before crucial events

The Lukan Jesus prays before significant events in his life. This pattern is so prevalent in Luke that it seems as if Jesus' prayers prepare the way for the work of God in salvation history. Jesus prays before he receives the Spirit at his baptism (3:22); he prays before choosing the disciples (6:12); he prays before the transfiguration (9:29); he prays before meeting his accusers in Gethsemane (22:39–46); and, even at death, Jesus commits himself to God in prayer (23:46).

Heroes in Luke's literary culture are also frequently seen praying or leading their people in prayer prior to significant events. Military leaders habitually offered prayers or sacrifices before a battle so that they might receive direction and favor from the gods. Xenophon records this practice: "And you observe, I suppose, that men engaged in war try to propitiate the gods before taking action."[9]

Plato's Socrates thinks that prayer should be given at the beginning of every event, small and significant. He thus asks Timaeus to invoke the gods before the immense task of discussing the nature of the world. Timaeus replies, "All men who possess even a small share of good sense call upon God always at the outset of every undertaking, be it small or great."[10]

Many ancient authors portray their heroes as people of prayer and people who pray prior to significant events in their lives. However, some—like the Lukan Jesus—also affirm the spiritual dependence of their heroes on the gods by linking their heroes' prayer habits with the idea that prayer is essential for spiritual growth. Xenophon, for instance, ties Socrates' habit of continual sacrificing to his claim to be guided by "the deity."[11] He also cites Cyrus's understanding of the connection between spiritual power and continual prayer.[12] Similarly Socrates' pattern of praying before every event, which includes his prayers for wisdom and inner beauty prior to discourses about philosophy, cannot be divorced from Plato's portrait of him as a man of eminent wisdom. The ruler Numa's legendary habits of solitary communion with the gods and his prayers for strength to transform his people into a peaceful community also cannot be seen apart from the habits of peace and worship that he instilled in his citizens and the renowned success of his reign.

Luke's auditors who possessed even a rudimentary understanding of the prayer habits of ancient heroes would therefore likely be able to see Jesus' prayer habits among those of the most legendary sages and kings. While they might expect Jesus to be a person who prayed, Luke's portrait of Jesus at prayer might lead ancient auditors to place Jesus in the company of the greatest ideal leaders, heroes who approached prayer as a means to nourish their connection to God.

The Purposes of Prayer

Jesus prays for many purposes in Luke, including for the ability to understand the divine will and for spiritual strength.

To understand the divine will

Jesus' understanding of God's will comes through prayer. His prayer at his baptism is met with a divine ratification of his person and ministry (3:22). Jesus prays for divine guidance before choosing his disciples (6:12). The Gethsemane narrative indicates that Jesus found the strength to embrace God's will while he was at prayer (22:39–46).

Many ideal philosophers and teachers in Mediterranean antiquity, like the Lukan Jesus, sought the divine will or divine wisdom through prayer. Xenophon refers to leaders who before warfare "with sacrifices and omens seek to know what they ought to do and what they ought not to do."[13] Cyrus's father tells him:

> Mere human wisdom does not know how to choose what is best. . . .
> But the gods, my son, the eternal gods, know all things . . . and if men
> consult them, they reveal to those to whom they are propitious what
> they ought to do and what they ought not to do.[14]

Cyrus listens to his father's words. He continually bases his actions on the omens that follow his prayers and sacrifices.[15] At the end of his life, Cyrus, an ideal king and person of prayer, thanks the gods for showing him through signs and wonders "what I ought to do and what I ought not to do."[16]

Plutarch records a narrative about Numa's determination to seek divine will. After being persuaded that accepting kingship will provide an opportunity for him to serve the gods and sway the people toward piety,[17] Numa declares that "his authority must first be ratified by Heaven." Then, he prays aloud and waits to learn the will of the gods.[18] Only after he receives favorable omens does he put on his royal robes.[19] After he assumes the throne, Numa continues to seek the divine will, in keeping with his nature and also his vocation. In keeping with the best examples of ideal heroes, Luke therefore portrays Jesus as one who is continually seeking the divine will.

To obtain personal strength

Many ancient heroes, like the Lukan Jesus, pray for personal strength. Plutarch's Lycurgus, after determining to bring about a spiritual revolution in his city, goes to Delphi to ask for the god's help.[20] Similarly, Numa "called in the gods to aid and assist him" in the task of moving his citizens toward peace and piety,[21] a task that he saw as his service to the gods.[22] The request for the ability to create a state that mimics a divine kingdom is similar to the Lukan request for the establishment of God's kingdom (11:2). Such a request is seen in Plato's *Laws*: "Let us invoke the presence of the God at the establishment of the State; and may he hearken, and hearkening may he come, propitious and kindly to us-ward, to help us in the fashioning of the State and its laws."[23]

Socrates believes in seeking divine aid in order to live up to his calling to be a true philosopher. Clearly acknowledging a divine hand in his gifts, he prays that his insight and beauty will grow: "Be kind and gracious to me; do not in anger take from me the art of love which thou didst give me, and deprive me not of sight, but grant unto me to be even more than now esteemed by the beautiful."[24] He describes the tasks of an ideal philosopher and states that that hypothetical person "is likely to be such as you and I might pray that we ourselves may become."[25]

In Luke's literary culture, ancient heroes seek divine aid to do their part in bringing about an ideal state or to receive divine wisdom to fulfill their callings or to achieve the ability to live a lifestyle of the highest virtue. While many leaders pray to receive divine favor in battle or for aid in the midst of a crisis, some pray in order to remain true to their calling to live a life of virtue and to encourage such a lifestyle in others. When Luke shows Jesus receiving divine wisdom, encouragement, and strength through prayer, his auditors might well see Jesus in the company of the greatest heroes of history, who also depended on prayer for the understanding and strength to do their part in bringing about a virtuous state or kingdom.

The Responses to Prayer

Jesus repeatedly tells his disciples to pray because God will answer. The Lukan narrative of what happens in response to Jesus' prayers affirms the truthfulness of his teachings. When Jesus prays, he, and sometimes those with him, often observes or hears God's response. Jesus' prayer at his baptism is followed by a dove alighting on him and a voice from heaven affirming him (3:21–22). Jesus' prayer at the transfiguration is met with his transformed appearance, heavenly visitors, and a verbal divine affirmation of his ministry (9:29–36). His prayer in Gethsemane brings help in the form of an angel (22:43). These observable, audible responses to Jesus' prayers have many parallels in the ancient Mediterranean world. When heroes pray, the gods respond in visible/audible ways.

Divine revelation

Many ancient heroes receive a divine revelation in response to prayer. In Xenophon's *Cyropaedia*, Cyrus prays before his expedition[26] and as he is on his way he sees thunder and lightning as a sign of the gods' favor. His father then says, "My son, it is evident both from the sacrifices and from the signs from the skies that the gods are sending you forth with their grace and favour."[27]

Plutarch similarly narrates the story of Camillus, who "was sacrificing and praying the goddess to accept of their zeal" "when the image, they say, spoke in low tones and said she was ready and willing."[28]

The prayers of Aeneas also are met with observable omens. Aeneas is praying when a magnificent serpent appears, a sight that energizes his prayers.[29] Later Aeneas prays for a sign:

> Scarce had he so said when under his very eyes twin doves, as it chanced, came flying from the sky and lit on the green grass. Then the great hero knew them for his mothers' birds, and prays with joy: O be my guides, if any way there be, and through the air steer a course into the grove.[30]

On another occasion, Aeneas prays and "[a]t this, the almighty Father thundered thrice aloft from a clear sky, and with his own hand shook forth to view from heaven a cloud ablaze with shafts of golden light."[31] Luke's audience, familiar with popular heroes who witness marvelous responses to their prayers, would have also had their expectations fulfilled by Luke's portrait of Jesus at prayer.

The Correlation of Life and Teaching regarding Prayer

The Lukan Jesus demonstrates a strong correlation of life and teaching in the area of prayer. For Luke, the miraculous responses to Jesus' prayers do more than affirm his prayer habits: they also support his teachings. Jesus' teachings about the graciousness of a God who answers prayer are supported by the phenomena that attend his prayers. The Spirit's presence at Jesus' baptism (3:22) proves his teaching that God will give the Spirit to those who seek him (11:13). Luke's well-placed comments about the power of Jesus' ministry (4:14) affirm his teachings that spiritual strength comes through prayer (22:39–46). The immediacy with which his prayers are answered and their direct fulfillment finally testify to the grace of God, which is so fundamental to the Lukan Jesus' understanding of prayer.

The correlations between the Lukan Jesus' prayer life and his teachings about prayer would provide a sense of satisfaction for Luke's auditors, who expected a unity of life and teaching among their heroes. Not only are Greco-Roman leaders continually portrayed as pious figures who regularly pray and sacrifice to the gods, but also ideal leaders show a correlation of life and teaching in this area.

Numa is a classic example of a pious hero whose religious teachings and deeds are in correspondence. He not only has a deeply rooted need for solitude in prayer but instills this need in his people as well. Numa, who "himself is said to have been the first" of the pontifices, regulates the worship of the people[32] by being able to "soften" the warlike nature of the city through his own example of worship:

> Numa, judging it to be no slight or trivial undertaking to mollify and newly fashion for peace so presumptuous and stubborn a people, called in the gods to aid and assist him. It was for the most part by sacrifices, processions, and religious dances, which he himself appointed and conducted . . . that he won the people's favour and tamed their fierce and warlike tempers.[33]

Through personal example, Numa, who loved to spend all his time in silent contemplation of the gods,[34] wandering alone in the country in the presence of the gods[35]—he who at first shunned the throne because of his love of peace and solitude[36]—teaches his citizens the same habits he cherishes. Plutarch notes that he also taught them to pay special honors to one Muse in particular, "the silent one," to whom he ascribed much of his teaching. Numa thus taught his citizens to practice the same patterns of withdrawal for private worship for which he was known:

> For, just as it is said that the Pythagoreans do not allow men to worship and pray to their gods cursorily and by the way, but would have them go from their homes directly to this office, with their minds prepared for it, so Numa thought that his citizens ought neither to hear nor see any divine service while they were occupied with other matters and therefore unable to pay attention.[37]

Instead, Numa instructed his people to seek the same isolation in prayer for which he was so famous.

Because of their tremendous respect of his own example of piety, Numa's citizens follow his teaching and worship practices.[38] Plutarch records:

> Not only was the Roman people softened and charmed by the righteousness and mildness of their king, but also the cities round about . . . and all of them were filled with a longing desire to have good government, to be at peace, to till the earth, to rear their children in quiet, and to worship the gods. . . . Honour and justice flowed into all hearts from the wisdom of Numa, as from a fountain. . . . Either fear of the gods, who seemed to have him in their especial care, or reverence for his virtue, or a marvellous felicity . . . made him a manifest illustration and confirmation of the saying which Plato, many generations later, ventured to utter regarding government, namely, that

human ills would only then cease and disappear when, by some divine felicity, the power of a king should be united in one person with the insight of a philosopher, thereby establishing virtue in control and mastery over vice.[39]

Just as Numa's own practice of prayer resulted in his legendary peaceful disposition, his teaching enabled the people to achieve the same level of peaceful worship in their own lives. Plutarch makes it clear that it was the unity of Numa's words and deeds that set him above all other leaders and proved that he was an ideal philosopher-king. So also, Luke's portrait of Jesus as a person whose own teaching regarding prayer flowed out of his lifestyle makes an important statement about how Luke's readers would have viewed Jesus. Luke's auditors would have received an image of Jesus at prayer that resonated with their images of legendary heroes at prayer. These parallels would likely have colored their growing perceptions of Luke's Jesus and fulfilled their anticipations for Jesus to be an ideal hero.

HUMILITY

Luke's portrait of Jesus as a person of humility finds company with descriptions of the lifestyles of the ancient Mediterranean's most admirable heroes. In Luke, Jesus corrects the prideful attitudes and behaviors of the religious leaders and his own disciples, while modeling humility in his own lifestyle. Luke's readers would then be led to the inescapable conclusion that Jesus himself is an ideal hero.

The Attitudes of the Humble

No desire for superficial or undeserved honor

Jesus chastises the prideful attitudes of both his disciples and the religious leaders when they demonstrate their overwhelming desire for superficial and undeserved honors (9:46–50; 14:7–14). When the disciples compete with each other for the place of preeminence as Jesus' best disciple (9:46), they are proving that their lack of humility aligns them with the standards of this world rather than with the kingdom of God. They desire the prestige of the position, not the true honor of righteousness.

The religious leaders in Luke also constantly seek recognition and honors. In Jesus' opinion, the honor they seek is completely undeserved. Not only do they seek honors based only on their position in society, but they also fail in

their task as religious guides. Jesus accuses them of having evil motivations and
not even knowing how to interpret the law (20:20, 41–44).

In contrast to the disciples and religious leaders, Jesus has no desire for
superficial honors. His interaction with the woman in Luke 11:27–28 demonstrates his humility. When the woman attempts to praise Jesus' person, he
deflects her praise and directs it instead to all those who obey God. Similarly,
in Luke 18:18, when the ruler addresses Jesus as "good teacher," he deflects
his compliment, declaring that only God is good (18:19).

Most ancient Mediterranean philosophers believed that an ideal leader
would have no use for superficial honors but would be a person who
was genuinely deserving. For Aristotle, the person who claims honor,
although he does not deserve it, is a fool: "[H]e who claims much without
deserving it is foolish, but no one of moral excellence is foolish or sense-
less."[40] Jesus' similar critique of the undeserving religious leaders highlights
their foolishness.

Many philosophers in Luke's milieu felt that a virtuous leader would not
seek praise and would deflect it away from himself if it was offered. Epictetus
thus notes that a virtuous leader desires to do good rather than to be honored.
He asks the imaginary virtuous person, "Do you wish to do good or to be
praised?" and responds, "Immediately you get the answer, 'What do I care for
praise from the mob?' And that is an excellent answer."[41] Likewise, he believes
that the virtuous person will not take praise seriously:

> Signs of one who is making progress are: He . . . says nothing about
> himself as though he were somebody or knew something. . . . And if
> anyone compliments him, he smiles to himself at the person compli-
> menting; while if anyone censures him, he makes no defense.[42]

The only form of praise that Plutarch admires is praise for virtuous
actions—and then that kind of praise is by definition that which is shared by
all people who act in like manner. He says:

> See whether the praise is for the action or for the man. It is for the
> action if they praise us in absence rather than in our presence; also if
> they, too, cherish the same desires and aspirations themselves and
> praise not us alone but all persons for like conduct; also if they are not
> found doing and saying now this and now the opposite.[43]

Jesus, too, prefers praise given for the action rather than for the person. When
the woman in Luke 11:27–28 attempts to praise Jesus' person, he deflects her
praise in favor of all who obey God's word. Similarly, Plutarch advises:

When the praise runs on the contrary to extravagance, as with the invidious flattery used by many, it permits one to say: "No god am I; why likenest thou me to the immortals? If you know me truly, commend my probity, temperance, reasonableness, or humanity." For to him who declines the greater honours envy is not displeased to grant the more moderate, and does not cheat of true praise those who reject what is false and vain.[44]

Like Jesus when he refused to accept the ruler's compliment in Luke 18:18, Plutarch distinguishes between flattery and the praise of virtuous action. He notes finally of superficial praise, "Such praise is best shown for what it is when true praise is set beside it."[45]

True sense of self

In Luke, Jesus teaches that self-delusion is an effect of the religious leaders' pride. The characterization of the religious leaders as self-delusional is affirmed in Jesus' parable of Luke 18:9–14. In this story, the Pharisee assumes that God will be as pleased with him as he is with himself. The Pharisee shows his pride by comparing himself with the tax collector, by his self-praise, and by expecting preferential treatment. The Pharisee's pride is proof of his unrighteousness, despite his external piety. He thanks God that he is not like "all other people" whom he classifies among the extortioners, unjust, and adulterers (18:11). However, he does not realize that he does the same things about which he judges others (11:39). Had he only shown the humility that he despised so much in the tax collector, he would have found favor with God. His lack of self-awareness deceives him into believing that he is more righteous than the tax collector. Jesus' parable shows that the Pharisee's pride results in his complete self-deception.

While Jesus criticizes those whose pride reveals their self-deception, he can also find examples of those whose humility is demonstrated in a true self-knowledge. Jesus affirms the centurion's sense of self in Luke 7:1–10. The centurion understands that personal worth comes not from society's standards but from God. Jesus also affirms the "prodigal" son's attainment of self in Luke 15:17. He "comes to his senses," realizing that he is unworthy even of claiming kinship with his family. He may be contrasted with his elder brother, whose pride leads him to betray himself as part of the family (15:28). The tax collector in Luke 18:9–14 also demonstrates a true sense of self. He realizes his sinfulness and comes to God in complete humility. Even his physical stance demonstrates his humility (18:13). Jesus therefore points to several examples of people whose humility is manifest in genuine self-understanding.

Many ancient Mediterranean philosophers assumed that those who sought honor undeservedly had a false sense of self. Just as the Lukan Jesus chastised the proud religious leaders for their hypocrisy and self-deception, Aristotle characterized the vain as lacking self-awareness:

> The vain on the other hand are foolish persons, who are deficient in self-knowledge and expose their defect: they undertake honourable responsibilities of which they are not worthy, and then are found out. They are ostentatious in dress, manner and so on. They want people to know how well off they are, and talk about it, imagining that this will make them respected.[46]

Both Jesus and Aristotle deemed such individuals "fools" for their pride, which stems from a lack of self-understanding.

Other philosophers also echo the thought that an ideal leader's humility should be rooted in a true sense of self. Epictetus thus instructs, "If someone brings you word that So-and-so is speaking ill of you, do not defend yourself against what has been said, but answer, 'Yes, indeed, for he did not know the rest of the faults that attach to me; if he had, these would not have been the only ones he mentioned.'"[47] Plutarch similarly demonstrates that a true sense of self can allow one to resist the temptations of pride:

> I urge . . . that we eradicate from ourselves self-love and conceit. . . . But if, in obedience to the god, we learn that the precept, "Know thyself," is invaluable to each of us, and if at the same time we carefully review our own nature and upbringing and education, how in countless ways they fall short of true excellence . . . we shall not very readily let the flatterers walk over us.[48]

Plutarch urges those who wish to develop humility to keep their own motivations in the forefront of their minds:

> And if we keep repeating to ourselves Plato's question, "Can it be that I am like that?" and turn our reason inward instead of to external things, and substitute caution for censoriousness, we shall no longer make much use of "righteous indignation" toward others when we observe that we ourselves stand in need of much indulgence.[49]

Jesus' own teachings similarly affirm that one of the consequences of pride is a lack of self-understanding. His interactions with people affirm that humility and self-awareness go hand in hand.

The Behaviors of the Humble

No focus on external status symbols

In Luke, Jesus criticizes the religious leaders for their focus on external status symbols. They love the clothing scribes wear; they love to be greeted in the marketplace; they take great pride in the external trappings of their religion; they love the best seats at a banquet and in the synagogue; they love the positions of power they hold in society (20:46). Jesus calls them "fools," since they have replaced God's system of worth with their own (12:20; 11:40).

Like the Lukan Jesus, many ancient philosophers expected that a true philosopher would not look to the outward trappings of the profession as a source of status. Epictetus thus complains that some love to adopt the dress and style of a philosopher without first digesting the virtuous lifestyle that should accompany such a profession:

> Immediately these men are off to the sceptre, to the kingdom. One of them lets his hair grow long, he takes up a rough cloak, he shows his bare shoulder. . . . Man, take a winter's training first. . . . Practice first not to let men know who you are; keep your philosophy to yourself a little while.[50]

Epictetus clearly states that one who values status is no philosopher:

> If it should ever happen to you that you turn to externals with a view to pleasing someone, rest assured that you have lost your plan of life. Be content, therefore, in everything to *be* a philosopher, and if you wish also to be taken for one, show to yourself that you are one, and you will be able to accomplish it.[51]

Plutarch notes that such concern about the external status symbols of the profession are the marks of a novice and will disappear in the life of one who truly becomes a philosopher:

> When men are being filled with the really good things, their conceit gives way and their self-opinion becomes less inflexible; and, ceasing to feel pride in their philosopher's beard and gown, they transfer their training to their mind, and apply their stinging and bitter criticism most of all to themselves, and are milder in their intercourse with others. They do not arrogate to themselves, as before, the name of philosophy and the repute of studying it, or even give themselves the title of philosopher; in fact, a young man of good parts, on being addressed by this title by another, would be quick to say with a blush: I am no god, I assure you; why think me like the immortals?[52]

The Lukan Jesus echoes this ideal that a true philosopher will not place store in externals but rather value his profession for its inherent attributes.

Focus on acquiring honorable behaviors

In sharp contrast to the religious leaders and disciples who seek superficial honors, Jesus does not value the pursuit of honor itself but rather the pursuit of honorable behaviors. Jesus' interaction with the woman in Luke 11:27–28 demonstrates that Jesus values honor that is directed toward an action rather than toward a person.

Like the Lukan Jesus, many ancient philosophers believed that an ideal leader would value the pursuit of virtue far above the esteem of his position. Epictetus, too, believed that an ideal philosopher would value philosophy for its practical effects rather than its accompanying honor. He saw the danger of pride in merely taking the name of philosopher: "On no occasion call yourself a philosopher, and do not, for the most part, talk among laymen about your philosophic principles, but do what follows from your principles."[53] Epictetus thus claimed of Socrates that "[h]e would not, I believe, have given way before anyone in—what do you suppose?—in proclaiming and asserting 'I am such and such a man.' . . . Far from it! but in being such and such a man."[54]

Plutarch agreed that the focus of the humble is the attainment of virtue, not the pursuit of prestige:

> It is therefore imperative that we consider carefully whether, as for ourselves, we employ our discourse for our own improvement, and whether, as it affects others, we employ it, not for the sake of momentary repute, nor from motives of ambition, but rather with the wish to hear and to impart something.[55]

Ancient philosophers thus expected a true philosopher to pursue philosophy without regard for the prestige or status that such a profession could bring. While many actual philosophers gloried in the clothing, lifestyle, and discussions of the profession, the ancients felt that true philosophers would seek such study for the practical results of virtue.

Self-praise

Jesus shows the folly of self-praise in his parable of Luke 18:9–14. The Pharisee begins his prayer like a regular thanksgiving prayer (18:11). One would expect him to continue in praise to God for God's good deeds. Instead, however, the Pharisee uses his prayer to expound on his own good deeds (18:11–12). He proudly lists his qualifications for acceptance before God, having no need to address God directly since he feels that, having already met God's requirements for righteousness, God owes him a favor.

While some public figures engaged in self-praise, many philosophers felt that an ideal leader would not praise himself. Plutarch, for instance, felt that self-praise was a shameful practice. He stated that "praise of ourselves is for others most distressing. For first we regard self-praisers as shameless, since they should be embarrassed even by praise from others; second as unfair, as they arrogate to themselves what is for others to bestow."[56]

Ancient philosophers believed that far from seeking praise for himself, an ideal leader would shun praise and be embarrassed by it. Plutarch therefore commented:

> For you should blush when praised, not be unblushing; you should restrain those who mention some great merit of yours, not find fault with them for doing you scant justice, as most do, going on themselves to recall and gorge themselves on other actions and feats of prowess until by thus commending themselves they undo the commendation of others.[57]

Jesus' critique of self-praise and personal example of humility therefore reflect the expectations for ideal leaders to be people who live lifestyles of humility.

The Correlation of Life and Teaching regarding Humility

Jesus teaches his disciples to be humble and himself exhibits an attitude of humility. Jesus tells his self-seeking disciples to imitate his own behavior: the attitude of a servant (22:27). Jesus places a child at his side, illustrating the level of status required by one who will be his disciple (9:47), and affirms this instruction by continually compromising his own status by associating with those of the lowest social status. When the disciples and religious leaders demonstrate their adherence to the honor system of their culture, Jesus rebukes their behavior (14:7–14) and refuses to become engaged in the exchange of honors expected in his society. While the Pharisee of Luke 18:9–14 praises himself at length, Jesus, who is fully deserving of praise, refuses to accept it even from another (11:27–28).

Ancient Mediterranean philosophers expected ideal leaders to demonstrate a correlation of life and teaching regarding humility and point out positive examples of this tendency. Epictetus thus recalls Socrates' attitude of humility: Listen, what does Socrates say? "Nor would it be seemly for me, O men of Athens, at my time of life to appear before you like some lad, and weave a cunning discourse."[58] Epictetus then notes the correlation of word and deed in Socrates' attitude of humility:

> And for that reason who ever heard Socrates saying, "I know something and teach it"? But he used to send one person here and another there.[59] Therefore men used to go to him to have him introduce them to philosophers, and he used to take them around and introduce them. But no, your idea of him, no doubt, is that, as he was taking them along, he used to say, "Come around today and hear me deliver a discourse in the house of Quadratus!"[60]

Plutarch further highlights the correlation of word and deed in Cleomenes' lifestyle of humility:

> In all these matters Cleomenes was himself a teacher. His own man-
> ner of life was simple, plain, and no more pretentious than that of the
> common man. . . . This gave him a great advantage in his dealings with
> the other Greeks. For when men had to do with the other kings, they
> were not so much awed by their wealth and extravagance as they were
> filled with loathing for their haughtiness and pomp as they gave offen-
> sive and harsh answers to their auditors; but when men came to
> Cleomenes, who was a real as well as a titled king, and then saw no
> profusion of purple robes or shawls about him, and no array of
> couches and litters; when they saw, too, that he did not make the work
> of his petitioners grievous and slow by employing a throng of mes-
> sengers and door-keepers or by requiring written memorials, but came
> in person, just as he happened to be dressed, to answer the salutations
> of his visitors, conversing at length with those who needed his services
> and devoting time cheerfully and kindly to them, they were charmed
> and completely won over, and declared that he alone was a descendant
> of Heracles.[61]

Plutarch clearly states that it was the instruction of Cleomenes' own humble lifestyle that led people to the inescapable conclusion that he was the most ideal sort of leader. In portraying Jesus as one whose teachings regarding humility flow from his own humble lifestyle, Luke is making a statement about the kind of leader that Jesus is also. In Luke, Jesus specifically aligns his purposes with God's instead of with the honor codes of the present world and invites his fol- lowers to do the same. Although he is worthy of all honors, he has no desire for status and expects no special treatment. He refuses praise and shames those who grant him superficial honors. Jesus uses his authority only to do good. Against the backdrop of the disciples' struggles for power and position, Jesus acts as their servant. The unity of his teaching and lifestyle is apparent in the fact that he points to his lifestyle as a model for their behavior.

As those who participated in the literary culture of Luke's day, Luke's audi- ence would have approached the Gospel with certain expectations for Jesus. They would have been accustomed to seeing their ideal leaders as people of prayer and humility. They would also have expected their ideal leaders to show a unity of word and action. By portraying his hero as a man of prayer and humility who demonstrates a unity of word and deed in each of these areas, Luke is portraying Jesus in the way that the greatest heroes of the ancient Mediterranean world were portrayed. Luke's readers would therefore have their expectations for an ideal hero fulfilled in his portrait of Jesus.

5

What Evangelicals Have to Do with Athens and Jerusalem

Stephen R. Todd

Stephen R. Todd is professor and chair of the Department of Classics at Samford University. He holds degrees from Furman University (B.A.) and Vanderbilt University (M.A., Ph.D.). Prior to coming to Samford, Todd taught at Baylor University, where he chaired the Department of Classics and directed interdisciplinary studies. He currently serves as president of the Alabama Association of Foreign Language Teachers.

In this essay, Todd extends the themes set forth by Catherine Wright into the patristic period, relating evangelical tensions between Christian theology and spirituality to Tertullian's famous question "What does Athens have to do with Jerusalem?" Todd argues that Christians, and not least evangelicals today, have much to learn from how early church believers appropriated classical paradigms. Todd uses Augustine's appropriation of Virgil as a major example of this kind of engagement.

Both chapters in this part of the book pose an important challenge to evangelical spirituality today. Evangelicals are frequently lured by a "Christ against culture" rhetoric that is often used to support an isolated, sectarian ecclesiology. These essays remind evangelicals that, as Todd puts it, "preserving and redeeming our culture is a crucial part of our calling as Christians."

✧✦✧ ✧✦✧ ✧✦✧

In his famous question "What does Athens have to do with Jerusalem?" Tertullian frames the challenge of uniting faith and reason, using Athens as a symbol of reason and Jerusalem to represent simple faith. Thus he sets the stage for the subsequent tension seen throughout the ages between Christian theology and spirituality, and he foreshadows the difficulties in bringing these two together and keeping them in harmony. Although the early church had not yet fully developed its theology, nevertheless the conflict had crystallized and battle lines were being drawn that would continue into the twenty-first century. Like the early church fathers, we today find ourselves facing the same critical challenge: How does one remain faithful to both Athens *and* Jerusalem in a culture that increasingly honors neither? Alan Wolfe, for example, in a recent article in the *Atlantic Monthly* (October 2000), notes that "evangelicals are trying to create a life of the mind at a time when secular America is questioning whether a life of the mind is worth having." Both Christianity and modern secular culture have their roots in antiquity, and during Christianity's first centuries the fundamental issues of being a Christian in the twenty-first century took shape at the intersection of early Christianity and classical culture. Accordingly, evangelicals today have important lessons to learn from those saints who have gone before us. An examination of the attitudes of the Greek and Latin Fathers toward their own secular culture not only can shed light on early Christianity and classical culture but also illuminate the way for evangelicals into the next millennium.

This chapter addresses both what the Greek and Latin Fathers have to say directly on these issues and also what their ideas, their methods of reasoning, and the form and style of their presentations demonstrate about the significance of their classical culture and education. Some, like Tertullian, were well endowed with classical culture but vigorously disapproved of any possible Hellenistic infiltration of Christianity. How did such individuals reconcile their own dependence on their classical heritage with their disapproval of much of its content? Modern research has shown that they were often far more indebted to their classical culture than any of them dared to admit. Other of the church fathers, such as the Cappadocians, defended their appropriation of their classical heritage, a heritage that in some aspects was clearly antithetical to their Christian beliefs. These and the other church fathers discussed below are selected because of the exemplary way they represent the range of ideas on this subject and also because they were pivotal in the development of the early church's position on these and related issues. In addition, we explore why such issues were so important to early Christianity and remain so for evangelicals today. For example, there was little alternative to classical learning for the early Christians, and some have argued that the survival of the church depended on the reconciliation of Christianity to the classical culture. But such was not necessarily the case, I suggest. Rather, is it not more likely that the lack of learning would not so much have directly impoverished the spirituality of the early Christians as threatened their witness, that is, their ability to argue and present the validity of their faith through their reasoned study of

God to those who did not value their spirituality but could value their use of reason? Likewise today, I propose, if we completely neglect the culture and learning of our contemporary world, we as individuals will not necessarily be impoverished spiritually, but collectively our ability to communicate the gospel message will be diminished, and this weakening of our ability to fulfill the Great Commission will, in turn, have important ramifications for our own evangelical spirituality.

Christianity emerged out of late Judaism into a world shaped and dominated by three centuries of the expansion of Greek language and culture. This unified atmosphere of Hellenistic culture greatly aided the Christian mission and Christianity's rise to prominence, but along with the Greek language and literary forms came Greek concepts and ideas that were inseparable from the language itself, and from the very beginning the opposition between Christianity and the classical pagan culture was apparent.[1] The early Christians had obvious objections to the Greek literature and learning that they inherited. The prose and poetry were full of polytheism and immorality, and rhetoric itself was widely criticized for its sophistic nature. The *Didascalia apostolorum*, a Syrian document from the early third century, offered what appeared to be a simple solution to this dilemma:

> But avoid all books of the heathen. For what hast thou to do with strange sayings or laws or lying prophecies which also turn away from the faith them that are young? What is lacking to thee in the word of God, that thou shouldst cast thyself upon these fables of the heathen? If thou wouldst read historical narrative, thou hast the Book of Kings; but if philosophers and wise men, thou hast the Prophets, wherein thou shalt find wisdom and understanding more than that of the wise men and philosophers. And if thou wish for songs, thou hast the Psalms of David; but if thou wouldst read of the beginning of the world, thou hast the Genesis of the great Moses; and if laws and commandments, thou hast the glorious Law of the Lord God. All strange writings therefore which are contrary to these wholly eschew.[2]

This expression of "better pious than learned" is typical of the attitude toward classical literature as expressed within the confines of the church, where one did not need to be so convincing; but such an attitude was not restricted to the unlearned. Both Tatian and Tertullian were strong anti-Hellenists. Tatian, a disciple of Justin, wrote Greek and was well heeled in Greek culture but vigorously disapproved of what seemed to him to be the Hellenistic infiltration of Christianity. He warned that "the future of their [the Christians'] cause did not lie in their gradual assimilation with Greek culture but would depend

entirely on their keeping it immaculately pure as a barbarous cult."[3] Tertullian
expressed a similar view:

> What indeed has Athens to do with Jerusalem? What accord is there
> between the Academy and the Church? Our instruction comes from
> the porch of Solomon, who has himself taught that the Lord must be
> sought in simplicity of heart. Away with those who have brought for-
> ward a Stoic, or Platonic or dialectic Christianity. As for us, we need
> not be concerned to know anything but the Gospel. Inasmuch as we
> have faith, we need not believe anything else.[4]

Tatian and Tertullian are exemplary of those who were trained by the liberal
arts but turned against them after conversion to Christianity. Tertullian
emphasizes the faith of the Christian religion as opposed to the "mere rational attitude" of the Greek philosophical tradition. He does not see Christianity as a philosophy and emphasizes the superiority of faith over Greek
philosophy, which always desired the support of reason. For Tertullian, there
should be no mixing of Christianity with philosophy but a radical separation
of the two. Tatian and Tertullian were extreme opponents of their classical
heritage and only grudgingly would admit that it had any value at all—they
conceded it could perhaps be used for understanding certain Christian truths.

There was, of course, a tide of opinion, particularly in the East, that ran
counter to the ideas exemplified by Tertullian and Tatian. The attitude of simple piety that was acceptable and convincing within the church itself could not
confute the reasoned argument of Christianity's opponents outside the
church. Further, there was no real alternative to the Greek and Latin literature and education that had trained the early Christian minds.

Accordingly, half a century before Tertullian raises the faith-and-reason
issue in the West, Justin joins faith and reason in his depiction of Christianity
as a philosophy. Justin expresses Christianity in Greek terms and, as an apologist, defends and depicts Christianity as playing an important role in the
Greek philosophical tradition. He has a very optimistic viewpoint of the harmony of Christianity and Greek culture. As a Christian, however, there are
some things in the Greek tradition that Justin must reject. He denounces all
religious syncretism with the Greek legends and gives credit to the pagans
themselves for casting out the evil demons of Homer, Hesiod, and the other
poets. Justin rejects any position incompatible with the Bible, but toward philosophy itself he is very positive. For him, both the gospel and Plato lead to
truth. The Greek philosophers, of course, made their errors, but Justin
approves of some of what he finds in Plato and the Stoics. He approves the
goal of philosophy as noble and valid, and he sees Christianity as the fulfillment of what the Greek philosophers (and the Old Testament) were seeking.

Justin contends, then, that the Hebrew Scriptures and Greek philosophy have common ground. This common ground that he found in the higher philosophical truths of the Greeks Justin attributes as coming either from Moses or through "divinely given reason." The antiquity of Moses, or the "loan theory," was an old theme: "Moses . . . is more ancient than all the Greek authors. And whatever philosophers and poets said about the immortality of the soul, or punishments after death, or contemplation of celestial phenomena, or other teachings of the same kind, they were able to understand and explain because they took up the suggestion of the Hebrew prophets."[5] Justin argued that the Hebrew Scriptures were older and that Moses therefore had the pure and authentic teaching. The Greeks also shared in these teachings, but in a corrupted form. The second explanation of the common ground between Christianity and the Greek tradition was Justin's theory of the *Logos spermatikos*:

> Each man [Justin is referring to the Greek poets and philosophers] spoke well according as he perceived, in proportion to his share in the seed-sowing divine logos, its resemblance. But men who contradict themselves on points of central importance do not seem to have attained an understanding of hidden things and an unshakable knowledge. Hence whatever things have been truly said among all men belong to us Christians. For after God himself, we worship and love the Logos who comes to us from the ingenerate and ineffable God, since he also became man for our sakes. . . . For all the Greek authors were able to perceive Reality dimly on account of the indwelling sowing of the Logos which is implanted in them. For the seed and likeness of something, given according to the capacity of the recipient, is one thing; and quite another is the thing itself, in which men share and whose likeness they possess according to the grace which comes from him.[6]

Thus, all can share in the divine Logos, though Christianity is certainly the superior path to it. In both this and the loan theory, Justin gives significant status to the Greek tradition and makes a crucial contribution to the assimilation of Christianity and Hellenism. His identification of Christ as the divine Logos extends Christ from the fulfillment of God's historical revelation to the Jewish nation to the fulfillment of God's revelation to the entire world. The advances made by the Greek tradition can now be seen as part of the larger providential plan for divine revelation of truth. Justin's adaptation of the Greek and Christian ideas of the Logos thus paves the way for a more complete blend of the two traditions.

The beginnings of this process of assimilation are seen in Justin, but it is in Clement and Origen that a successful and permanent blend of Christianity and Greek ideas develops. The Greek Fathers at this time continue to reject anything that they see as nonbiblical, so the pagan religious values must be rejected, but there is a profound attempt made to harmonize the best of pagan thought with the Bible. In this way Clement and Origen develop a very complex synthesis of Greek and Christian elements that can be challenging and confusing for the outward observer but apparently presented no conflict at all for its originators.

Clement, for example, clearly rejected the pagan religious values of Greek culture, and his respect for the liberal arts was never unqualified. Although his outward acceptance may seem more reserved than Justin's, his inward appreciation and use of Greek culture goes much deeper. Like his contemporaries, Clement used the Greek forms of literature and language as well as the classical ideas. His use of Greek culture earned the disapproval of some of his contemporaries, and he had to justify his literary and philosophical allusions in answer to their criticisms. He responded with the Pauline "become all things to all men" (1 Cor. 9:22) and argued that it was indeed possible for a Christian to have knowledge of the best of the contemporary philosophical thought, including Stoicism and Platonism, and not be drawn away into unorthodoxy. When not answering his critics, Clement praised philosophy as a gift from God and emphasized its value as a preparation for Christianity. He compared its role among the Greeks with the role of the Law for the Jews:

> God is the cause of all good things; but of some primarily, as of the Old and the New Testament; and of others by consequence, as of philosophy. Perchance, too, philosophy was given to the Greeks directly and primarily, till the Lord should call the Greeks. For this was a schoolmaster to bring the Hellenic mind, as the law the Hebrews, to Christ.[7]

When faced with the high standing of Plato, Clement turns to the theory of plagiarism by the Greeks. He, like Justin, assumes that it all must be derived from Moses. For Clement, his Christian faith is primary and the Greek culture is supplementary. He sees the usefulness of the Greek forms and ideas, and perhaps even the education as a preparation for Christianity, but he is clearly bringing a new substance into these old forms—the new wine of Christianity into the old skins of classical culture. Clement does not deny the value of the Greek tradition where it is not harmful, but he proclaims that it has been eclipsed by Christianity, which has achieved everything the Greek tradition had attempted. The elements in Clement that seem so Hellenistic to the outside observer apparently came very naturally from the Alexandrian, who probably never saw anything in them foreign to Christianity.

Origen represents possibly the greatest attempt made to his day to bring Christianity and classical Greek culture together. Origen gives the Christian religion its own theology and in doing so creates a complicated blend of Christianity and Greek culture. As in Clement, the resulting Hellenization was not necessarily intentional, for though his mind was filled with Greek culture, the subject of Origen's quest was clearly Christianity. Origen did with the Bible what the Greeks did with Hesiod and Homer. Using the methods of the Alexandrian tradition—critical editions, commentaries, scholia, dialogue—he translated the religion of Jesus into theology in the Greek manner.[8] He interpreted Christianity in Greek philosophical terms, with the result being fully biblical, at least in his own eyes, yet full of what his opponents saw as Hellenistic ideas. Greek *paideia* filled his thinking, providing the framework for Origen's systematic theology and the background for his ideas on the doctrine of divine education.

Porphyry, the Neoplatonist opponent of Origen, emphasizes Origen's double life, how he was brought up Greek, with Hellenistic views, but lived as a proponent of Christianity. Origen himself apparently saw these not as two but as one, joining the two in a way that disturbed even the pagans. In addition, one of Origen's students gives evidence for his broad use of the best of the liberal arts—including rhetoric, the sciences, and ethics—to form a foundation for the study of Scripture: "No subject was forbidden us, nothing hidden or inaccessible. We were allowed to become acquainted with every doctrine, barbarian or Greek, with things spiritual and secular, divine and human, traversing with all confidence and investigating the whole circuit of knowledge and satisfying ourselves with the full enjoyment of all pleasures of the soul."[9]

Marcellus of Ancyra alleged that Origen "began to teach and preach too soon after he had been studying philosophy and was led astray by the Platonists with which his mind was filled."[10] Indeed, Origen at times made vast concessions to Platonism in *De principiis*, but though deeply influenced by the Platonism and Greek culture that permeated the thinking of his day, Origen endeavored to be a Christian. Although he could not deny the value of the Greek tradition, he rejected those things he judged contradictory or damaging to Christianity. At that time there was no serious alternative to Greek culture and the education it provided. Origen could not imagine any other tradition, but as a Christian he saw Christianity as the superior fulfillment of everything to which Greek culture had aspired. The result is Origen's complex blend of Christianity and Greek culture. Origen, in providing Christianity with theology, also left the indelible marks of his Hellenism.

With Justin's Logos as a decisive point of unity, the Alexandrian school in their development of theology had brought Christianity and Greek culture together, with Origen representing a polished blend of these two systems of thought. It is with the Greek Cappadocians, however, that Christianity faced Greek culture as a whole and began the development of an entirely new civilization under Christian leadership. Up to this point there had been a great deal of sharing between Christian thinkers and Greek culture in language, literary form, and philosophy, and this sharing came to a climax in Origen. The merger brought with it the realization that Christianity and its Greek heritage did have much in common. By taking this common ground and making it their own, the Cappadocian Greek Fathers made a positive move toward the goal of a Christian civilization.[11]

Christianity had yet to win over the well-educated pagan population, who still held to their classical culture as if to a religion. With the growth and assertion of a Christian civilization came the cultural reaction in defense of the classical heritage. In the West the leaders were Symmachus and the other conservative senators who fought the removal of the altar of the goddess Victoria from the Curia. In the East was Julian with his systematic effort to destroy Christianity and to bring back the Hellenic culture, including the cults of the pagan gods. Even the well-educated Christians, including the Cappadocians, had to reject this reestablishment of the pagan religion and culture in this form. Yet the Cappadocians, while dismissing the pagan religion, had the foresight to seek out and develop their distinctively new kind of "Hellenism" instead of simply rejecting the old culture. Christianity was now in a position to take over the cultural and intellectual leadership, and this it did by adapting the defeated pagan heritage to its own use.

In the Cappadocians, Christianity acquired "everything in the Greek tradition that seemed to them worthy of survival," thereby fortifying its own position as well as preserving the Greek cultural heritage.[12] Each of the Cappadocians had a full classical education—Basil and Gregory of Nazianzus in Athens itself—and was therefore well versed in the liberal arts. Their attitude toward classical culture is reflected in their widespread use of the Greek tradition, and they were criticized for "interpolating a foreign philosophy into the Bible."[13] The way in which they answered such criticism further expresses their attitude toward their Greek learning. Gregory of Nyssa's *De vita Moysis* is perhaps a response to such accusations. In it Gregory gave an allegorical interpretation of the life of Moses and explained that as Moses learned and used the Egyptian wisdom, so could the classical Greek culture be used. The basket in which Moses floated in the Nile was the "composite classical *paideusis*" and the wisdom of the Egyptians was the "spoils of the pagans."

Gregory of Nazianzus is also full of classical allusions, philosophy, and rhetorical devices that he must defend as follows:

> I take it as admitted by men of sense, that the first of our advantages is education; and not only this our more noble form of it, which disregards rhetorical ornaments and glory, and holds to salvation and

beauty in the objects of our contemplation; but even that pagan culture which many Christians spit upon, as treacherous and dangerous, and keeping us afar from God. For as we ought not to neglect the heavens, and earth, and air, and all such things, because some have wrongly seized upon them, and honour God's works instead of God: but to reap what advantage we can from them for our life and enjoyment, while we avoid their dangers; not raising creation, as foolish men do, in revolt against the Creator, but from the works of nature apprehending the Worker and as the divine apostle says, bringing into captivity every thought to Christ: and again, as we know that neither fire, nor food, nor iron, nor any other of the elements, is of itself most useful or most harmful, except according to the will of those who use it; and as we have compounded healthful drugs from certain of the reptiles; so from secular literature we have received principles of inquiry and speculation, while we have rejected their idolatry, terror, and pit of destruction. Nay, even those have aided us in our religion, by our perception of the contrast between what is worse and what is better, and by gaining strength for our doctrine from the weakness of theirs. We must not then dishonour education, because some men are pleased to do so, but rather suppose such men to be boorish and uneducated, desiring all men to be as they themselves are, in order to hide what is appropriate to them among the common mass and escape the detection of their want of culture.[14]

In this account, Gregory of Nazianzus warns against its dangers but assures us of the usefulness of the pagan culture—if nothing else, it shows us its own shortcomings. His statement shows not only that many Christians had reservations about the use of the pagan culture at this time but also assures us of the free use of the Greek tradition by Gregory Nazianzus, since he required such a defense.

Basil's essay "To Young Men, on How They Might Profit from Pagan Literature" embodies the standard view held by the Cappadocians, and which became "the charter of all Christian higher education for centuries to come."[15] In this essay Basil states that pagan literature is inferior but not without value. That which illustrates good men of the past and teaches good principles is worthy of study. Some of it even conforms to the gospel teaching, such as the idea of the superiority of the soul over the body. The Christian can profit from the pagan tradition as Daniel did from Babylonian wisdom and Moses did from the Egyptians. The warning that Basil gives is to guard against the immoral and religious content that must be rejected. This "enlightened" view of the Cappadocians reasonably accepted the traditional educational system and, in its revival of the Greek tradition, exhibited the capability to capture the contemporary mind. In their presentation of a new Hellenism and development of the new Christian civilization, the Cappadocians made a subtle distinction between paganism as a religion and Hellenism as culture. They could reject much of the content of the Greek tradition, but its form and especially the ideas that gave it its universal appeal Christianity found very useful.

Justin opened the door for the blending of Christianity and Greek thought in the theology of the Alexandrian school through his exposition of the divine Logos. Justin, Clement, and Origen exhibited the profound influences of their Greek tradition in spite of an outward reserve. They were Christians who naturally brought their Hellenic culture into their learned presentation of Christianity. Their Christianity was always primary, however, and they recognized the Christian faith as the ultimate source of all truth. The Cappadocians seized the blend of Christianity and Greek culture that they found in Origen, and grasping the universal ideals of the Greek tradition, they fortified the development of a Christian civilization, while preserving and revising the best of the Greek classical tradition. The Cappadocians, seeing beyond the pagan religion of Hellenism, developed a distinctively new "Hellenism" in terms of a Christian civilization. They clearly recognized the value of the underlying ideas that had infiltrated the Christianity of Justin, Clement, and Origen, and they even accepted the modified classical educational system. In the end, their attitude toward their classical Greek tradition seemed very reasonable: provided that the dangers were avoided, they saw Greek culture as quite valuable—it indeed lived on in much of the Christian tradition that they were developing.

The pathways that we find connecting Athens and Jerusalem eventually turn toward the West and Rome. The central figure of Western Christianity in the process of conciliation between Christianity and its classical background is Augustine. Augustine's primary devotion is clearly to the Christian faith, but that Augustine brought his classical heritage into his Christianity is also indisputable, and his appropriation of the writings and thought of the Roman poet Virgil are striking. Augustine, too, was born into an age when all educated men were steeped in the classical tradition. If one received an education, from one's childhood one would be instructed in the pagan writers. An important part of this education was Virgil, the most influential poet of his own day, who continued to be held in high esteem throughout the Middle Ages. Virgil was the supreme authority on matters of language, and all grammarians had a thorough knowledge of his works. The first book a child was given was written by Virgil, and his writings were the staple not only of elementary education but of the advanced rhetorical education also.[16]

Augustine himself records his love for Virgil in his early schooldays, which deeply ingrained the Roman poet into his thinking and character. Augustine also recalls how, in the school of rhetoric, his renditions of Virgil brought great applause. As a teacher as well, Augustine was certainly immersed in Virgil, and even after he left his chair at Milan, he continued to expound on the poet among his friends—as seen in his dialogues, where Augustine affectionately refers to Virgil as "our poet" (*poeta noster*). Augustine continued to be influenced by Virgil throughout his career. However, after his conversion, Augustine fell under the influence of the traditional Christian opposition to pagan culture. From the eve of his baptism, Augustine recorded three prayers in *De ordine* that he used as an expression of his religious sentiments. Remarkably, these prayers for such an important occasion were borrowed directly from Virgil, where they originally had been addressed to Apollo. With his baptism and ordination as a presbyter (388 C.E.), however, came a decisive change in his attitude toward his beloved poet. From that time forward, as his literary activity as a theologian began, Augustine submitted himself to the church, and use of Virgil's works came to be conspicuously different.[17]

In 394, Augustine announced the principle that "classical authors deserve mentioning only in matters of language (*de verbo, non de re*)."[18] This principle obviously limited Augustine's use of pagan authors, but the use of Virgil in accordance with this principle is seen throughout Augustine's work. Virgil was especially authoritative about matters of language and style. Along with Cicero, he was an important source for Augustine concerning syntax and meanings of words. Virgil was cited frequently for interpretation and definition of words in Scripture. The poet also provided Augustine with a model of literary adornment. In the *Contra Iulianum*, Augustine presents an especially embellished argument in answer to criticism that had been given in like form. Here it seems that Augustine was making an effort to show his pagan opponents that he, too, had such learning and ability.

Augustine borrowed some of Virgil's lines and applied them directly to the Christian sphere. Although Augustine did find some passages that he thought were in agreement with biblical opinion (usually wrongly, misunderstanding Virgil's meaning), generally Augustine realized that he was using Virgil's lines differently from how the poet had intended. Thus he gave the words a new sense, alien to Virgil's original meaning but useful in the Christian sphere. Through this process of *interpretatio Christiana* Virgil's poetry is "christianized," but only superficially, for Augustine never supposed that Virgil could have been a Christian.

After his announcement in 394 that classical authors deserve mention only in matters of language, there is evidence of a growing indifference in Augustine's attitude toward Virgil, as Roman paganism became more and more an object of Augustine's criticism. This attitude reached its hostile climax in book 1 of the *Confessions*, where Augustine fervently expressed contempt for the early instruction that polluted his mind. He now preferred reading and writing to "worthless" instruction in literature. Strongly influenced by the

Christian prejudice against his pagan literary heritage, Augustine at this point designated Virgil as "their poet" *(eorum poeta)*."[19]

In spite of this aversion, Augustine made considerable use of Virgil in his *magnum opus, De civitate Dei*. Careful analysis has demonstrated that Augustine's work on *De civitate Dei* was accompanied by extensive rereading of Virgil's poetry.[20] This great increase in Augustine's use of Virgil does not indicate a change of attitude, however. The wide use of Virgil in *De civitate Dei* illustrates one of the chief applications that the early Christians found for the pagan literature—that of polemical material to use against the pagans. Throughout Augustine's career, the use of Virgil and other pagan literature is conspicuously absent from two groups of his writings—the dogmatic and exegetical works for fellow believers and the polemical pamphlets against those who claimed to be fellow believers. In both instances Augustine's audience was made up of nonpagans, to whom the authority of pagan literature would mean relatively little. When he addressed a pagan audience, however, as he did in *De civitate Dei*, Augustine found it necessary to draw from pagan sources, and especially from Virgil. In such a "documentary exposition" of Augustine's estimation of pagan culture as opposed to the claims of Christianity, Virgil would, of course, be one of the principal authorities. Augustine systematically quoted Virgil to provide useful information for his argument, using Virgil as "his guide" in his description of Roman character. He used his learning here not to impress fellow Christians but to reach out to non-Christians in fulfilling the mission of his faith, to proclaim the "kingdom of God" to the "kingdom of this world."

Virgil, therefore, provided the basis for Augustine's criticism of the Roman ideals, especially of Roman religion and the Roman national spirit. Augustine's criticism of Roman religion was founded on Virgil. Using the poet's works, Augustine pointed out the immorality of the pagan gods and the inconsistencies between the various contradictory interpretations of these deities. Augustine therefore cited from Virgil information on magic, miracles, demons, and life after death. Virgil is also the obvious authority on Rome's national spirit— and thus an important part of Augustine's "theology of history." Augustine argued that Virgil's goal for Rome was "an encroachment upon the power of God."[21] Augustine found abundant material in Virgil to cite against Roman imperialism.

In his presentation of the Roman national spirit, however, Virgil provided Augustine with more than just information, for it is Virgil's vision for Rome that both inspired and challenged Augustine. Virgil had presented eternal Rome as the product of divine providence. This idea provided Augustine with part of his historical and divine perspective, as well as providing the foil for his *City of God*. Virgil had provided a *moral* view of history: providence had brought Rome to the climactic peace under Octavian. Augustine came to share this view of Rome, although he saw its purpose in a different light. Virgil's formulation of the *Pax Romana* had certainly impressed on Augustine the sense of mission behind Rome's rise. It was Virgil's statement of the divine mission of Rome that provided the background for Augustine's great defense of Christianity.

Implicit in Augustine's vast use of Virgil is praise for a poet of such magnitude and authority. Here we see the ambivalence of Augustine's attitude—"the conflicting tendencies of the literary man brought up in the classical tradition and the man of the church."[22] An important distinction can be made, however, between Augustine's appreciation of Virgil as a poet and his attitude toward Virgil's culture. Virgil was a master of language for Augustine, but not of thought. Although he admired the poet greatly, he rejected and consistently criticized his culture and thought. The conscious use of Virgil's thought that Augustine exhibited was the use of his lines for a Christian purpose, with a meaning different from their original. Not only Virgil but the whole of the classical tradition found expression in Augustine in this way: "remodeling the thought and transferring it to the Christian sphere is a characteristic feature in his dealing with the classical literature."[23]

This remodeling and transferring of Virgil's thought is, I think, one of the fundamental issues involved in understanding the process of the Christianization of the empire. Virgil was unquestionably one of the central figures of Roman civilization. By looking into his past, he presented Rome in such a way as powerfully to express and embody the hope of the Roman Empire. Virgil blended his past with the present by adapting the ideals of his heritage and making them his own—civilizing them in the process. "Vergil had a providential mission to prepare the world for Christianity. He gave Christianity a challenge to accept, and to change, as he accepted and changed inherited thoughts and phrases from the Greeks."[24] Albert C. Outler terms this process the "transvaluation of classicism." Augustine appreciated his heritage and perhaps wished to conserve it, but as a Christian first and foremost, his attitude had to be one of criticism of the paganism of his heritage. As he borrowed from the classical tradition, everything had to be completely subjected to his Christian faith: "Thus, pagan literature, philosophy, and history can be transvalued and conserved." To remain true both to his past and to his Christian faith, Augustine was faced with one solution—the transvaluation of his heritage.[25]

Virgil and his tradition had thus presented Augustine and early Christianity with a critical dilemma: Could Virgil's thought and poetry be used for the expression of Christian values, or even values acceptable to Christianity? The use of Virgil's works would certainly present many difficulties, for the *Aeneid* could not be totally acceptable to the Christian faith. Was it even compatible?

This question is the essential issue faced by every generation, including our own, concerning the importance and use of its past. Here the question is so critical because these individuals stood between two vastly different cultures, both of which made serious claims to their attention. Here was an entire generation with pagan roots and upon whose shoulders the developing Christian civilization would stand. Just as the Homeric hero was no longer acceptable to Virgil in his day, so also the hero created by Virgil was not acceptable to the Christian tradition. Virgil had taken the cultural tradition of Greece and Homer, as well as the epic genre, and had made it his own, choosing what he found acceptable and compatible with his ideals. The Roman poet related these two cultures in such a way as to combine them in Roman civilization and define them in terms of Roman destiny. Augustine, in turn, was faced with a similar process, and the influence of Virgil on this process is indisputable. Virgil had not only presented Augustine with the most important expression of the Greco-Roman tradition but also showed him how to relate to it and adapt it to his own Christian tradition.

As one of the important civilizing influences of his day, Virgil had an impact on the newly developing Christian civilization. As a model for language, literature, and thought, the poet not only defined the classical heritage of the early Christians but also showed them how to adapt it and to make it their own. Like the Cappadocians in the East, so Augustine in the West was doing more than just continuing an old cultural tradition; he was developing the foundation for a new Christian civilization. Virgil was no doubt an inspiration for this new culture, both directly, as can be seen in Augustine's *De civitate Dei*, and indirectly, as part of that underlying fabric that went into the making of the new civilization.

Let me close, then, by reflecting on the example of these saints who have gone before us. The neglect of the culture of our world—including the best of its learning and the life of the mind— may not directly impoverish our own spirituality but does affect our ability to communicate the gospel and therefore our ability to fulfill great commission. This is a most significant issue because it involves the central mission of why Christ came into this world and has important ramifications for the vitality of the Christian life. Therefore, preserving and redeeming our culture is a crucial part of our calling as Christians. There are dangers involved any time we attempt to be *in* but not *of* this world, but we do have abundant resources to help us keep before our minds the distinctions between those two prepositions and what they represent. Would Christianity have survived and continued without the undergirding and the preparation of the classical world? Yes, I suggest, it would have, though God in his providence provided that particular foundation. But would the classical world, its literature, culture, and thought, have survived? The answer to that, perhaps, is more doubtful. We today find ourselves once again at such a crossroads, and the issue at hand is not so much will Christianity survive as will Christianity once again step into the gap, redeem the time and the age, and administer the saving grace of God to the world, including the best of its culture, and bring this place while we are here, more in line to what God intended.

FOR FURTHER READING

Ancient Sources

Justin Martyr. *First Apology; Second Apology.*
Tertullian. *Apology; De praescriptione haereticorum.*
Clement of Alexandria. *Exhortation to Conversion; Miscellanies.*
Basil. *To Young Men, on How They Might Profit from Pagan Literature.*
Augustine. *Confessions; On the City of God,* book 8; *De ordine.*

Bibliography

Chadwick, Henry. *Early Christian Thought and the Classical Tradition.* New York: Oxford University Press, 1966.

Cochrane, Charles Norris. *Christianity and Classical Culture.* New York: Oxford University Press, 1957.

Comparetti, Domenico. *Vergil in the Middle Ages.* Translated by E. F. M. Benecke. Hamden, Conn.: Archon Books, 1966.

Dodds, E. R. *Pagan and Christian in an Age of Anxiety.* Cambridge: Cambridge University Press, 1965.

Hagendahl, Harald. *Augustine and the Latin Classics.* Göteborg: Stockholm Universitetet, 1967.

Hatch, Edwin. *The Influence of Greek Ideas on Christianity.* 1957. Reprint, Gloucester, Mass.: Peter Smith, 1970.

Jaeger, Werner. *Early Christianity and Greek Paideia.* Cambridge, Mass.: Harvard University Press, 1961.

Laistner, M. L. *Christianity and Pagan Culture in the Later Roman Empire.* Ithaca, N.Y.: Cornell University Press, 1951.

Marrou, Henri Irénée. *A History of Education in Antiquity.* Translated by George Lamb. New York: Sheed and Ward, 1956.

Nock, A. D. *Conversion.* New York: Oxford University Press, 1933.

Norris, R. A. *God and World in Early Christian Theology.* New York: Seabury Press, 1965.

Outler, Albert C. "Augustine and the Transvaluation of the Classical Tradition." *Classical Journal* 54 (1959): 213–19.

PART 3

Critique

6

Outward Faith, Inward Piety: The Dependence of Spirituality on Worship and Doctrine

Ralph C. Wood

Ralph C. Wood is University Professor of Theology and Literature at Baylor University. He holds degrees from East Texas State University and the University of Chicago (Ph.D.). Before coming to Baylor, Wood taught for many years at Wake Forest University and also spent one year as Distinguished Professor at Samford University. A prolific author, Wood has written numerous essays and reviews, many of them published in the *Christian Century*, for which he serves as an editor-at-large. He is also the author of *The Comedy of Redemption: Christian Faith and Comic Vision in Four American Novelists* (Walker Percy, Flannery O'Connor, John Updike, and Peter DeVries).

In this chapter, Wood explores the dilemma of evangelical spirituality caught, as he suggests it is, between the dogmas of secular rationalism on the one hand and an undoctrinal, sentimental pietism on the other. Wood draws from the writings of Karl Barth, Gerard Manley Hopkins, and John and Charles Wesley to present countermodels of spiritual mentors for whom private piety was rooted in the life of public faith. Like McGrath earlier in the volume, he also finds deep spiritual wisdom in Isaac Watts's hymn "When I Survey the Wondrous Cross."

৯৯৯ ৯৯৯ ৯৯৯

The contemporary obsession with spirituality, among Christians and pagans alike, surely betokens something worthy of the church's attention. I am not convinced, however, that the current vogue for spirituality should be embraced without making important historical and theological distinctions. I contend, moreover, that these distinctions will lead us to prefer the term *piety*

91

over *spirituality*. Such inward piety, I argue, springs from the outward life of faith as it is lived in the church, especially through doctrinal preaching and sacramental worship. Only when it is thus focused and grounded and transformed, I conclude, can the church benefit from the resurgent spirituality of our time.

THE DANGEROUS VAGUENESS OF SPIRITUALITY

The term *spirituality* is perilously vague. It is an abstract noun that has become so devoid of theological content that it can be attached to almost any modifying phrase. An electronic Web search for the word *spirituality* received ten thousand responses. Even when the genitive *of* was added, there were still several hundred sites. Here are but a few of the many "spiritualities" advertised on the Internet: the spirituality of unity, the spirituality of work, the spirituality of simplicity, the spirituality of intimacy, the spirituality of nonviolence, the spirituality of the body, the spirituality of imperfection, the spirituality of perfection, the spirituality of indigenous cultures, the spirituality of food, the spirituality of letting go, the spirituality of the feminine, the spirituality of the good herb, the spirituality of aging, the spirituality of the religious educator, and—perhaps most revealing of all—the spirituality of wildness.

This last sort of "spirituality" is described rather ungrammatically as follows: "religion that is lived, felt, and experienced—rather than simply believed—real and ecstatic and visceral. Wicca, neo-paganism, ecospirituality, shamanism, totemism, shapeshifting, therianthropy, nature magic, animal and plant lore, and earth-based spirituality of all kinds." Surely the one thing missing from this sorry litany is the spirituality of abortion. Once spirituality is made but another shopping item in the spiritual bazaar of self-interest, it can be put to purposes that are truly demonic. Hence the confession of a wise and skeptical friend: "Whenever I hear the word *spirituality*, I grab first for my wife and then for my wallet."

With uncanny prescience, C. S. Lewis anticipated what is potentially perilous in the current vogue of spirituality. In his space novel of 1944 titled *Perelandra*, Lewis depicts a demonic scientist named Weston as an advocate of an immanentist life worship that has remarkable parallels to contemporary spirituality. Weston has contempt for the transcendent God who creates and judges and redeems the world. He will have nothing to do with the incarnate Lord who requires that we worship him rather than his creation, who commands that we live not for this world alone but also for the Life beyond life. Weston's anti-Christian philosophy proves predictably antihumanistic, as the denial of the God who has become human issues finally in a hatred of humanity itself. Weston worships the dynamic and impersonal life process instead. He scorns "mere humanity" in the name of a vitalism as vacuous in its rhetoric as it is vicious in its ethics:

> The majestic spectacle of this blind, inarticulate purposiveness thrust ing its way upward and ever upward in an endless unity of differenti- ated achievements towards an ever-increasing complexity of organisation, towards spontaneity and *spirituality*, swept away all my old conception of a duty to Man as such. Man in himself is nothing. The forward movement of Life—the growing *spirituality*—is every- thing. . . . To spread *spirituality*, not to spread the human race, is hence- forth my mission.[1]

No such monstrous imprecision attends Paul's use of the word *spiritual* in the New Testament. He sets up a clear contrast between the life of the flesh (*sarx*) and the life of the spirit (*pneuma*). The conflict lies not between the body (*soma*) and the soul (*psyche*), but rather between a way of life confined to the earthly horizon of human self-seeking, on the one hand, and the heavenly life dedicated utterly to the Spirit of God, on the other. Hence Paul's straight- forward declaration: "The mind of sinful man is death, but the mind con- trolled by the Spirit is life and peace" (Rom. 8:6). Far from exalting the incorporeal world at the expense of the corporeal, Paul makes clear that the deadliest "acts of the sinful nature" are not only outward and bodily but also—and chiefly—inward and spiritual: "idolatry and witchcraft; hatred, discord, jealousy, fits of rage, selfish ambition, dissensions, factions and envy . . . and the like" (Gal. 5:20–21).

Nor does Paul ever regard the gifts of the Spirit as something that can be acquired by human yearning or native capacity. The natural human desire for God given in the created order of things has been perverted and forfeited in the Fall. The *Book of Common Prayer* (1549) puts our condition pungently: "There is no health in us." Our *salus* can be restored only through the salva- tion offered by the gift of God in the life, death, and resurrection of Jesus Christ. Union with God and participation in the divine life, by way of the ascending and reigning Christ, occurs only through the gift of the Spirit called faith. And this total entrustment of one's life *to* God is itself enabled *by* him. It is a faith *in* Christ that is worked through the faith *of* Christ:

> Some biblical scholars point out that the Greek preposition connected to the word "faith" [e.g., in Rom. 3:21 and Phil. 3:9] can be translated "of" as well as "in." . . . The two possible translations are comple- mentary. . . . The gospel leads to faith in God that comes, not through the law of Moses, but through the faith of Jesus. Jesus trusted God. Jesus obeyed God. Though Jesus was crucified because of his trust in God, God raised Jesus from the dead, thereby vindicating Jesus' trust

in God and vindicating God. God's power to restore life and to restore fellowship with those from whom Jesus had been alienated is now revealed.[2]

The objective and totally finished character of Christ's already-accomplished act makes possible our own subjective and partial appropriation of it. Thus do the New Testament words *spirit* and *spiritual* refer primarily to the life of Christian faithfulness—a faithfulness that is inseparably outward and inward. It is noteworthy that these words do not produce a biblical term akin to our "spirituality."

SPIRITUALITY AND PIETY

Declan Marmion points out that Jerome, in the fifth century, was the first Christian theologian to use the word *spiritualitas*. "So act as to advance in spirituality," Jerome advised recently baptized believers. He used the word to mean very much what Paul meant—to advance in a life of total devotion to the Spirit received in baptism, and thus in opposition to the life of sinfulness. Between the sixth and eleventh centuries, the word took on a decidedly supernatural sense. Spirituality referred to a life lived not according to nature but according to the counsels of perfection contained in the Beatitudes and omitted from the Commandments. *Spiritualitas* was thus put in contrast with *corporalitas* or *materialitas*. By the twelfth and thirteenth centuries, a further shift had occurred. The opposition between "spirituality" and the ordinary meanings of the word *flesh* had become virtually complete. *Spiritualitas* was now a monastic word set over against *carnalitas* and *mortalitas*, even *brutalitas* and *animalitas*. It referred to the incorporeality and eternality of the soul, while the latter words described the consequences of original sin.[3]

These changes in the various meanings of spirituality were accompanied by another and even more consequential shift. Jacques Leclercq observes that two kinds of theological schools had developed in the High Middle Ages, with two kinds of theology as the result. Schools for clerics were situated in cities and near cathedrals. With a curriculum based on the seven liberal arts, they sought to train future clerics for the "active" pastoral life. Such "school" theology was centered on an oral style of education based principally on the question-and-answer method. A problem was propounded, various authorities were adduced, and a solution was thus found. The intention was to inculcate clear, impersonal, unambiguous knowledge—even if it meant recourse to jargon. Magnificent though its accomplishments were in such theologians as Aquinas and Abelard, "scholastic" theology became gradually equated with rote learning and specialist argot.[4]

Over against it there arose a monastic theology that was tied to a rigorously ascetic life of prayer and worship and work. Because the monasteries were located in rural retreats that revered silence, it became a written as much as an oral style of theology. It was taught not by schoolmasters but by abbots or abbesses, who sought to tutor their monks and nuns in the "contemplative" life. This intensely personal kind of theology was based more on spiritual desire than on intellectual inquiry. It thus had recourse to poetry and metaphor rather than to precise technical terms. Monastic theology did not seek to cultivate the *knowledge* of God through abstract reasoning so much as the *experience* of God through concrete imagination. As with the ancient desert saints, so with these medieval monastics: they were concerned less with routing heresy than with overcoming temptation. They wanted to honor and praise God by means of an ever-enlarged participation in God's own life. Mystical union with God rather than propositional understanding of God was their goal. It is noteworthy that the most famous of these monastic theologians, Bernard of Clairvaux, made his motto *Credo ut experiar* rather than *Credo ut intelligam.*[5]

It is also noteworthy that, in his *Institutes of the Christian Religion,* John Calvin cites Bernard of Clairvaux more than any other theologian except Augustine of Hippo. Not at all the desiccated logician of divinity that he is often made out to be, Calvin called prayer "the central practice of the Christian life," and the longest chapter in the *Institutes* is devoted to prayer. Yet Calvin did not share the monastic conviction that the heart's desire is a sure guide to life in God. Calvin starchily declared the heart to be a factory for idol building. Perhaps this explains why Calvin chose the word *pietas* rather than *spiritualitas* to describe the Christian life of total devotion to God. The old Roman word, redolent with rich social and political connotations, helped guard against a potentially delusory inwardness. It connoted instead a sense of duty and responsibility, even patriotism; a deep devotion and loyalty to one's family and homeland; but also a kindness and tenderness toward others in need. In every case, *pietas* pointed the Romans to a reality beyond themselves—namely, to a huge sense of indebtedness to their country, to their parents, and of course to their gods. Calvin insisted, therefore, that a truly inward piety has its grounding in such outward acts of faith.

Both English and American Puritans followed Calvin's practice by employing the word *piety* for their own devotional practices. They, too, knew the perennial human temptation to confuse our fallen longings with the motions of the Holy Spirit. They thus insisted that life in Christ takes us *out* of ourselves—out of our pathetically small subjectivities—into the grand objective realm of the *not merely me*: into the eternal world of God's own justifying grace and sanctifying holiness. In the Puritan tradition, prayer itself was not understood as an entirely inward act of private and personal devotion. As the Westminster Shorter Catechism makes clear, prayer is one of the three "outward and ordinary means whereby Christ communicateth to us the benefits of redemption." The other two "outward means" are the Word truly preached and the sacraments rightly celebrated. In all three activities, Christians are recipients of theological gifts that make the life of piety inseparable from the life of worship and doctrine.

Their deadly separation occurred only during the Enlightenment. I believe that it is a mistake, therefore, to regard the current fashion for spirituality as a reaction against the cerebral kind of deistic theology that arose with the Enlightenment. Certainly, the seventeenth and eighteenth centuries marked a new turn to the outward and observable world that can be known rationally and scientifically. It is also true that a deistic theology followed from it. Yet even this empiricist turn was not purely outward and objective; it was also deeply inward and subjective. The notion that nature can be viewed neutrally was an intellectual deceit. It was but another lensed way of seeing, a new kind of subjectivism now disguised as pure objectivity. Even Descartes's famous formula—*Cogito, ergo sum*—is marked by its emphasis on the thinking subject: *I* think. Surely this highly individualized, subjective, autonomous, and reflexive self is the chief creation of the Enlightenment.[6]

It is no accident that a new and often nondoctrinal kind of pietism arose alongside the new secular rationalism as its close cousin. The Age of Reason was also the Age of Piety. It was the epoch not only of Gottfried Leibniz and Pierre Bayle, John Toland and William Paley, but also of Charles Wesley and Nikolaus Zinzendorf, the Freemasons and the Rosicrucians. They were all marked, albeit in different ways and degrees, by the modern turn to the sovereign subject whom Karl Barth calls the Absolute Man:

> [Enlightenment] man knows that he is linked with, and ultimately of the same substance as, the God significant for him in this double function. God is spirit, man is spirit too. God is mighty and so is man. God is wise and benevolent, and so is man. But he is all these things, of course, infinitely less perfect than God. Man's way of being these things is confused and fragmentary, but it *is* the same way. . . . Has not [this Enlightenment] man in fact asked himself and himself given the answer he apparently wished to hear from some other source? This is the question of which, thus expressed, man in the eighteenth century was not aware. This was the absolutism also inherent in his inner attitude to life; he assumed it to be self-evident that in taking himself into account, and himself answering the account, and then acting in obedience to it he was also showing the existence of God. . . . He believed—even in this inmost place we find him prey to a strange vicious circle—that by virtue of the reality of

his own existence he could vouch for God and in so doing for the possible existence of God.[7]

SPIRITUALITY AS SANCTIFICATION

I believe that much of contemporary spirituality is an extension of the delusory sovereignty that characterized Enlightenment mentality. Such pernicious self-referentiality can be overcome, I believe, only if we learn to cultivate a theologically grounded piety. At its best, the new concern with the spiritual life reflects a laudable desire to make Christian faith a matter of the heart no less than the head, a discipline of devotional practices rather than a repetition of doctrinal propositions. J. I. Packer, citing Henry Rack, offers a helpful definition of a distinctively Christian spirituality: it is an "enquiry into the whole Christian enterprise of pursuing, achieving, and cultivating communion with God, which includes both public worship and private devotion, and the results of these in actual Christian life."[8] Diogenes Allen makes a similar reading of spirituality as an attempt to deal seriously with the church's primary concern for holiness of life: "Christian spirituality concerns sanctification . . . the work of God the Holy Spirit, bringing to fullness the work of Christ, in the church, the body of Christ. Sanctification runs through the entire work of all the great theologians of the past and colors virtually *everything else* that they wrote."[9]

Anything less than a rigorous spirituality will make for a subjectivism that turns us into caricatures of ourselves rather than the Christian persons we are meant to be. The Greek *persona* means "mask." We cannot be persons at all without wearing masks, for masks enable us to assume our rightful roles. The poet W. H. Auden once observed that there is no real distinction between the sincere and the insincere, only between the sane who know they are wearing masks and the insane who do not. This is especially true of Christians. We perform our various earthly callings and tasks only as we wear one mask above all others: the mask of Christ. To wear any other is to ignore Luther's warning: "The moment I consider Christ and myself as two, I am gone." John Fletcher of Madeley, an eighteenth-century Anglican who quotes this saying of Luther, makes clear what is at stake in "putting on Christ." It requires, says Fletcher, a renunciation of

> all separate existence in Adam and from Adam. You will take Christ to be your life, you will become his members by eating his flesh and drinking his blood, you will consider his flesh as your flesh, his bone as your bone, his righteousness as your righteousness, his cross as your cross, and his crown (whether of thorns or glory) as your crown. You

will reckon yourself to be dead indeed unto sin, but alive unto God, through his dear Redeemer. You will renounce propriety, you will heartily and gladly say, "Not I, but Christ liveth, and only because He lives I do, and shall live also."[10]

The Pauline insistence that we "put on Christ" accounts, I believe, for the apostle's strange admonition that we not be caught naked at the Second Coming (2 Cor. 5:3). To wear the *persona* of Christ, Paul indicates, is to be clad with the garments of righteousness. The metaphor of clothing as a covering for sin runs throughout the Bible, from the moment the Lord God replaces the first couple's pathetic fig leaves with leather skins, to the proper dress that Jesus requires for those who are driven in from the streets to feast at the king's banquet (Matt. 22:11–14). If nakedness is a metaphor of our fallenness, then dress becomes something other than mere protection from the elements. We make theological no less than sartorial statements with our attire.

It is noteworthy that many highly spiritual folks in our time do not find anything extraordinary about their outward personification of Christ. Convinced that only the inward and spiritual truly matter, they enter the presence of the Lord wearing backward baseball caps, thigh-high skirts, muscle-preening polo shirts, and knockabout shoes. Thus do they make unconscious declarations that, for them, the act of worship is nothing extraordinary. It requires no drastic reclothing. Black Christians deny this false distinction. They worship God in the beauty of their best apparel. They want their clothes to reflect God's own glory. They have no dress-down days at their churches. They approach God, instead, in the splendor of their dress, outwardly embodying the claim that we are meant to be God's own well-clothed royalty, enjoying the marriage feast of the Lamb in *style*.

It has now become almost a commonplace to observe that, unlike these faithful black Christians, many people now identify themselves as "spiritual" but not "religious." Robert C. Fuller is one of their chief defenders. In a book titled *Spiritual, but Not Religious: Understanding Unchurched America*,[11] Fuller praises the spirituality that rejects the special authority of the Bible, the unique divinity of Jesus, the fallenness of humanity, and especially the church as a corporate community wherein sin is overcome and lives are reconformed to the image of God. Doctrines and institutions are moribund and stifling for such spiritual people.[12] Robert Wuthnow keenly disagrees. He shows what is almost inevitably self-centered about the contemporary turn to the inner self as the ultimate locus for an encounter with God. He quotes Thomas Moore's immensely popular *Care of the Soul* as evidence of the literal *self*ishness that underlies Moore's call for people to cultivate the sacred in everyday life and thus learn to be content with themselves. "Dropping the salvational fantasy," says Moore, "frees us up to the possibility of self-knowledge and self-acceptance."[13] No longer is the soul regarded the transcendent, unitary seat of selfhood implanted by God; it has become what Wuthnow calls the "dispersed self." Rather than defining itself in relation to received teachings and doctrines and social institutions, this new sort of soul creates its own ever-fluid identity through "a wide variety of encounters and experiences, including moments of interaction with sacred objects, such as trees and automobiles. Broadly speaking, it is a dispersion of experiences, themselves widely separated in space and time, with different people, and of varying significance."[14]

FORMALITY AND SPIRITUAL FORMATION

Ours is hardly the first age to have contested the relation of the subjective and the objective, the inward and the outward. It was a much-agitated issue between Puritans and Anglicans in the seventeenth century. Preaching at St. Paul's Cross in London during 1625, John Donne responded to Puritan critics of the Church of England: "[I]f I come to extemporal prayer, and extemporal preaching, I shall come to an extemporal faith, and extemporal religion; and then I must look for an extemporal Heaven, a Heaven to be made for me." "Let us not *pray*," Donne concluded, "not *preach*, not *hear*, slackly, suddenly, unadvisedly, extemporally, occasionally, indiligently. Let all our speech to him, be weighed, and measured in the weights of the *Sanctuary*."[15] An ad hoc kind of Christianity leads, so Donne contends, to a faith that is so self-absorbed that even Paradise must exist primarily for him alone.

Donne and his fellow establishmentarians were accused of stifling the Nonconformist freedom to cultivate an inward and personal piety, replacing it with a stiff and unfeeling adherence to the *Book of Common Prayer*. Ramie Targoff demonstrates that the *Book of Common Prayer*, a work that has influenced worship in the Anglophone world perhaps more than any other, was much more than Thomas Cranmer's clever theological compromise between Romanists on the right and Calvinists on the left. It was the product, instead, of the Church of England's deliberate insistence that carefully scripted public worship shapes and transforms Christian worshipers in indispensable ways. Without such formal rigor and beauty, the spiritual life can dissipate into chaos and inconsequence.

Sixteenth-century Anglicans hardly came upon their conviction afresh. Aristotle had insisted a millennium earlier that there is a causal link between ethics and habits. Moral virtue depends, according to Aristotle, on practices that we carefully learn and often repeat. As important as doctrinal orthodoxy always remained, the early church agreed with Aristotle, insisting that its public liturgy formed the character and lives of Christian worshipers. Gradually, especially in the late Middle Ages, this link between the public and the personal was obscured. As the Latin mass came to be celebrated behind the rood screen, so that parishioners could neither see it nor even hear it in their own language, the Catholic Church supplied them with *Lay Folks' Mass Books.* These worship guides, Targoff shows, encouraged individual worshipers to undertake their own meditations and examinations of conscience as the monks said and sang the service beyond the wall. Catholics rejected a common liturgical text, even in the vernacular, on the grounds that it would distract laypeople from their private devotions.

The Anglicans regarded the Puritan exaltation of original prayers and extemporaneous sermons as an odd return to Catholic practice—insofar as it made worshipers into virtual nonparticipants at a service that itself lay at the mercy of the minister. Like Luther, these Anglicans exalted the aural over the visual. When we worship, Luther insisted, we should stick our eyes in our ears. Richard Hooker, the chief defender of the *Book of Common Prayer,* also agreed with Calvin that human nature is far too weak and fallible ever to rely on a spontaneous spiritual life: we always need external props and aids. Yet Hooker was not concerned only about religious order and control. The bookless and unreading masses convinced him of their need for standardized liturgical practices that would deepen devotion to God in ways that private promptings of the Spirit do not.

Like the Puritans, the Anglicans sought the transformation of the human heart. Yet the heart remains a notoriously invisible and unreliable thing, whereas outward postures and gestures and enunciations can be both seen and measured, as can communicants kneeling at an altar or serving each other bread and wine. The Puritans charged that such public repetition of *Prayer Book* confessions and litanies encourages hypocrisy. Donne and a host of other Anglicans rejected this easy divide between the authentic and the theatrical. We become the things that we perform, they argued, for it is the outward life that shapes the inward. The Lutheran theologian Joseph Sittler advised the church to watch her language. Sloppy worship produces sloppy existence before both God and our neighbors. Stanley Hauerwas and William Willimon make the link between liturgy and ethics far more drastic: "You begin by singing some sappy sentimental hymn, then you pray some pointless prayer, and the next thing you know you have murdered your best friend."[16]

THE OUTWARD SHAPING OF THE INWARD LIFE

I confess that my own heroes in the faith are men and women whose outward and public faith exhibited their inward and private piety. C. S. Lewis is altogether typical. Once when two of Lewis's friends came to collect him for a day's trip away from Oxford, they noticed that Lewis was walking up and down in his garden while they sat impatiently in the car. When Lewis finally joined them, his friends demanded an explanation. Lewis replied that he must say his prayers before departing. Prayer, for C. S. Lewis, was an outward, even visible habit that shaped his inward and spiritual life. His prayer life was also rooted in hard study. When Lewis was asked what kind of devotional reading he most favored, his interlocutor perhaps assumed that he would answer by naming something like Oswald Chambers's *My Utmost for His Highest*. Instead, Lewis replied that his spiritual life was enriched by such theological treatises as Athanasius's *On the Incarnation*. Lewis was not preening. He was making the salient point that a piety that is not based on—and that does not lead to—a profounder *knowledge* of God is a bogus and bankrupt piety. It comes as no surprise that Lewis opposed innovations in worship. The moment our attention is drawn to the service itself, rather than the God whom we are meant to serve, worship is broken:

> Every service is a structure of acts and words through which we receive a sacrament, or repent, or supplicate, or adore. And it enables us to do these things best—if you like, it "works" best—when through long familiarity, we don't have to think about it. As long as you notice, and have to count, the steps, you are not yet dancing but learning to dance. . . . The perfect church service would be one we were almost unaware of; our attention would have been on God.[17]

Piety is rooted in action as well as prayer and worship. Gerard Manley Hopkins, the great Jesuit poet of nineteenth-century England, was once asked by his friend Robert Bridges for advice about overcoming his inveterate unbelief. Bridges expected Hopkins to reply with a lengthy theological treatise. He received, instead, a two-word reply: "Give alms." Hopkins's point was simple: the Christian faith requires our habituation to self-giving outward practice in order for it to issue in a life of God-loving inward belief. This is hardly to suggest that Hopkins found his ethical and spiritual life easy. On the contrary, it was often agonizing. His "dark" or "terrible" sonnets, as they are often called, declare the awful otherness and hiddenness of God, no less than the wondrous nearness and dearness of God. The heavenly Father and Lord of Jesus Christ, as Hopkins understood profoundly, is not our heavenly chum. He is the sovereign, free, and living Lord who comforts only as he also frightens. Hence Hopkins's fearful question in his sonnet that begins "Thou art indeed just, Lord": Could God's love do him any greater harm than the depredations of his worst foe?

> Wert thou my enemy, o thou my friend,
> How wouldst thou worse, I wonder, than thou dost
> Defeat, thwart me?[18]

Hopkins insists that the gospel is never something that we can comfortably *assume* to know in advance, something that we need only *apply* either here or there. On the contrary, the gospel always awaits our astonished rediscovery, indeed, our constant and trembling reconversion. The reason is not hard to find. The Christ's cross is at once the place of God's supreme light as well as his complete darkness. To bear it faithfully is to be vexed no less than cheered. Bishop Kallistos Ware thus sums up the fearful wisdom of Abba Agathon, one of the desert saints of ancient Egypt: "Prayer is the hardest of all tasks. If we do not find it difficult, perhaps it is because we have not really started to pray."[19]

Hopkins was so convinced of the link between the outward and inward life that he joined his friends at Oxford in practicing what they called "the discipline of the eyes." They believed that what we *see* shapes our souls. To behold ugliness and vulgarity and crudity—whether on television or billboards—is to risk the twisting and perversion of our very lives. Karl Barth also believed that what he *heard* shaped his soul. He began every day by listening to Mozart for an hour and then praying for another hour.[20] Barth was not seeking to put himself into something as silly as "the mood for prayer." He wanted instead to hear earthly echoes and musical parables of the heavenly kingdom, so that when he prayed he might participate in the very life of God. In order that his prayers not become mere subjective meanderings among his own small-minded concerns, Barth always prayed aloud, even though he prayed alone. Only in prayer, Barth observed, do we not wear masks. There we stand naked before God. Because such nakedness cannot be publicly displayed, Barth was loath to exhibit his own piety:

> The witness of the disciple consists in the fact that he refrains from attesting his piety as such. If he is to display the Kingdom of God, and proclaim it from the housetops (Mt. 10:27), he will not make a show of his own devoutness but keep it to himself, allowing God alone to be the One who judges and rewards him. This restraint will be a witness to the pious world with its continual need to publicise itself, and perhaps even to the secular world. It will speak for itself—or rather, it will speak for that which does seriously and truly cry out for publicity.[21]

THE WESLEYS AS EXEMPLARS OF TRUE PIETY

What, then, are we to conclude from these distinctions and examples about the outward and visible faith in Christ that forms the basis for an inward and invisible piety? I believe that the resurgent interest in the life of prayer will prove itself lasting rather than faddish only if it issues in a renewed emphasis on doctrinal preaching and liturgical worship. These are the places *par excellence* where we become public Christians of the kind whose devotional life is not subjectively self-serving. Hence my disagreement with Alister McGrath's commendation of Archbishop Donald Coggan's claim "The journey from the head to the heart is one of the longest and most difficult that we know." This may have once been true of those who espoused a certain kind of Catholic or Protestant scholasticism, but I do not believe it to be true today. "Theological correctness" is a problem only to a minuscule minority. There may be few remaining dispensationalists who open their Scofield Bible every morning to trace the divine ordering of the successive ages, even as I suppose there is a tiny tribe of Calvinists who ponder the Canons of Dort every night before bed. But surely the chief difficulty of our time is that our piety is too little rooted in theology, not that it is dominated by doctrinal considerations.[22]

The journey from the heart to the head is not only the most difficult but also the most necessary in our subjectivist and emotionalist age. We need to balance Bernard's *Credo ut experiar* with Augustine's *Fides quaerens intellectum*. Experience of God will be something other than terrible self-delusion only if it is grounded in *intellectum*—in an ever-greater knowledge and understanding of God. The terrible Christian scandal of our time, as I have sought repeatedly to emphasize, is that a sappy sort of spirituality overemphasizes the heart at the huge expense of the head. I concede that there is legitimate worry about a false emphasis on knowledge. Yet learning becomes a temptation to arrogance and a distraction from true piety only when it is disordered—that is, when it is loved more than God and thus when it becomes a substitute for the love of God.

From the medieval monastics to Wesley in the eighteenth century, this has not been the case. The great devotional writers of the West have all stressed the interstitial relationship of knowledge and piety: *the love of learning and the desire for God*, as Leclercq titles his splendid book. "From his arrival at Clairvaux to his entry into Heaven," Leclercq writes, "the real, the only Bernard was, indissolubly and simultaneously, a learned man and a man of God, a thinker and a saint, a humanist and a mystic."[23] Our best Protestant pietists are agreed. "It is a fundamental principle with us," John Wesley declared, "that to renounce reason is to renounce religion, that religion and reason go hand in hand, and that all irrational religion is false religion."[24] Thus did he write and publish digests of several major Enlightenment thinkers, including David Hume and John Locke. Wesley wanted his followers to engage their piety with the most rigorous philosophical thought of their era. He sought also to master the best science of his time, convinced that "the book of nature is written in an universal character, which every man may read in his own language."[25] Nor did Wesley ever stop emphasizing the importance of what

George Whitefield called the "externals"—the ordinary (and often uninspiring) daily practice of self-denial, the routine doing of good for people in trouble, the sometime dutiful observance of prayer and fasting.

For both of the Wesleys, private piety is rooted in the life of public faith. "There is no holiness," John insisted, "that is not a social holiness." He and his brother were profoundly concerned with the amelioration of human suffering—poverty and illiteracy, sickness and criminality, hunger and homelessness. Yet they were not romantic about God's "preferential option for the poor." Sin infects the penniless no less than the rich, even though it does greater harm in the wealthy than the poor. Poverty can be the occasion for a terrible envy, just as prosperity can induce an even more damning complacency. Both rich *and* poor need saving. Charles Wesley's hymn gets the matter exactly right: it is not the poor who are God's "preferential option" as such, but the "humble poor" whose neediness has opened them to the grace of God as the cushioned and comfortable are not. Two of my former students who serve as copastors of an inner-city Baptist church in Trenton, New Jersey, happily confess that they are never laden with the unhappy suburbanite task of persuading their parishioners that they need God.

The Wesleys learned, to their pain, that the path of radical Christian practice is strewn with hazards and threats. It is a lesson easily forgotten among suburban Christians. Charles and John did not speak of their Christian "walk," therefore, but employed far more militant metaphors: "struggle," "contest," "battle," "warfare." "Soldiers of Christ, Arise," Charles Wesley cries out in one of his best hymns, "and put your armor on." "Wrestle and fight and pray," he adds, "tread all the powers of darkness down and win the well-fought day."[26] This call to Christian arms was no idle analogy. The Wesleys repeatedly stirred up riots in places where they were preaching. In a town called Devizes, for example, the local Anglican ministers were so riled by their influence on the masses that they aroused a mob against them. These ruffians first stoned and then flooded with firehoses the house where the Wesleys were staying. The hooligans ripped off the shutters and drove the preachers' horses into a pond. Local Methodist leaders were ducked in this same pond; others had bulldogs set on them, their homes looted, their businesses ruined.

Charles Wesley is not to be compared with the composers of contemporary praise songs, whose poetic worth is negligible if even detectible. That Charles stole his hymn tunes from the drinking ditties sung in taverns is a canard. He was a poet of the first rank who was ever so careful to fit his text to appropriate music. That the two Wesleys often made their witness in public houses—outraging their owners—has contributed to this popular misconception, as has a certain confusion over the musical term *bar tune* or *bar form*, which has nothing to do with inebriating liquor. One of Charles Wesley's most remarkable hymns, "Jesus, Lover of My Soul," may have been written, in fact, in response to the frightening incident at Devizes. It is a deeply mystical, even a spiritually erotic hymn; for it speaks openly of Jesus as the spouse and lover of Christians. Yet there is nothing smarmy about the intimacy with Christ that Wesley enjoins. Set to a minor key by Joseph Parry, it has a haunting quality that makes one tremble at the thought of fleeing to Christ's breast as our only security in the midst of life's floods and storms, whether human or natural. We are naked to evil, Charles Wesley confesses, unless Christ shields us:

> Other refuge have I none, hangs my helpless soul on thee;
> leave, ah! leave me not alone, still support and comfort me.
> All my trust on thee is stayed; all my help from thee I bring;
> cover my defenseless head with the shadow of thy wing.[27]

The revival led by the Wesleys did so much to relieve human misery that they may well have prevented the political violence that devastated France in 1789 from occurring in England. Yet, while they were opposed to the American Revolution, the Wesleys were far from political conservatives. John especially abominated the institution of slavery. One of his last acts before dying was to call the abolitionist William Wilberforce to his bedside, encouraging him in his battle against the slave trade. Earlier he had written Wilberforce a letter declaring slavery to be "that execrable villainy which is the scandal of religion, of England, of human nature."[28] Two days before his death, Wesley penned his final letter, again to Wilberforce: "Reading this morning a tract wrote by a poor African, I was particularly struck by that circumstance, that a man who has a black skin, being wronged or outraged by a white man, can have no redress; it being a *law* in our Colonies that the *oath* of a black man against a white goes for nothing. What villainy is this!"[29] It would be a sign of true Christian seriousness if our contemporary advocates of spirituality were to condemn elective abortion and capital punishment with equal vehemence.

THE CENTRALITY OF PREACHING
AND HYMNS FOR WORSHIP

The Wesleys, like their medieval counterparts, understood that preaching helps guarantee the reciprocal relation of heart and head. Instead of constantly asking, what can God do *for* us?—how we might come to feel more pious or to be more holy or to act more spiritually—doctrinal preaching enables us to ask the far profounder question: What does God want to do *through* us? The good news of the gospel is that God is determined to create a radically redemptive community, a new people whose benefits are not meant primarily for themselves but for God and the world. This transformed body is sustained by wisdom that the world regards as folly—the preaching of Christ crucified (1 Corinthians 23). Hence Paul's insistence that the gospel is not something to be preached so much as it is preaching itself. "Faith comes from hearing the message," he declares in Romans 10:17: *fides ex auditu*.

The Shema calls Israel not to *see* God but to *hear* him, for hearing is the organ for receiving and obeying commands. The eyes have lids that can gaze or blink back or shut out; they are the organs of vision and surfaces. The ears have no such flaps; they are pierced with truths that require heeding or spurning. This is not to discount vision, even though Scripture constantly stresses the priority of faith over sight: Jesus congratulates those who have not seen but nonetheless believe, even as Paul declares that "we live by faith, not by sight" (2 Cor. 5:7). The eyes provide vision that leads to understanding, and thus are they ever so important. But understanding follows from faithful obedience, rather than being a prior condition for it. *Credo ut intelligam*, declared St. Anselm; he believed in order that he might understand. Saving faith cannot do without understanding, but it is often enabled and perennially sustained by faithful proclamation, by preaching that issues in transformed personal and communal life.

The preaching that engenders authentic piety must be founded on the bedrock claims contained in the great confessions of the church. They are not only reflective distillations *of* Christian experience but also a powerful spur *to* Christian experience. The larger our theological claims, the larger our encounter with God, both communally and personally. Charles Spurgeon once declared, for example, that anyone having a small creed also had a small church. Heresy is deadly, among other reasons, because it leads to counterfeit religious experience. For a religious person to have a false idea of God, William Temple once observed, is to be worse off than having God not at all: it would be better to be an atheist. Contemporary Christian spirituality could be rescued from an enormous vapidity by learning even such basic doctrines as justification by grace alone and sanctification through faith alone. Both doctrines teach that what God in Christ has done *for* us, God insists also in doing *in* us.[30] So would a renewed emphasis on the doctrine of the Trinity help overcome our pernicious individualism. Only because we believe that God has a rich and complete life unto himself—as the three persons of the Holy Trinity give themselves utterly without stint to each other—do we also believe that the communal God is free to act in our behalf, delivering us from our present misery. Such deliverance comes only as our communities of faith enable us to participate in God's own triune life of total, self-surrendering love.

Good preaching and teaching will sustain Christian piety only as they are inseparably tied to good worship. As I have sought repeatedly to show, such worship must rely more on ceremony than spontaneity. Liturgical worship need not be highfalutin and altogether solemn. It can often be quite simple and uncomplicated and joyful, as the worship of the Taizé community demonstrates. Yet it must be ceremonial if it is to avoid the shallowness of spontaneity that we have heard John Donne complaining about. Ceremony, by reaching deliberately for the artificial, can plumb the depths of genuine significance, as Thomas Howard explains:

> Through the imposed, we meet the natural. Through the prescribed, we meet the sincere. This is always and everywhere true. No tribe, culture, civilization, or society has ever operated on any other assumption.
>
> Birth rites, puberty rites, marriage rites, death rites: no one gives the back of his hand to these things. Huns, Florentines, Saxons, Watutsis, and Athenians all agree here. If you are approaching something significant, or *if you want to discern the significance of an event*, you must submit to ceremony.[31]

Contemporary spirituality can also be given dignity and depth through the quality of church music as well as the character of the preaching and praying. Especially for those of us who stand in the noncreedal traditions, the heart of our theology lies in our hymns. They are our sung creeds: they often set forth what we believe and practice more sharply and freshly than either our prayers or our sermons. Yet in many evangelical churches, our richly theological hymns are being rapidly replaced with religiously vacuous praise songs. As far as I can see, these choruses are useful mainly in helping young Christians memorize Scripture. Yet they threaten to arrest believers in a perpetual milk-drinking adolescence, since these praise songs are very rapidly becoming standard fare for adult worship. Let it be clear that I am not making an elitist call for high-toned anthems and complex cantatas, nor for a return to hymns with archaic words and unsingable tunes. But I do believe that we must reclaim the imaginatively rich theology that characterizes the greatest of both our ancient and modern hymns.

Consider, for example, four works that few of my students know—including, alas, few of the seminarians whom I teach: "A Mighty Fortress Is Our God," "Love Divine, All Loves Excelling," "When I Survey the Wondrous Cross," and "Come Ye Sinners, Poor and Needy." Then consider a praise song that they *all* know: "Majesty." The three hymns and the one gospel song, both in their lyrics and their melodies, make us shudder with awe, tremble with thanksgiving, stand aghast at Golgotha, mark the wonder of Christ's intimacy with us, and ponder the cost of our glad surrender to the God who has yielded himself up for our sake. The praise song, by contrast, has rhymes that are banal, a tune that is saccharine, and a meaning that is sentimental, if it is discernible at all. The authority that supposedly flows from the heavenly throne, rather than being clearly defined, is murkily praised. There is no christologi-cal link, for example, to the Son who rules at his Father's right hand, nor to the Scripture and the Tradition that remain the real authorities of the one holy catholic and apostolic church.

A serious case can be made for Isaac Watts's "When I Survey the Wondrous Cross" as the sublimest hymn in the English tongue.[32] It is indeed a poignantly introspective and "I"-centered hymn, combining deep theology with deep piety. Yet the original words even of this unsurpassed poem have been doc-tored. It originally began with these lines: "When I survey the wondrous cross,/Where the young Prince of glory died." Watts was willing to confess—at least in his bravest moments—that Jesus did not die as a tired old codger, full and weary of years, but as a man on the very threshold of adult achieve-ment. Thus did Watts emphasize, in single word, both the horror of Christ's early death and the wonder that the gospel is meant for all—for the exuberant young no less than for the exhausted old. Even worse damage has been done to Watts's great hymn by squeamish spiritualizers—from the eighteenth cen-tury to our own time—who have excised its most vivid stanza. There Watts links the outward gruesomeness of Christ's saving act with the drastic inward effects that it works in us:

> His dying crimson, like a robe,
> Spreads o'er his body on the tree:
> Then I am dead to all the globe,
> And all the globe is dead to me.[33]

The gore that drenched Christ's naked body became his gown of glory. Here was no noble martyr's death. Here the King of the cosmos bore our sin away in the stream of his own blood. Nothing other than such love can demand our bodies and souls, our minds and hearts, our very lives, our all. Nothing else can rescue us from a vague and often heretical spirituality, prompting a strong outward faith that sustains a vital inward piety. Nothing less can constitute the basis of a Christian culture that might invigorate the life of the church and its academies, and thus the life of the world as well.

7

Union and Communion:
Joining the Fellowship of Heaven

Gerald Bray

Gerald L. Bray is the Anglican Professor of Divinity at Beeson Divinity
School of Samford University. A native of Canada, Bray was trained in
Classics at McGill University, took a degree in Russian literature in London, and holds both master's and doctoral degrees from the University
of Paris–Sorbonne. Before coming to Beeson, Bray was tutor in Christian doctrine and philosophy at Oak Hill Theological College in London. He is an ordained priest in the Church of England. A prodigious
scholar and linguist, Bray has written numerous articles and books,
including *The Doctrine of God* (1993), *Documents of the English Reformation*
(1994*), Biblical Interpretation: Past and Present* (1996), and *The Personal
God* (1999). He has also edited *Tudor Church Reform* (2000) and three volumes in the *Ancient Christian Commentary* series (1998–2000).

In this chapter, Bray examines the way in which the spiritual experience of Christians is rooted in the biblical revelation of God as the
Father, the Son, and the Holy Spirit. Working from New Testament
and early church texts, Bray explores the themes of adoption and
assurance as they are related to the revelation of God as a Trinitarian
community of holiness and love. Although evangelicals are formally
orthodox in the acceptance of the doctrine of the Trinity, this fundamental Christian teaching is in fact frequently ignored in evangelical
piety. Many contributors to this volume have called for a more fully
Trinitarian spirituality, and Bray shows why this is so important for
Christian faith and life.

࿐ ࿐ ࿐

Knowing God is the heart of our spiritual experience as Christians, and the God
whom we have come to know is a Trinity of three coequal persons, revealed to
us as the Father, the Son, and the Holy Spirit. If we do not understand this, then

109

there is something vital to our lives about which we are unclear. Of course, by itself, that does not call our faith into question, since there are obviously many things we experience of which we have little or no real understanding. But it does handicap us if we are trying to grow in our knowledge of God, since unless we have some grasp of the basic principles on which that knowledge is based, we are likely to mistake what is happening to us and perhaps even go astray as we try to interpret it. Certainly our growth will be stunted in ways that can and should be avoided by a careful study of how God has revealed himself to us.

To help us understand the importance of this, and at least one way in which we can take the concept of the Trinity on board, let us look at the New Testament evidence. We shall take this in stages—first a single verse, then a paragraph, then a whole chapter—but each of these stages marks another step in our growth toward a deeper understanding and experience of the God who has redeemed us in Jesus Christ and united us to God in the power of the Holy Spirit.

GALATIANS 4:6—THE IMPORTANCE OF ADOPTION

Let us begin by remembering that we are *sons* (i.e., children and heirs) of God. What difference does this make? We are adopted children, of course, because spiritually speaking, our birth parents are Adam and Eve. Being adopted by God does not change that, and as long as we live, the sin we have inherited from them will continue to affect our lives. But if this is true at one level, it is also true that because we are sons, God has put the Spirit of God's Son into our hearts, crying *"Abba,* Father" (Gal. 4:6). Do you see the Trinity in this verse? Spirit, Son, Father—all three are intimately involved in what happens to us thanks to our adoption by God.

To put it a different way, we are now "seated . . . in the heavenly realms in Christ Jesus" (Eph. 2:6). The barriers that once cut us off from God have been broken down, and we have been given access through Christ to the Father, in the Holy Spirit (Eph. 2:18). In the Old Testament, God was present among God's people but dwelt in a kind of box. This might be the ark of the covenant or the Holy of Holies in the Temple, but either way, God lived in a sacred space that was barred to ordinary people. Only the high priest could go into that holy place, and then only once a year, when he made the sacrifice demanded on the Jewish Day of Atonement. But when Christ died on the cross, making the one, perfect, and eternal sacrifice for our sins, the veil in the Temple that separated the Holy of Holies from the people was torn in two, giving us free access to God's presence and inner life.

In a way, it is rather like experiencing an atom, if you can imagine that for a moment. On the outside, the atom is one—simple and stable. But cut it open, and inside you have a dynamic life of protons, neutrons, and electrons so powerful that it can blow the whole world to bits. This is something like the transformation that has occurred in our lives. When we received Christ into our hearts, the way into God was opened up, and our old lives were blown away, to be replaced by his presence in our hearts. You can call this being "born again" or "dying and rising with Christ," but however you describe it, the old has passed away and all things have become new in him. We are now walking with God as he is in himself.

Christ's sacrifice is made real for us in and through the Holy Spirit, whom God has put in our hearts to teach us what God is like. The Spirit makes it possible for us to be united with Christ, so that like him, we too can pray "*Abba, Father.*" Paul's use of the Aramaic word *Abba* is a deliberate reminder that this was the way that Jesus prayed to God, and the way in which he taught his disciples to pray too. Jews did not normally do this, and when Jesus began to speak of God as his Father, they were scandalized, because it appeared to them that he was making himself equal to God (John 5:18).

Jesus is God, of course, and as the Bible tells us, he is the Father's only begotten Son (John 1:14). In other words, Jesus was the only man in history whose birth father was God. But we who have been adopted as sons and therefore as brothers of Christ enjoy the same privilege of a direct relationship with the Father as the birth Son has always enjoyed. Like him, we too can pray *Abba*, not in our own strength but by virtue of the Spirit, who aids our weakness and who prays for us even when we cannot pray for ourselves. This is the greatness and the glory of adoption by God—the most important single thing that can ever happen to any one of us, and at the heart of our adoption is this intimate experience of the Trinity, the inner life of God.

PHILIPPIANS 2:5–11—THE IMPORTANCE OF ATTITUDE

Once we have got the concept of adoption under our belt, it is time to move on to the next stage—the problem of attitude. Anyone who has teenage children knows exactly what this is all about. For some reason, it seems that younger children generally obey their parents and often have quite a positive outlook on life. But when the teen years hit, rebellion and lethargy have a way of setting in. Nobody really understands why young people, at the height of their physical strength and mental agility, so often insist on trying to deny everything they have been given thus far in life. Older people would give anything to have those advantages back again, and it puzzles them to see teenagers react in this way— even if it is also true that they were once like that themselves.

Christians can also go through a spiritual form of adolescence and lose that freshness that the Bible describes as their "first love." They can become rebellious and resentful of the demands their Christian commitment seems to be making of them. Outsiders may think that all is well and that these Christians are enjoying the best years of their lives, but inside there is a spiritual turmoil and dryness that makes them unhappy with their lot. When this happens, we need to learn again the importance of attitude, and few biblical texts are more helpful in this respect than Philippians 2:5–11.

From this passage we learn first that Christ is equal with God. This equality is fundamental, because it is that which gives him the freedom to deny himself and to submit voluntarily to the will of the Father. This point needs to be emphasized, particularly at a time when it is widely believed that equality and submission are mutually contradictory. If a woman is equal to her husband, we are now being told, then she should not be expected to submit to him, and the apostle Paul was wrong to teach people otherwise. Reasoning of this kind sounds very persuasive, but it ignores the fact that submission is only possible on the basis of fundamental equality—otherwise, it would not be submission but subjection, leading directly to domination and tyranny.

Submission is the very opposite of this. Far from being an invitation to domination, it is a means by which the bond of love is strengthened. By submitting himself to the Father, Christ made it possible for the Father to show the true extent of his love for his Son—by raising him from the dead. What would have happened if Jesus had taken the attitude that as he was equal to the Father, he did not have to submit to his will? The glorious work of human salvation would never have taken place, and we would be dead in trespasses and sins. The Son's attitude to his relationship with the Father is not a minor point that can be glossed over—it is the very heart and foundation of the gospel message.

Notice carefully what Paul says in Philippians. The Son of God chose to submit to the Father by assuming the role of a servant. In that role, he became a man. The order here is very important. Some people are tempted to say that Jesus was equal to God in his divinity but inferior to him in his humanity, as if the man Jesus of Nazareth had no choice but to do what God told him. This way of thinking can be justified if we think of divinity and humanity as things or substances. Divinity as a quality is obviously superior to humanity, and in that sense the traditional expression is correct. But Jesus was never a man without also being God at the same time, and so it is misleading to say that during the time of his incarnation he was "inferior" to the Father. His incarnation was not the cause but the consequence of his servanthood, which he had already taken on beforehand. If the immortal Son of God was to suffer and die for the sins of the human race, he had to acquire a means by which he could do that, and so the incarnation became logically necessary. But we must never forget that the one who learned obedience in the school of suffering was not a man striving to measure up to the demands of God, but God himself submitting in the fullness of divine power to the Father's will, which was that we should be saved from our sins.

In reminding us of this, the apostle Paul takes us right to the very heart of God, which is the relationship of love between the Father and the Son that has made such an act of self-sacrifice both possible and productive. But the apostle reminds us of this in order to tell us that we, too, must have this attitude in us. To be a Christian is to submit to the point of self-sacrifice, to die with Christ in order that we might also rise with him into a new and better life. We cannot do this by ourselves, of course, and this is why God has put the Spirit of God's Son into our hearts. Paul does not mention the Holy Spirit explicitly in this passage, but the Spirit's presence and work in our hearts is the context of everything that he says. He begins the passage by telling us to have the mind of Christ in us, and that is possible only by having his Spirit—and by listening obediently to him.

Today it is common to hear people talk about the fullness of the Holy Spirit and the need for us to experience this fullness in our lives, but unfortunately they do not always connect this to that attitude of humble obedience to the will of God that is such a fundamental feature of the Christian life. It sometimes seems as if these people have been beguiled by great expectations of some extraordinary spiritual gift, when in fact they need to learn the simple steps of daily obedience. Instant gratification replaces steady growth and the way to lasting happiness, with the inevitable result that many people are "burned out" and disappointed in their hopes. There is no need to deny the miraculous or say that moments of exaltation do not occur—they clearly do. But they are by definition exceptional, and the Christian life is a full-time occupation in which an attitude of submissive obedience, not an expectation of exceptional blessing, is the chief hallmark. And as soon as we talk about obedience, we are back to the Trinity—the Holy Spirit who makes it possible for us to be conformed to the attitude of the Son in fulfilling the will of the Father.

ROMANS 8—THE IMPORTANCE OF ASSURANCE

Obedience is foundational to our spiritual lives, but how can we prevent a life of daily obedience from becoming a form of spiritual drudgery? Many people do God's will as they see it for years, and yet do not seem to reap any tangible reward. This is not a new problem, of course—long before the coming of Christ, the psalmist complained to God that the wicked prosper and the righteous seem to do nothing but suffer (Psalm 73). How is it possible to accept this apparent injustice, without rebelling against a God who seems to bestow divine favors so unfairly? Christians who are called to endure a life of hardship need to have a good reason for it if they are going to keep going, and this is where the importance of assurance comes in. Like submission, assurance is often misunderstood, and so we need to clear the ground a bit first. To know that we are saved and going to heaven when we die is not a form of pride or presumption, although many people seem to have this impression. Christians have no business going around boasting that they are somehow better (or better off) than other people, and very few in fact do. The reason for this is that our assurance of salvation is not based on anything we have done but on what God has done for us—a very different thing. Sinners who are saved by grace have not accomplished anything, and it becomes them to be correspondingly modest. If we boast at all, then we should boast about what God has done for us, in spite of ourselves. And when we do that, we shall soon find that we are face to face once again with the doctrine of the Trinity.

The logic of Christian assurance is spelled out with the greatest clarity in Romans 8, and the Trinitarian implications are there for all to see. God the Father has condemned human sin in the sacrificial death of the Son. That death has the power to take away the burden of sin and the sentence of death that once hung over us. The result of this is not that we have gone back to the state of Adam in the garden of Eden (something that would merely have exposed us to the possibility of sinning again) but that we have been born again into a new life in Christ. This is the work of the Holy Spirit in our hearts. As the Spirit of Christ, he makes us righteous in God's eyes. What we could never do or be in ourselves, the Spirit has provided for us, by uniting us with Christ and thereby shielding us from the wrath of God poured out against sinners. Paradoxical as it may sound, a Christian who sins is drawn closer to Christ, because he or she becomes more dependent on him for redemption. Growth in the Christian life is seen most clearly in the way in which an awareness of this dependence develops in us. The apostle Paul, for example, was more conscious of his sinfulness toward the end of his life than he was at the beginning. Writing to the Ephesians, sometime in the last phase of his earthly ministry, he had to stretch the Greek language in order to express it, by calling himself "less than the least of all God's people" (Eph. 3:8). But far from despairing at his apparent lack of progress in spiritual things, Paul was reassured by this, since he also knew that God had given him the grace to preach among the Gentiles the unsearchable riches of Christ.

The Holy Spirit, as the Spirit of the Father, gives life to our mortal bodies. Only God can give us life, and it bubbles up inside us like a spring in the desert. One of the greatest testimonies to the reality of this is the sight of Christians rejoicing in the midst of pain and suffering. It happens all the time, in every part of the world. Visitors to churches in the slums of third-world cities are always struck by the tremendous joy that exudes from those congregations. Time and again, individuals who have been struck down by some debilitating disease impress others by the calm acceptance with which they deal with this apparent tragedy. Those who are bereaved grieve, but not as those without hope, because they know that their loved ones, however much they miss them, have gone to a better place, where we shall one day be reunited with them. And last but not least, those who have sunk to the bottom are turned around and given a second chance. One way or another, every Christian knows this from experience, and when things look bad for us we always have that to hang on to. As the psalmist put it: "Weeping may remain for a night, but rejoicing comes in the morning" (Ps. 30:5).

To have the Spirit of Sonship is to know that we are children of God the Father. This means that we have the guarantee that where God is, we shall be also. In the longer term, we know that when we die we shall go to be with God in heaven. But in the shorter term, and this is what matters here and now, we enjoy the "first fruits" of eternal life already. The concept of "first fruits" may be unfamiliar to those who are not engaged in agriculture, but a little thought will tell us what they are: the first signs of the blessing that is to come. They may not be as ripe as the later harvest, but they often taste sweeter, just because they are fresh and new. We may compare them to a warm day in spring. The temperature may be a long way off what the hot summer days will bring, but somehow we appreciate the spring day more, because of the freshness and the promise of future hope that the returning sun brings. We do not judge the first fruits by the objective reality but by the subjective experience we have of them. In spiritual terms, they give us an assurance of blessings to come that will far surpass the objective reality of the present, and it is because of this that we rejoice.

The Holy Spirit in our hearts gives us the strength to pray when words fail us. It is the Spirit who nourishes and maintains our relationship with God, guiding us through the twists and turns of daily life and showing us at each bend in the road how all things work together for good to those who love God and who have been chosen according to his purpose. The Christian life is nothing less than the fellowship of the Trinity, in whom we live and move and have our being. Let us pray that as we go along the road that leads to the heavenly city to which we have been summoned, that we shall know God the Father, Son, and Holy Spirit more deeply, and rest in God's love more securely with every step that we take.

8

Growing in the Grace and Knowledge of Our Lord and Savior Jesus Christ

Mark R. Talbot

Mark R. Talbot teaches philosophy at Wheaton College. He is a graduate of Seattle Pacific College (B.A.) and the University of Pennsylvania (Ph.D.). He has written *The Signs of True Conversion* (2000) and coedited *Limning the Psyche: Explorations in Christian Psychology* (1997). He is the vice chair of the Council of the Alliance of Confessing Evangelicals and an executive editor for *Modern Reformation* magazine.

In this chapter, Talbot locates the discussion of spirituality in the context of human development, arguing that all human beings have a general orienting perspective on life, a "spirituality" that he defines as "any more-or-less coherent and complete way of looking at and evaluating everything." The burden of Talbot's essay involves identifying an authentic Christian spirituality amid the many competing and conflicting alternatives in today's pluralistic postmodern context. Genuine Christian spirituality, as Talbot presents it, is based on the divinely inspired written revelation of God in Holy Scripture. Christian theologians, Talbot suggests, are "the church's sewage specialists." Their charge is to safeguard the sacred deposit of faith so that it may be passed on intact to the rising generation.

✧✧✧ ✧✧✧ ✧✧✧

The letter inviting my participation in the conference underlying this book stated that its purpose was "to emphasize the coinherence"—that is, the permanent and inseparable linkage—"of theological integrity and spiritual vitality." This needs emphasis because theology and spirituality "are frequently pulled in opposite directions, particularly within contemporary evangelicalism."

It is true that many evangelicals think that careful theological study is

116

unnecessary for true spirituality or even that it tends to kill spiritual life; and indeed, eager Christians can be ruined by college and seminary theology courses. But I want to show why authentic Christian vitality and real theological integrity are inextricably intertwined.

I start by making some observations about the term "spiritual." Today, lots of non-Christians call themselves "spiritual." In the New Testament, to be "spiritual" means to be indwelt by God's Holy Spirit, which happens only as we accept by faith what Jesus has done for us. This seems to exclude non-Christians from being "spiritual" in any authentically Christian sense. Yet a Hindu *sannyasi* who renounces everything so that he can wander through the world unencumbered by anything other than his desire for the release of his self from the cycle of transmigration seems to be unquestionably spiritual. So what does being "spiritual" mean?

Answering this question and some other questions arising from it will allow us to understand not only how non-Christian and Christian spirituality relate but also exactly how evangelical theology and Christian spirituality are linked.

WHAT DOES IT MEAN TO BE "SPIRITUAL"?

A couple of years ago, I saw a rock musician on television who had just won a music award. His music was, by every reasonable standard, immoral. Yet, as he accepted his award, he declared that he was "a very spiritual person." As a philosophy professor who is interested in how people use words, I wished I could have asked him exactly what he meant.

Can someone who encourages immorality be "a very spiritual person"? Is there a sense in which all human beings are "spiritual" creatures? And in what sense is a Hindu *sannyasi* "more spiritual" than almost all the rest of us?

Even trying to define the term *spiritual* is complicated. The term can imply a state of being spiritual. It can refer to the incorporeal, the nonphysical nature, the mind, and even simply to religious objects or concepts. Yet there is one use of the term *spiritual* that allows us to answer all our questions while tying all these ideas together.

This use recognizes that we human beings are "spiritual" creatures in this sense at least: our "psychologies" are not nailed down to our "physiologies."[1] We are capable of being much more than just the sum of our physiological drives. We can be—and as we mature, we inevitably are—occupied with much more than our immediate physical wants and needs. I may be rested, well fed, and physically satisfied right now and yet be concerned about what will happen to me in twenty years. You may be plagued by your poverty-stricken past, even though right now you live in the lap of luxury.

Part of what it means to be human is to be capable of living—and indeed, to be encouraged by other human beings to live—in a world that stretches back into a more-or-less distant past and that anticipates a yet unrealized future. Mommy tells Matt that Christmas is coming and that he may get the bike he wants, especially if he is good. Sarah considers her family's illustrious history at Wheaton College and finds herself moved to work hard while she is there so that she may do well, too. This is what distinctively human life is all about—and it depends on our "more spiritual" qualities. Once the cat is fed, she doesn't have a care in the world; we don't encourage our dogs to behave better by promising them Milk-Bones for Christmas; and a great ape is not motivated to make something of himself by remembering who his great-grandfather was. All of us who are capable of developing normally are capable of becoming "spiritual" in the sense of learning to look up from our immediate physical environments and beginning to live in a world that is larger than the one we currently see.

WHAT ACCOUNTS FOR OUR BEING "SPIRITUAL" IN THIS SENSE?

When we encounter spoiled children—say, a little boy throwing a temper tantrum in the grocery store aisle because his mother won't buy him the candy he sees—we recognize that this is not the way it ought to be. Bobby's life isn't likely to be very good if he thinks he can get everything he wants on demand. He needs to learn sometimes to settle for "delayed gratification."

Learning to say no to our immediate physical wants and needs is part of the "socialization process." Becoming socialized is the main way in which we become "spiritual" in the previously specified sense. It happens primarily by others *addressing* us in various ways.

This begins at a very early age. Fourteen-month-old Rachel has just begun to slap at those who are holding her, and so they start "civilizing" her by intercepting her arm as they sternly say, "No!" Rebekah's mother sees her eyeing her younger friend's new red ball as he plays with it, and so she helps her three-year-old to check her impulse to snatch Caleb's new toy by saying to her in a certain tone of voice, "Rebekah, that's Caleb's."

The forms of address become more sophisticated as we grow older. Yet they persist because we all need reminders of how we ought to behave. When the state trooper pulls me over to tell me that I was doing seventy-three miles per hour in a fifty-five-mile-an-hour zone, then even if he lets me off with a warning, I know my driving has been addressed in an unmistakable way.

Usually we address others by speaking to them. When Mike gets a little out of hand at the party, Lisa may remind him to restrain himself simply by touching his hand. Yet that touch's effectiveness depends on her previously having spoken some words to him.

Language is especially effective in enabling us to think more expansively because it allows us to represent unseen realities. Matt's mom encourages him to be good by talking to him about his desire for a new bike and explaining to him how his getting it is linked to his behaving in praiseworthy ways. My exercising before dinner and then refusing dessert is prompted by my having read another magazine article emphasizing how important exercise and weight loss are to avoiding heart disease.

WHAT FOLLOWS FROM OUR BEING "SPIRITUAL" IN THIS SENSE?

Many animals can communicate in primitive ways: the baby seal's cry tells her mother that she is under threat, and some primates seem to be capable of learning a rudimentary language from human beings. Yet we alone of all visible creatures can communicate sophisticatedly enough to enable us to live in a world where the here-and-now can be dwarfed by the there-and-then.

If the ability to live beyond the present is taken to be integral to human spirituality understood generically, then someone who encourages immorality can indeed be "a very spiritual person." Hitler was "spiritual" in this sense, since he anchored his Third Reich in an ancient mythology and portrayed it as lasting a thousand years. And insofar as this generic human capacity also enables us to choose to live "above" or "apart from" ordinary life, the Hindu *sannyasi* who renounces nearly everything that the rest of us hold dear has indeed chosen to be "more spiritual"—in the sense of more ascetic—than we.

This generic human capacity means that we are not physiologically "hardwired" to live in a particular way. Consequently, we must learn to make sense of things. Animals have to learn some things. For example, cheetah cubs must be taught to hunt. But while there is some learning particularly among the "higher" animals, most animal behavior is hard-wired in the sense that it is governed by instinct. Hummingbirds and monarch butterflies don't learn to fly south for the winter. They don't need to be told to flee the killing cold, for their flight is triggered automatically by the decrease of sunlight per day. Human beings, by contrast, must learn most things. Initially, the hungry baby must be guided to its mother's breast. Little boys must be taught not to run out into busy streets. As Monica Lewinsky has shown, sometimes young single women need to be told—and sometimes strongly reminded— that older married men are off-limits, no matter what those men may think.

Most crucially, we must learn to orient ourselves in human life's "evaluative space." When we move to a new area, we tend to get lost until we have learned to make sense of our new geographical space. But the fact that we are not physiologically hard-wired means that we can get lost in a much more fundamental way—we can become uncertain about who we are, what we value, and where to find it.

When Matt's mother, Kim, encourages him to be good so that he may get the bike he wants for Christmas, she is engaged in the process of helping him to become a full-fledged *person*. Persons are *agents* who perform *actions* that are not reducible to mere bodily behaviors or even to the instinct-prompted behaviors of the higher animals. When agents act, their behavior is *significant*. In other words, an act has, for the agent performing it, a particular *meaning*. For example, Kim's addressing Matt is meant by her to help socialize him. She aims to help him develop into a mature human being who has learned to shape his behavior in socially acceptable ways. If she is successful, then Matt's good behavior will have its own significance. He will intend it as a means of pleasing his parents so that they will be more inclined to give him a bike for Christmas.

When they are acting as agents, Matt and his mother also understand themselves in particular ways. Kim sees herself as Matt's mother with a duty to help him become a well-behaved human being. Matt, in turn, sees himself as her little boy who aims to please her both just for itself and for the reward that his good behavior may bring.

Their views help to orient them in human life's evaluative space. Kim has identified one of her roles and considered what her having that role should mean to her life today. She knows that a significant portion of her time right now ought to be aimed at giving Matt a proper upbringing—and that means she sees herself as occupying a very different position in life than she did when she was still footloose and fancy free. Her life thus takes on a particular aim, and she charts her days' courses accordingly. Matt is still young enough that his values are pretty much set for him. As with most little boys, he loves his mother more than anything else; and so his world revolves around her. As he grows, his values will expand and change. In adolescence he may struggle with "finding himself," which really means finding his own place in life's evaluative space. Granted, he will always need to eat and sleep and find physical satisfaction—and his drive to satisfy these physiological needs will do something to orient him and give his life some particular aims. Yet merely being rested and well fed is not enough to fulfill a normal human being. If he develops normally, then Matt will someday need and want to acquire an understanding of himself and his values that gives his whole life meaning and aim.

WHAT IS "A SPIRITUALITY"?

Adolescent identity struggles accentuate the truth that human beings cannot thrive unless they know who they are in the sense of knowing what they value and where to find it. In fact, our quest to get what we value motivates even our attempts to locate ourselves in physical space. I am not likely to be out driving around exploring my new neighborhood unless there is something that I value that I have gone out to get. My desire to obtain specific goods prompts me to try to make sense of my new geographical space. If the gas hasn't been turned on in my new house, then I may seek out one of my new neighbors in order to ask for directions on where to find the nearest place to get something to eat.

Supermodel Linda Evangelista once bragged that it took $10,000 to get her out of bed. We all need something to get us out of bed. Physical discomfort or the need to eat or relieve ourselves may do it temporarily, but ultimately our physiological needs and wants do not supply us with a reason for living.

We must have a reason for living if we, as human persons, are to flourish. We must possess some interpretation of life that orients us and gives our lives meaning and purpose. Fully fledged persons do more than perform individually meaningful actions; their lives make sense. We at first get a fix on life by riding piggyback on those around us who already have a clear sense of where they are going in evaluative space. Matt's young life takes its direction from the way it is caught up in his parents' lives. Yet there should come a time when Matt will want to step out on his own; and then he will need to make sense of life for himself. Then he will avoid aimlessness only if he thinks he understands his particular place in life. He will need to feel that he has some worthwhile long-range goals. The fact that he is not physiologically hard-wired to pursue any particular way of life means that when this time comes, he will need to face a certain range of questions—questions about how he will lead his life; questions about what he will take to be of ultimate value; questions about where life's varied valuables can be found; and questions about what life's different experiences mean. He will need to answer these questions to his own satisfaction in order to get himself usefully oriented in human life's evaluative space. Answering them will situate him in life by clarifying for him what his aims are and how he should go about trying to meet them. Answering them will identify for him the goods he is seeking. In fact, it will tell him who he really is. For to know who I am is, as Charles Taylor has observed,

> a species of knowing where I stand. My identity is defined by t￼
> mitments and identifications which provide the frame or ￼
> within which I can try to determine from case to case what is g￼
> valuable, or what ought to be done, or what I endorse or oppo￼

In short, someday Matt will need to get an orienting perspective on life; he will need to find a way of looking at things that helps him to make sense of it all.

Let us call such an orienting perspective "a spirituality." Both the possibility and the necessity of having such a perspective arises out of what I have called human spirituality understood generically. Having "*a* spirituality" in this sense really does distinguish us from the animals, because "we, in contrast to our fellows in the animal world, live by adopted *conceptions* of what our life is and ought to be. We *impose order* on ourselves and our world by the way we 'picture' things."[3] There are many different orienting perspectives and so there are many different spiritualities, including New Age spirituality, Theravada Buddhist spirituality, Muslim spirituality, Wicca spirituality, Native American spirituality, postmodern spirituality, vegetarian spirituality, Christian spirituality, and even Oprah spirituality. Each comes to us as a different "word" on what human life is and ought to be. "A spirituality" is any more-or-less coherent and complete way of looking at and evaluating everything. It gives us a way of understanding the past and anticipating the future. It equips us to live in a world that is larger than the one we currently see.

Different spiritualities produce different lives. For instance, James Houston has noted that "[t]he endless vigil, the extreme asceticism, and the simplicity of a mullah, guru, or fakir seem to excel any standards of ascetic spirituality in the West," and indeed, "Hindu people"—not Christians, mind you—"are often looked upon as the most prayerful of people, whose whole lives are made up of prayer."[4]

As paradoxical as it seems, there is even a Western materialist spirituality. If this is Linda Evangelista's spirituality, then what gives her life purpose and meaning is the prospect of acquiring more money, more fame, and more things.

DO MULTIPLE "SPIRITUALITIES" IMPLY THAT CHRISTIANITY IS NOT UNIQUELY TRUE?

So far I have claimed that human beings are naturally "spiritual" creatures who are not physiologically hard-wired to approach life in any particular way. This means that we must orient ourselves in life by adopting some particular "spirituality." There are many to choose from, and because each involves a different way of life, they can be irreconcilable, with outlooks on life that actually conflict. For instance, Wicca bills itself as a pagan spirituality. It has been revived in deliberate opposition to orthodox Christian spirituality; and so one must decide between being an orthodox Christian or a witch.

Much intellectual effort has been expended in attempting to articulate and defend the varied conceptions of what human life is and ought to be, sometimes with explicit reference to some of the rival possibilities. For example, the ancient Epicureans had one "take" on the meaning of life and their rivals, the Stoics—a conflicting one. Theravada Buddhists want their lives to end in nirvana—the extinction of desire—while Muslims want theirs to end in a paradise where all their desires will be catered to with fruit, ease, sexual partners, and plenty of water, milk, honey, and wine. Plato wrote about as many words as we find in the Christian Bible articulating and defending his "word" on reality, which converges and diverges from the Bible's "word" in various ways.

Right now, Matt is oblivious to differences like these. He just soaks in his family's Christian perspective. Someday he will realize that Bobby's family sees things quite differently. This may lead him to wonder why he should take his family's perspective as true or best. If he suffers a full-blown identity crisis, then that will show that he has come to think that his family's "take" on things is not the last or only word about getting oriented in evaluative space.

Whole cultures can also be more or less aware of rival spiritualities. Until Columbus discovered America, Native Americans were unaware of Christian spirituality. Until the United States began to receive a lot of Asian immigrants, most Americans had no chance to know a Buddhist or Hindu or Muslim personally.

Today, however, it is hard for most human beings to be oblivious to such differences. This is especially true in societies as well traveled and information-rich as ours. This has led us into a kind of cultural identity crisis, where our society's primary opinion makers are no longer certain why they should take their own spiritualities to be any better or truer than those found elsewhere. This crisis is aggravated by our awareness of value conflicts within our society. Black, white, and Hispanic Americans often have significantly different evaluative standards and dreams. GLAAD—the Gay and Lesbian Alliance Against Defamation—has a vision for America that clashes with the vision that the conservative Family Research Council has been formed to project.

Evangelical Christians have historically believed that it is only through hearing the gospel preached that human beings can come to know what true spirituality is (see Rom. 10:9–15, 17; 1 Pet. 1:18–25; 1 John 1:1–3). But today our awareness of different spiritualities is often taken to discredit any claim that one spirituality is truer than the rest. Christians of earlier times—it is now argued—may have been sufficiently ignorant of rival spiritualities to have found it plausible to maintain that faith in Jesus is the only way to God, but our increased awareness of other religions proves that this cannot possibly be the case.[5]

Initially, this argument can seem quite convincing, especially when someone is becoming significantly aware of other spiritualities for the first time.

Thus an eager Christian's confidence in what Scripture itself claims (see, for instance, Acts 4:12 and 1 Tim. 2:5) can indeed be undercut by what he or she learns in the course of a good college or seminary education. Getting educated is then often made to take the rap. This, I shall show, misplaces the blame, but right now I note just one weakness in the foregoing argument.

It misrepresents the facts. Christians of earlier times—the argument maintains—were sufficiently ignorant of rival spiritualities to have found it plausible to maintain that faith in Jesus is the only way to God. It is assumed that if they had been more aware of rival spiritualities, then they would not have been inclined to make such an exclusivistic claim. That assumption is false. The earliest Christians were quite aware of irreconcilable spiritualities because Christianity arose in a world chock-full of rival religions. Our Lord and his apostles preached that the gospel reveals the only true way to God in opposition not merely to various kinds of misguided Judaism (see Mark 2; Acts 2:22–4:30; Gal. 1:13–24; 2:11–4:7) but also to the full pantheon of Greco-Roman gods (see Acts 17:16–31).

As Nikolai Nikolaievich, Yurii Andreievich Zhivago's maternal uncle, notes in his diary in Boris Pasternak's *Doctor Zhivago*,

> Rome was a flea market of borrowed gods and conquered peoples, a bargain basement on two floors, earth and heaven, a mass of filth convoluted in a triple knot as in an intestinal obstruction. Dacians, Herulians, Scythians, Sarmatians, Hyperboreans, heavy wheels without spokes, eyes sunk in fat, sodomy, double chins, illiterate emperors, fish fed on the flesh of learned slaves . . . all crammed into the passages of the Coliseum, and all wretched.

"And then," he continues, "into this tasteless heap of gold and marble," Jesus Christ came,

> and at that moment gods and nations ceased to be and man came into being—man the carpenter, man the plowman, man the shepherd with his flock of sheep at sunset, man who does not sound in the least proud, man thankfully celebrated in all the cradle songs of mothers and in all the picture galleries the world over.[6]

The earliest Christians were anything but ignorant of conflicting spiritualities. Yet this did not intimidate them or lead them to soften Jesus' own claim that he is "the way and the truth and the life" and that no one comes to God except through him (John 14:6). They eagerly aimed their message that faith in Jesus Christ is the only way to be truly reconciled with God at this panoply of rivals.[7]

It is legitimate to doubt whether there is one truest and best spirituality, but this doubt should not be based on a false assumption. Evangelical Christianity's historic claim that human beings can only come to know what true spirituality is through hearing the gospel message about what God has done through Christ's earthly work can be maintained even by those who are well aware of the world's many other spiritualities. In fact, we will see why this is so only by thinking more deeply about specifically Christian spirituality.

WHAT IS UNIQUE ABOUT CHRISTIAN SPIRITUALITY?

Spirituality is not a biblical term. There is no direct equivalent to it in biblical Hebrew or Greek. In fact, the word has only recently become popular. Sometimes it stands for something like what has been suggested above. For instance, Gordon Wakefield says it refers to "those attitudes, beliefs and practices which animate people's lives and help them to reach out towards super-sensible realities."[8] James Houston defines it more theologically as the "state of deep relationship to God."[9] He says "interest among evangelical Christians in spirituality is new." Formerly,

> expressions such as "holiness, holy living, godliness, walking with God, discipleship" seemed more acceptable because they emphasized a formal commitment, a deepening relationship with Christ, and a life of personal obedience to the word of God.

I think these expressions remain preferable because their use in Scripture puts some constraints on how they are understood. "Spirituality," as Houston notes, is more abstract. This makes Christian use of it both attractive and risky. It is attractive because using it can emphasize legitimate similarities between Christian faith and other faiths. Understood as one "word" on what human life is and ought to be, Christian spirituality—like Buddhist spirituality or Hindu spirituality or Western materialist spirituality or postmodern spirituality—is just one among many "spiritualities," and so there is nothing that formally disqualifies it as one option among others, but talking about "Christian spirituality" in this way risks obscuring what is unique to Christian faith.

For our society sees "being spiritual" as a generically good thing. It takes the *kind* of spirituality someone practices to be less crucial, although in some social settings Eastern spiritualities clearly get the edge. Yet "being spiritual" shouldn't be praised as such, because there are good and bad spiritualities.

Even more crucially, Christians should be careful when they talk about "Christian spirituality," because merely putting "Christian" in front of "spirituality" does not mean that we thereby know what makes Christian spirituality unique. As Wakefield observes:

People may be deceived about the real sources of their spirituality. Consciously and outwardly they may be committed to Christ, convinced that he is the power of their lives and the motive of their actions, whereas they are merely the children of their times . . . if not indeed governed by self-interest and evil desires, which masquerade as Christian.[10]

So what is authentic Christian spirituality?

The great early American theologian Jonathan Edwards helps us here by noting that something is called spiritual in the New Testament when it proceeds from God's Holy Spirit. As Edwards says,

[I]t is with relation to the Holy Ghost, or Spirit of God, that persons or things are termed spiritual, in the New Testament. "Spirit," as the word is used to signify the third person in the Trinity, is the substantive, of which is formed the adjective "spiritual," in the Holy Scriptures.[11]

This is a different definition of "spiritual" than any we have considered so far. As Edwards insists, this definition does not take something to be "spiritual" merely because it is concerned with "things that are immaterial, and not corporeal." Nor does it "signify any relation of persons or things to the spirit or soul of man, as the spiritual part of man, in opposition to the body, which is the material part." Consequently, it does not warrant calling some human qualities "spiritual" qualities "because they have their seat in the soul, and not in the body." It also does not condone our calling something "spiritual" simply because it is religious. Something is called "spiritual" in the New Testament when it is related to the Holy Spirit—and especially when it is related to the Spirit in particular ways. For instance, persons are called "spiritual persons" only when "they are born of the Spirit, and because of the indwelling and holy influences of the Spirit of God in them" (see 1 Cor. 2:14–15; John 3:1–8). Things such as "spiritual truths" and "the fruits of the Spirit" are called "spiritual" because they get their character from the fact that through them the Holy Spirit is mediating God's saving grace to human beings (see 1 Cor. 2:13; Gal. 5:22–25). And even things such as the "spiritual gifts," which can be possessed by those who have not been born of the Spirit,[12] are called "spiritual" because it is the Spirit who gives them to human beings (see 1 Cor. 12:1–11).

Authentic Christian spirituality is, then, genuinely supernatural. It is not something we can produce for ourselves. It arises only when God sends his Holy Spirit to do what only God can do, bless and save and sanctify human beings. In Old Testament times, God promised to pour out God's Spirit on people (see Joel 2:28–29; Isa. 44:3) so that they would follow God's decrees and keep his laws (see Ezek. 36:24–27). God said he would do this when he made his new covenant (see Jer. 31:31–34). This covenant was effectuated by the work of God's Son, Jesus Christ, during his earthly incarnation—through what he did once and for all for sinful human beings by living a perfectly sinless life and dying a sacrificial death (see Heb. 7:11–8:13 with Rom. 3:21–26, 5:12–19; and 2 Cor. 5:21). Now the resurrected Christ lives to intercede for those who come to God through him (see Heb. 7:25). He has asked his Father to send the Holy Spirit to be with his disciples forever (see John 14:16). The world, Jesus told the apostles, cannot accept the Holy Spirit "because it neither sees him nor knows him" (John 14:17). Yet his disciples know the Spirit, because the Spirit lives with and in them. The Spirit testifies to them about Jesus (see John 15:26) even as he convicts the world "in regard to sin and righteousness and judgment" (John 16:8; cf. 16:7–11). As the very Spirit of truth, he guides those who believe in Jesus into all truth (see John 14:17, 26; 16:12–15). As a life-giving Spirit, he frees Christians to fulfill the righteous requirements of God's law (see Rom. 8:1–4). Thus they become increasingly conformed to Christ's likeness (see Rom. 8:29; 2 Cor. 3:3–18). They also become ministers of God's new covenant (see 2 Cor. 3:6). They become "Christ's ambassadors" (2 Cor. 5:20) who, "by setting forth the truth plainly," commend the Christian way of life to every person's conscience (2 Cor. 4:2; cf. 5:11). Through Christians, God makes his appeal to other human beings to be reconciled to God through Christ (see 2 Cor. 5:20, 21). Those who believe this appeal thus come to receive God's Spirit (see Gal. 3:1–5, 13–14) and thus come to know and practice true spirituality.

True spirituality, then, really is unique. In the last analysis, it is not as if Christian spirituality and Buddhist spirituality and Hindu spirituality and Western materialist spirituality and postmodern spirituality are all just different varieties of some more general thing, like different kinds of pine trees. If the Bible's claims are true, then Christian spirituality, and the spiritual life arising from it, is related to other "spiritualities" and other kinds of "spiritual life" like a living pine tree is related to artificial Christmas trees—the faux trees just mimic the real tree. Artificial Christmas trees can look real, and they perform an important function: for many people, they give Christmas its focal point by being the place where they hang their ornaments and place their gifts. In other words, neither artificial Christmas trees nor non-Christian spiritualities are useless. Yet each must ultimately be acknowledged to lack true life.

Scripture presents us with just two ways of living: there is a way leading to life and a way leading to death (see Deut. 30:15–20; Matt. 7:13–14). In our now-natural, unredeemed state, each of us is already on death's pathway—indeed, already dead (see Eph. 2:1–3). No matter which of the world's non-Christian spiritualities we have embraced and no matter how "religious" that way of life is (see Acts. 17:22; Matt. 23:15, 23–32; cf. 2 Kings 18:25–29; Isa. 1:10–15), we need redemption from it. It is essentially a futile and false spirituality (see Eph. 4:17–18; 1 Cor. 3:18–21), notwithstanding the fact that it may have been handed down to us by our forefathers (see 1 Pet. 1:18), with a long history (see Isa. 19:11–13; Rev. 12:9) and much thought invested in it (see Acts 17:16–21; Luke 11:46, 52; cf. Acts 7:22). Every spirituality promises real life; in fact, it is primarily the plausibility of a spirituality's promises that leads human beings to embrace it. But biblical Christianity claims that it is only by being reborn of God's Holy Spirit through faith in Jesus Christ that we come to possess real life—eternal life—with the God who actually has made and rules and judges all things (see John 3:3–8; Titus 3:3–7; Rom. 1:18–2:5). If this is true, then only one spirituality gives to its possessors what all of them promise, and there is only one true spirituality among many shams.

WHY MUST EVANGELICALS DO THEOLOGY?

As I have said, evangelical Christians have historically believed that it is only through the preaching of the gospel that human beings can come to know what true spirituality is. Perhaps only a few of them could have done more than quote a Bible verse or two to support this belief, but until quite recently almost all of them would have maintained that explicit faith in Jesus is the only way to secure eternal life with God. Today, however, confidence in this Christian truth is waning.

When critics attack historic evangelicalism, they often call it a variety of "religious exclusivism." A defense of the historical position is impossible here. It would have to address questions such as these: Why should the reception of God's life-giving Spirit depend on preaching? Isn't God unfair if God does not make true spirituality available to those who never hear the Christian message? Can't people of other spiritualities somehow be saved through faith in Christ's work even though they never actually hear his name?

Today, even some evangelicals claim that true spirituality can be achieved independently of actually hearing the gospel. They maintain that it is possible for people to avail themselves of Christ's saving work even though they don't know his name. Often they are moved to embrace these positions because they think that if it were otherwise, then God would be unfair. There are still excellent reasons to maintain the historical position, but that is not my concern right now. My concern is for those evangelicals who hold that vital Christian living always includes evangelistic and missionary impulses. These Christians may sense some real link between authentic Christian vitality and the historical evangelical position. Yet they may also be leery of theology precisely because they have seen too many theology students lose their eagerness to witness. To these evangelicals I would say this: today, the only way to defend the historical position effectively is through careful theological reasoning. Those challenging the historical position have already done their homework. They have thought through the issues carefully enough that merely citing Bible verses against them is ineffective, since they have plausible reinterpretations of many of those texts.

Etymologically, the term *theology* is derived from two Greek words: *theos*— or "God"—and *logia*—"oracles" or "words" or "messages." In other words, theology is "words or discourse about God." It studies God and the things of God. Evangelical theology is the branch of it that takes with utter seriousness the Bible's claim to be God's own words written, the completely true, fundamentally self-consistent, and utterly sufficient source of all that we need to know for Christian life and godliness (see 2 Pet. 1:3, with 2 Tim. 3:14–17). It studies the Scriptures as representing the final "word" on how we should consider and evaluate everything.

When some spirituality's truth is challenged, its adherents need to defend it by thinking through those challenges so that they can answer them in careful and credible ways. With spiritualities where God has little or no place, we wouldn't want to call this thinking theology. Yet for those spiritualities where belief in God is central, *theology* is exactly the right word for describing the kind of thinking that must be done if they are to remain viable options. This is as true for historical evangelicalism as it is for any other form of theism, even if we recognize, as evangelicals should, that saving faith in Christ's work is itself God's gift (see Eph. 2:8–10, with Matt. 13:11 and John 6:44). Ultimately, all the praise for anyone's salvation must be given to God; but this is not to say that God works independently of human effort (see 1 Cor. 15:9–10; Phil. 2:12–13).

Any evangelical who is inclined to condemn theological thinking needs to read the book of Acts again. There Luke tells us that while Paul was in Thessalonica, he "*reasoned* . . . from the Scriptures, *explaining and proving* that the Christ had to suffer and rise from the dead" (Acts 17:2–3); that every Sabbath when he was in Corinth, "he *reasoned* in the synagogue, *trying to persuade* Jews and Greeks" (Acts 18:4); and that in Ephesus, he "spoke boldly . . . for three months, *arguing persuasively* about the kingdom of God" (Acts 19:8). And this was not just Paul's practice. Luke reports that Apollos "*vigorously refuted* the Jews in public debate" in Achaia, "*proving* from the Scriptures that Jesus was the Christ" (Acts 18:28); and what he preserves for us of Peter's speech on the day of Pentecost (see Acts 2:14–41) shows that Peter proceeded in similar ways.

HOW ARE WORDS AND LIFE LINKED?

If Matt suffers a full-blown adolescent identity crisis, then his Christian parents will be remiss if they do not talk to him in various ways. Scripture makes it utterly clear that godly parents will teach their children about God and his great deeds from their children's earliest days (see Deut. 4:9–10; 2 Tim. 3:14–16). Moses instructed the Israelites to impress God's commands on their children by talking about them continually (see Deut. 6:4–7). Peter charges Christians with an even greater task: we are always to be prepared to give an answer to anyone who asks us why we have the hope we do (see 1 Pet. 3:15). Matt's parents are responsible before God not only to counsel him about the way that leads to life; they are also charged to have thought through their faith thoroughly enough to be able to address his doubts and questions credibly.

In Deuteronomy, the Israelites stand at the edge of the promised land. As Moses anticipates their entering it without him, he encourages them to remain faithful to the God who had delivered them from Egypt and sustained them in the wilderness for forty years. This leads him to emphasize the importance of his words—which are really God's words—again and again.[13] In a crucial passage he says:

> Be careful to follow every command I am giving you today, so that you may live and increase and may enter and possess the land that the LORD promised on oath to your forefathers. Remember how the LORD your God led you all the way in the desert these forty years, to humble you and to test you in order to know what was in your heart, whether or not you would keep his commands. He humbled you, causing you to hunger and then feeding you with manna, which neither you nor your fathers had known, to teach you that *man does not live on bread alone but on every word that comes from the mouth of the LORD* (Deut. 8:1–3; my emphasis).

When the devil tempted Jesus in the desert after he had fasted forty days, he answered the devil's temptation to turn stones into bread with this passage's final words (see Matt. 4:1–4) and thus emphasized that, in a very real sense, human beings are *verbivores*—word eaters (see Ps. 119:103; Jer. 15:16). This is what made God's declaration that he would send a word famine on Israel so frightening. Without words, human beings are indeed condemned to "stagger from sea to sea and wander from north to east," searching for meaning without being able to find it (Amos 8:11–12).

Most of what I have said about human spirituality supports the claim that human beings cannot get properly oriented in life without "digesting" words. Our lives take on significance and meaning only as we take in some particular perspective on life. We do this by believing some "word" about what human life is and ought to be. In this way, distinctively human life is both created and sustained linguistically.

The psalmist assumes this when he warns us not to be like horses and mules that lack understanding and thus must be controlled by bit and bridle (see Ps. 32:8–9). He declares that he will instruct, teach, and counsel us in the way we should go. Instructing, teaching, and counseling are primarily linguistic activities. They convey to us ways of looking at and evaluating things so that we can make the sorts of thoughtful and uncoerced decisions that are part and parcel of our humanity.[14] Thus Scripture recognizes that language is among human life's most distinctive features, and that without it human life as we know it would not exist. So, as we might expect, it emphasizes the importance of words again and again. In fact, Jesus takes words so seriously that he declares we will have to render account for each careless one on the judgment day, and it will be by our words that we will be either justified or condemned (see Matt. 12:36–37; cf. Prov. 10:14).

Solomon declares that it is by accepting the right words that we can live good and godly lives (see Prov. 2:1–22); and, indeed, our lives take on the character of the words we digest. Getting oriented in life's evaluative space requires our digesting some particular set of words—some particular series of *stories* that enable us to understand who we are as well as where we have come from and where we are going, some particular set of *evaluative categories* by which to judge what is true and false and good and bad, and some particular pattern of *metaphors* and *explanations* that helps us to construe our lives in meaningful ways.[15]

HOW ARE AUTHENTIC CHRISTIAN VITALITY AND REAL THEOLOGICAL INTEGRITY INEXTRICABLY INTERTWINED?

As God's special written revelation to us of what we must know to think and to live truthfully and righteously before him (see 2 Pet. 1:2–3), Scripture identifies itself as the means by which we can acquire the true stories (see Rom. 15:4; 1 Cor. 10:1–11), the right evaluative categories (see Ps. 19:7–11; Matthew 5; 1 Corinthians 13; Gal. 5:19–23), the correct metaphors (see Ps. 23:1–4; Isa. 53:6; Eph. 4:17–24; 6:13–17) and explanations (see Deut. 6:20–25; Rom. 5:12–21; 7:7–25; Hebrews 9) for properly understanding and ordering our lives before the only God who actually exists (see 1 Chron. 16:23–26; Isa. 42:17; 45:5–7).

But Scripture goes further than that. It assumes that real life—eternal life—depends on hearing or reading God's words (see Deut. 32:45–47; John 6:68;

1 Cor. 2:11–13). When the apostle Paul wrote to the Galatians in order to urge them not to desert authentic Christian spirituality (see Gal. 1:6–9), he asked them this: "Did you receive the Spirit by observing the law, or by believing what you heard?" (Gal. 3:2). In other words, Christian faith is not just another spirituality. It is not just one more orienting perspective on life. It is the means by which God brings his life-giving Spirit to human beings (see 1 Pet. 1:22–25 with John 3:1–8). Such faith comes to us through our hearing the Christian message, and we hear that message through the preaching of Christ (see Rom. 10:17, RSV).

Christians have "the word of life" (Phil. 2:16), which we are to preach to everyone so that no one will lack the opportunity to embrace true spirituality. Yet we will not do this accurately and effectively without the aid of evangelical theology, as J. I. Packer shows in the opening chapter of his *Hot Tub Religion*.[16]

Starting from the claim that theology is "simply God-talk—or, more fully, thoughts about God expressed in statements about God," Packer goes on to claim that our thoughts and words about God will be right only when they track God's own thoughts and words. For Christians, who have always taken the Scriptures to be God's word written,[17] this means that good theology must be evangelical, for evangelical theology—as it has been bequeathed to us by the Reformation[18]— takes the Bible's claim to be God's own words most seriously. The Westminster Larger Catechism, which was first published in 1647, puts historical evangelicalism's view of Scripture like this: "The holy Scriptures of the Old and New Testament are the word of God, the only rule of faith and obedience."[19]

Theology should be then, as Packer observes, first of all "an exercise in listening"—primarily, as the Westminster Confession puts it, an exercise in listening to "the Holy Spirit speaking in the Scripture." Yet this must include a kind of collaborative listening. For while the Scriptures contain "the whole counsel of God" (Acts 20:27, RSV), each of us tends to distort God's counsel, sometimes by our not knowing enough to hear a text accurately, sometimes by our not remembering what Scripture says elsewhere, and sometimes by our reading our particular sins or limitations into a text. Yet we do not all distort the same texts; and so we can help each other hear more accurately. Each of us needs to listen to others who have also listened to God speaking through God's Scriptures; and we should listen especially carefully to those who have worked hardest to understand what the Scriptures say. Since, moreover, only born-again Christians have received God's Spirit, and "no one knows the thoughts of God except the Spirit of God" (see 1 Cor. 2:6–16, with John 3:1–8), collaborative theological thinking among those who have been enlightened and enlivened by God's Spirit is clearly our best hope for handling correctly God's life-giving word of truth (see 2 Tim. 3:10–11, 14–16).[20]

In this regard, as Packer says, well-versed theologians can be thought of "as the church's sewage specialists." Just as an ordinary sewage treatment plant may stand beside a pristine lake to safeguard the health of its waters, so the role of Spirit-enlightened and -enlivened theologians "is to detect and eliminate intellectual pollution and to ensure, as far as [human beings] can, that God's life-giving truth flows pure and unpoisoned into Christian hearts." Christian theology exists to test our thoughts and words about God in order to find "and filter out anything . . . that confuses minds, corrupts judgments, and distorts the way that Christians view their own lives." For evangelical theologians in particular, with their special commitment to the Scriptures as God's completely true, fundamentally self-consistent, and utterly sufficient written word, theology centers on clarifying that word to those who are confused about its meaning, helping those who are straying from it to get back on track, and assisting the doubtful to find their certainty in it, just as Packer's claims imply.

If this is evangelical theology's task, and if my previous claims about Christian spirituality are true, then it is not hard to see how evangelical theology and Christian spirituality are linked. For the Spirit in authentic Christian spirituality is the Spirit who speaks in the Scriptures (see 2 Pet. 1:20–21; 1 Pet. 1:10–12; Acts 1:16). He continues to accompany those writings whenever they are studied and preached. Authentic Christian spirituality is thus naturally allied with evangelical theology because evangelical theology emphasizes the Spirit-inspired Scriptures to an unparalleled degree.

It is also not hard to see how authentic Christian vitality and real theological integrity are inextricably intertwined. As the church's sewage specialists, Christian theologians must safeguard God's words (see 2 Tim. 1:14). This means that they are to contend for "the faith that was once for all entrusted to the saints" (Jude 3). This is the faith that is found in the Bible's Old and New Testaments. So Christian theologians should measure a theology's integrity by its fidelity to biblical faith (see 2 Thess. 2:15).

Because of our unparalleled commitment to the Scriptures, evangelicals, of all Christians, should strive for real theological integrity so that God's life-giving Word will be accurately read and effectively preached. Whenever this happens, we can expect that God's Spirit will accompany God's Word, bringing all who are appointed to eternal life to believe (see Acts 13:48; 1 Thess. 1:4–5; 2 Thess. 2:13–14). These believers will then possess authentic Christian vitality—which is real or true spirituality.

At the end of his second letter, Peter commands us to "grow in the grace and knowledge of our Lord and Savior Jesus Christ" (2 Pet. 3:18). Growth in Christian grace is equivalent to growth in true spirituality (see Gal. 5:16–26; Heb. 10:29). Growth in Christian knowledge involves becoming both more aware and more certain of "the depth of the riches" that God has given us through the work of God's Son, Jesus Christ (Rom. 11:33).[21] By now it should be clear, especially to those of us who identify ourselves with historical evangelicalism, that spiritual vitality and theological integrity really do coinhere. They are permanently and inseparably linked. Indeed, the health of evangelicalism depends on our not pulling them apart. Careful Spirit-enlivened and Spirit-enlightened theological study not only will not tend to kill spiritual life; it is absolutely essential to preserving and promoting true spirituality.

PART 4

Applications

9

Practiced Theology—
Lived Spirituality

Marva J. Dawn

Marva J. Dawn, who serves churches transdenominally through Christians Equipped to Ministry in Vancouver, Washington, is a Lutheran minister who is both an experienced church musician and a theologian (with a Ph.D. in Christian Ethics and the Scriptures from Notre Dame). A popular speaker and writer, she has emerged as a major voice in the Christian community calling for spiritual renewal and authentic worship based on the warranted wisdom of the church's historic Trinitarian faith. Among her many writings are *Truly the Community*, *Keeping the Sabbath Wholly*, *Reaching Out without Dumbing Down*, *A Royal "Waste" of Time*, and *Unfettered Hope: A Call to Faithful Living in an Affluent Society*.

In this chapter, Dawn explores the fusion of theology, spirituality, and ethics. She notes that evangelicals have sometimes produced unbiblical spiritualities when ethical ways have been reduced to moral tightness rather than justice. Drawing on the work of Jacques Ellul, Dawn explores the themes of generosity and peacemaking as two ways Christians can overcome the idolatries of greed and violence through faithful discipleship to Christ.

꧁ ꧁ ꧁

Let us think about a Trinitarian fusion of three things: theology, spirituality, and ethics. I first learned the tight correlation (which this conference volume is intending to recover) from Roger Brooks, a devout Jew and one of my professors in my Ph.D. program at Notre Dame. When I asked him, as part of my study for comprehensive exams, how Jews saw the correlation between spirituality and ethics, he reacted with disgust. He asked why one would ever consider splitting them and continued, "There is no difference between spirituality and ethics. They're both obedience to Torah."

137

Why do we divide the dimensions of faith into compartments? We should be ashamed if we bifurcate—as does much Christian literature—spirituality and ethics, ethics and theology, theology and spirituality. When I was appointed Teaching Fellow in Spiritual Theology at Regent College, I felt that I had finally come home. This was a title that described the kind of connecting I've been trying to do in all my teaching. All these dimensions are one. All come out of desiring to know God and to live in obedience to God. It is a holistic—and holy—way of life.

My goal in this chapter is to recapture the Hebrew unity, but also to recognize a crucial ordering with inextricable connections. Let us think about doctrine/theology as the bones of the body, of spirituality as the enfleshment in a way of life, and of ethics as the reaching out from that enfleshment. The ultimate question is how these enfleshed bones of doctrinal faith reach out to the world.

Such an image has very practical implications. For example, if spirituality is the entire enfleshment, then we cannot reduce it merely to feelings, as many contemporary versions of spirituality do.

DOCTRINAL BONES AND
SPIRITUALITY'S PROPER SHAPE

As a first point, let us think about the critical importance of understanding doctrinal bones as one aspect (but an indispensable one) of the entire shape of our spirituality. Some of us perhaps grew up in churches where faith was understood solely as intellectual agreement with doctrinal propositions. Some denominations' catechism classes required that teenagers be able to spit back the right answers to doctrinal questions, and then it was assumed that they had faith.

On the opposite side of the spectrum, perhaps some of us had a more liberal background in which doctrine did not much matter. The assumption was that there is no difference between Christianity and every other religion in the world—all of them are expressions of the same religious emotion. Of course, Muslims wouldn't agree with that claim. They are quite particular about their particularity, and true Christianity is, too.

In *The Nature of Doctrine*, George Lindbeck insightfully proclaims that Christianity is not merely cognitive (solely intellectual assent to a set of doctrinal propositions), nor is it simply experiential-expressive (engaging in, and articulating common, uplifting religious experiences). Rather, Christianity is a cultural-linguistic system, a practicing of the language of faith.[1]

Consider how you learn a language. You practice it—speak, listen, read, write it. One of the troubles with graduate school languages is that we usually learn only to read them—and thus don't really *know* them because we don't *live* them.

Doctrine got a bad name when we forgot that it is enfleshed in the faith life. And faith, as a language, is learned by engaging in its practices. We exercise faith and learn its language when we engage in worship, Bible reading, prayer, meditation, Sabbath keeping, giving money, hospitality, and all the other practices of true Christianity.

When I am asked to give children's sermons, for example, I always end with a prayer in which I say a phrase and have the children repeat it. That way they practice the language of faith. They learn to pray. The value of prayer books is that they widen our language, teach us other ways to pray. When we use rote prayers to train our children, we also free them eventually for a greater fullness in spontaneous prayers.

The person who introduced the workshop session that undergirds this chapter ended with a prayer that I have known since childhood, since it is centuries old and also appeared in the hymnal our congregation used every week for worship. To pray such a prayer at the beginning of that time made me feel right at home in faith in the midst of the people assembled. We used a language of faith together that I have spoken for many years.

Such prayers provide doctrinal bones. The central example is the Lord's Prayer, which Jesus gave the disciples to teach us to pray aright. When we invoke it together, it structures our faith around solid doctrine, knits us as a people, and reminds us that we are part of the whole company of saints. If I pray, "*Ojcze nasz, którys jest w niebie,*" I am linked to my friends in Poland as they entreat the same Father in heaven. When I pray the same prayer in Malagasy or Norwegian, I am linked to past students south and north and engage in the same practices with them that unite us in the same global family.

This recognition of the universal Christian faith is essential because we live in an age of so many ambiguous and indeterminate spiritualities, as several plenary addresses in this volume have noted. Surf the Web, and you find tons of the stuff. We have to discern the dangers of such spiritualities, intensely private and concocted from an eclectic mixture of sources and leading us away from the only One who is Truth.

Robert Wuthnow has documented the movement in United States culture from the "dwelling spirituality" of the 1950s to the "seeker spirituality" of the new millennium.[2] My objection to many contemporary spiritualities is not that I am trying to recover the "religious" organizations and ethnic loyalties of spirituality in the "dwelling" era just after World War II. These tend too easily to become small boutiques offering spiritual goods and services. My concern is for a spirituality that will not slither off because its enfleshment is secured to straight, sound doctrinal bones.

Wuthnow charts the first shift from the mid-century "at home" spirituality in the rebellions of the 1960s and early 1970s, when many rejected the simple religious truths of their childhood in order to be free to express their own subjectivities. At this point, the former deep commitments to truth were turned to greater concern for feeling good.[3]

This was modified further in the late 1970s-1980s, when people recognized the danger of the 1960s rebellions and began to desire disciplines, though these were commonly reduced to therapeutic devices. Wuthnow compares them to what Jacques Ellul called "Technique," quick-fix methods that wouldn't interrupt one's busy lifestyle and wouldn't interfere with being a normal person. Unlike a monk's practices, undergirded by obedience to hierarchy and personal sacrifice, this kind of discipline became detachment, a cheery attitude, reassurance, faith in goodness and common sense and not requiring knowledge or training, and fundamentally getting what one wants.[4]

No doubt you have seen books that describe these easy disciplines. They seem not to correlate with the recognition that "the sacred is always too powerful to be tamed by simple formulas and techniques."[5] I am concerned about this problem whenever I am asked to suggest spiritual tools, for sometimes people think that if they use just the right devotional book, it will solve their problems of not feeling close to God or not living as they would like. Good devotional tools are never techniques, but rather mentors from the larger Church, guides, sources of ancient wisdom, conversation partners.

The late 1980s and 1990s were characterized by a growing interest in miracle and mystery in the attempt to make sense of a world that was becoming increasingly dangerous and chaotic. This was the time when angels suddenly appeared in the secular market—in pins, books, decorations, even a new journal. Remarkably, these angels are usually cute and cozy—hardly the sort of appearance that would necessitate saying, "Fear not!" Angels who do what one wants and appear when one wants never inspire terror.

These angels represent a larger phenomenon, that people seek some sort of religious spectacle that doesn't cost them much in order to feel confident about the existence and presence of God.[6] As Wuthnow explains, this acquisitive spirituality can be understood best by paying attention to the implicit conversations people have with their own past. They know that religion played an important part in their forebears' lives, and "without necessarily wanting to live in that world, they nevertheless worry that something important has been lost." This leads to various attempts to sacralize some small aspect of everyday life, to read some spiritual significance into it to find more meaning.[7]

The period of the late 1980s and 1990s produced what Wuthnow calls a

"Spirituality of the Inner Self."[8] This might compare to what Robert Bellah called "Sheila-ism" in *Habits of the Heart*, a spirituality that is "Sheila's own."[9] This spirituality has no objective truth but finds its unity in the midst of the practitioner's psychological polytheism by means merely of focused attention on the present moment.

I have sketched Wuthnow's analysis so extensively because these movements demonstrate many of the dangers in spiritualities without adequate doctrinal bones and ecclesiological muscles. One insufficiency is that they lack "an interpretive framework providing coherence to individual biographies."[10] Another is that without a "more orderly, disciplined, and focused approach to the sacred,"[11] they are overly influenced by moods, circumstances, or exposure to constantly changing ideas. Consequently generally superficial, they deprive their practitioners of the depth and confidence of biblical spirituality, focused as it is in the confidence of relationship with the One who is the Way, the Truth, and the Life.

By contrast, evangelicals also produce unbiblical spiritualities when ethical ways are reduced to moral tightness rather than justice, when doctrinal truths are reduced to jargon, and when the Christian life is put on as a (hypocritical) Technique rather than gained by character formation.

There is an even deeper danger to spiritualities composed of bits and pieces gathered from various religious traditions. I have a friend who grew up in a strong denominational church but has become involved in all sorts of spiritual practices, including techniques with crystals. She is also profoundly depressed.

Recently, a text assigned by my prayer book for the daily reading made me very concerned for her. Beginning with Isaiah 8:11, the Lord criticizes Israel for turning away from the true God and toward such things as "mediums and spiritists" instead. Verse 22 prophesies that those who do this will "look toward the earth and see only distress and darkness and fearful gloom, and they will be thrust into utter darkness." I wondered if the "fearful gloom" of severe depression my friend is experiencing is related to her dabbling in the practices of other gods.

Moreover, it is not merely one's "personal choice" to confuse spiritualities. The resultant crooked bones affect the whole community. The darkness and gloom spread—in her case, to her family, friends, church, and work colleagues.

There is always hope, of course. Isaiah 9 goes on to assure us that "the people walking in darkness have seen a great light; on those living in the land of the shadow of death a light has dawned." This will happen because "to us a child is born, to us a son is given" who was called "Wonderful Counselor, Mighty God, Everlasting Father, Prince of Peace." I continue to pray and work toward the end that she would give up those fragments of other spiritualities and return to a faith grounded solely in the light of Christ.

However, my concern here is simply to accentuate the necessity that we always be vigilant. Historian Martin Marty emphasizes that we are in very much the same situation as the early Christians. The world is just as pluralistic as it was in the first three centuries of Christianity before the "Constantinian Fall." "Who Jesus Christ as Lord was had to be determined among many altars and shrines, many banners and advertisements, many pitches and preachments, among the so-called gods and the many gods and lords."[12] In the midst of all the postmodern choices, we need a strong skeleton for faith, firm theology at its center, a core in our spirituality with its axis in Jesus Christ.

THE IMPORTANCE OF STRAIGHT DOCTRINAL BONES

Another great danger for theology as the undergirding of spirituality is the tendency to take seriously only certain parts of the Scriptures instead of the whole counsel of God. Frequently in evangelical churches I hear benedictions that end only in the name of Jesus. Why don't the leaders say, "In the name of the Father and of the Son and of the Holy Spirit"? That is the faith into which we have been baptized.

Do we realize how rarely we are Trinitarian? If we focus only on Jesus, we might not have a comprehensive doctrine of creation and its goodness. We might inadequately trust the Lord's sustaining of creation or might not marvel at how God continues to create.

To avoid offensive patriarchal images of God the Father, some denominations choose to avoid that name altogether. Other churches have a deficiency of the Holy Spirit, while the charismatics perhaps underestimate other persons of the Trinity. It seems that almost every church group is a bit lopsided in one direction or another. Perhaps we don't recognize how very practical the doctrine of the Trinity is.[13]

I have two illustrations so that you will not forget the crucial importance of straight doctrinal bones—and of *each* biblical bone. I have to wear a strong plastic brace on my leg if I want to walk. Twelve years ago a doctor misdiagnosed when my foot was broken and I was told to walk a lot, which led to its shattering. A specialist rebuilt my foot by removing the shattered bones and screwing my metatarsals to the heel—but that took away the arch and changed the angle of my body, so my leg broke soon after I started walking on my nice little foot. My leg healed with a bend in it, which is now held in place (that is, crooked) by my brace. Without the brace, my leg would snap at the bend if I put full weight on it—just as our churches snap if they come under pressure at the points of crooked doctrine.

We also need the second illustration, however, because some think that it is sufficient merely to brace up doctrinally crooked churches with a bit of "plastic" from the outside. We have discovered with my leg that crooked bones coming close to the skin and hard plastic immediately on the other side of the skin leads to ulcerated wounds. Perhaps the most obvious example of this problem in churches occurs when they have an inadequate doctrine of community and thus let conflicts fester rather than work on rebuke, reconciliation, and restoration.

Our goal in spirituality is for straight doctrinal bones to provide a strong skeleton on which our character is enfleshed. An example of crooked bones and a resultant crash was provided several years ago when prominent televangelists were caught in adulterous relationships. That was not surprising, however, for they had actually fallen long before when they and their ministries had problems with "Mammon." They had already succumbed to the temptation of instant gratification; it was already part of their character.

A speaker earlier in this conference said, "A thief is not someone who steals but someone who could." Similarly, one who has allowed self to become central in terms of an idolatry of money can more easily fall prey to sexual attractions. Every dimension of doctrine and ethics matters for the development of Christian character.

One key doctrine that frequently gets distorted is that of grace. Recently I preached for a clergy conference on Mark 7:31–37, the healing of the deaf and mute man in the region of the Decapolis. Verses 34–35 tell us that after putting his fingers in the man's ears, Jesus said, "'*Ephphatha*' (which means, 'Be opened!')" and the "man's ears were opened." I emphasized in my sermon for the pastors that they had come to this retreat and that Christ also was there to heal. Jesus does the opening. We don't have to crank it out, scramble for it.

These were pastors discouraged because the severe farm crisis is forcing many farmers in their churches to give up their vocation. My husband asked me that night on the telephone what I had said to them, so I reported that I had kept emphasizing, "Jesus heals. He is present here and in your parishes. When you preach that Jesus heals, don't preach that the farmers have to open themselves up to it." My husband groaned—because that was exactly what he had heard that morning.

I find it necessary constantly to warn pastors against such preaching of "how we should be open." I have heard far too many sermons that turn the Gospel into Law, turn grace into what *we* have to do. Jesus doesn't heal "if we are open." He heals. Of course, we *want* to be open to whatever God wills to do, but let us who teach and preach be very careful how we articulate the connection of the Gospel and God's grace with how we respond.

When we turn the Gospel into Law, our life becomes a "try harder" spirituality, rather than the "gift of God" spirituality that receives grace. Gospel must be the core of all our teaching in the Church.

The Law is important. It drives us to the gospel, shows us how much we need a Savior, guides us to live in response to grace, helps us to be disciplined. But the core of the Christian life is the good news that God has done everything necessary for our spiritual lives. Let's make sure that every sermon, every educational endeavor, clearly proclaims the Gospel. It will make ulcerated wounds if we try to prop up a lack of Gospel with outside "plastics" such as more rules.

THE WHOLE METANARRATIVE

The core of all doctrine, spirituality, and ethics is the whole metanarrative of the Bible. One of the reasons that I love using the *Revised Common Lectionary* to guide our choice of texts for Sunday worship is that in the course of its three years, it introduces worshipers to a much larger proportion of the Church's Scriptures.

I have been curious for a long while and have never gotten a good answer to this question: Why is it that evangelicals, who claim to be the most Bible-centered, read the least of it in worship? Mainline churches use a First Testament[14] lesson, perhaps a psalm (often sung), an epistle lesson, and a reading from the Gospels. In contrast, many evangelical churches might have no other readings and cite only a verse or two for the sermon.

I'm not arguing that every denomination should share with the churches usually called "liturgical" in their lectionary series, but I do insist that every congregation should give its people a full sense of the whole Bible over the course of the church year.

BIBLICAL INTERPRETATION

Then we must ask the larger question of how we interpret the Scriptures we read, for this connects our theology to its enfleshment in spirituality and ethics. The Scriptures must be understood as a master story with multiple narratives that form us as we are immersed in them. We become part of this genuine story as we then live out of the character shaped by all of God's revelation.

One of the largest differences between liberals and conservatives arises in methods for interpretation of the Scriptures, and it seems to me that often both are wrong in applying them to daily life. The hermeneutical battles develop because we have to ask how something written two thousand years ago can apply now in vastly dissimilar circumstances. Aren't biblical passages archaic, old-fashioned, not commensurate to our times?

Jacques Ellul, French sociologist and lay theologian, offered a superb response to this question in 1968, in his ironically titled "Innocent Notes on 'the Hermeneutic Question.'"[15] In that article, Ellul combined the insights of a sophisticated biblical scholar conversant with linguistic theory and the "innocent" forthrightness of a resolute believer to demonstrate that the hermeneutical gap does not lie between the culture of two thousand years ago and the present world. Do you think the people around Isaiah understood Isaiah? Did the folks with Jesus understand Jesus? Isn't the gap rather between those who believe and those who don't?

Ellul's "innocent notes" turn the whole hermeneutical argument on its head. He insists that you can't comprehend "le Révélation" unless you receive and believe "le Révélé." We put too much of the wrong burden, then, on our hermeneutical skills, for we must begin instead with the Revealed One and then be formed by faith in Jesus Christ to live out the Revelation, which is the Word of God.

Conservatives often define how we *live* the Word with a simplistic slap-dash—my phrase for a method of application that does not take into any consideration the cultural circumstances in which a text was written, but instead insists "it says this, so therefore it means this." As one prime example, some say, "Women should never teach because Paul says he doesn't permit it in 1 Timothy 2:12." But this doesn't take into consideration 1 Corinthians 11:5, which mentions women praying and prophesying, or Romans 16:1, which names Phoebe a "deacon" (the Greek noun is in the masculine form, so it seems to signify a title, since Paul didn't use "deaconess" or another word for female servant). Furthermore, the slapdash prohibition does not seem consistent with Paul or the entire corpus of 1 and 2 Timothy, with its heavy emphasis on *false* teaching. It seems to me that Paul does not mean women can't teach ever, for all time, but that the situation in Ephesus at the time of his writing prevented it.[16]

Liberals, by contrast, frequently make the opposite mistake in interpretation if, instead of slapdash, they use a throwaway method. I've had people tell me concerning 1 Timothy 2, "Paul wrote that, and he was a male chauvinist, so I just don't pay attention to it." Excuse me?

By this contrast we can see how right Ellul was in calling our attention to our presuppositions. Do we believe this is the Revelation of God rather than the work of human authors whose prejudices got in the way? Do we believe God used human writers with their own personalities, but whose work was directed by the Spirit's inspiration to rise above those cultural conditionings?

APPLYING THE SCRIPTURES: "IMPROVISATION"

This, however, still leaves us with the particular issue of how to interpret and "apply" such passages, and for that problem N. T. Wright offers what I believe is a very helpful method.[17] Let us imagine that we have just found an incomplete manuscript of a William Shakespeare drama. How would we perform it?

Imagine that we have uncovered the first five acts of this play and the last bit of the seventh.[18] How could we produce it? We could try to write the missing parts, but we are not as wise as Shakespeare, or as clever, or as insightful into human personality. We could never be sure if we captured very well his intentions—and we could not check out our attempts with the author.

Instead, we would try to find actors who were highly experienced in the theater, who knew Shakespeare's work inside and out, who understood all his writings and his life and his personality. Then they would have to immerse themselves in the acts of the new play that had been found. With this basis, they could improvise the missing parts, and their improvisation would be different at every performance because of variations in the audience and their reactions.

The key is the actors' immersion in what had already been written. Similarly, we immerse ourselves in the Word of God that is written—the commandments, narratives, poetry, prophecy, drama—and that forms us to be a certain kind of people, Christians, who live in certain ways. The advantage of this schema for application of the Scriptures is that it doesn't limit us merely to the rules that have direct application (and rules can even be modified by the larger narratives in which they occur). And our Author is still alive and present in our midst! Let us look at the acts in God's Revelation and consider how they might form us.

Act 1: Creation

Creation accounts are not limited to Genesis 1 and 2 but include Psalms (such as 8 and 104), Romans 8, Colossians 1, and numerous other passages that discuss God's creation. If we immerse ourselves in these, we are formed to have the kind of character that will improvise faithful caring for the creation and rejoicing in it. For example, Genesis 1:29–30 tells us that God created enough green plants for all the creatures to have food. If I am formed by Act 1, I will develop my life toward feeding everyone. God's creation design is that no one would be hungry, so it is obviously the result of the Fall (see Act 2) that many people in the world are starving. As part of the New Creation made possible by Jesus (see Act 4), we will respond (in Act 6) by working to eliminate poverty and hunger.

The creation account in Genesis 1 also tells us that we have dominion *with* the creatures. My visual limitations prevent me from being a scholar of

Hebrew, yet it seems to me that we should translate the ב in 1:26 and 28 as "with" instead of "over." Many good theological works on the environment are now recognizing the misuse of Scripture involved in past justifications for human destruction of the earth. True immersion in the biblical narratives would form us, instead, to care for the earth for the sake of itself, as well as for the sake of future generations.

Genesis 1 also begins our theology of male and female relations, for it emphasizes that both equally bear the image of God. Furthermore, we don't have to be characterized by our culture's silly stereotypes of masculinity and femininity, for who I am as a woman is defined by how I image God. I find that extraordinarily freeing. It also prevents us from many of our culture's rebellions against God's creation of male and female, for the way we live our own unique creation as imagers of God must be in accord with who God truly is.

Act 2: The Fall

This part of the play is crucial in shaping us because it helps us understand why we can't be what we want to be (e.g., Romans 7), why so much of life is broken (Genesis 3), why various forces constantly pull us away from God (Revelation 12–14, 20), why we have to be vigilant against them (Jesus' warnings in the Gospels).

Martin Luther summarized the effects of the Fall on our lives as constant battle against "the devil, the world, and our flesh."[19] We can't help but be formed to be more watchful against this triumvirate's destructions if we immerse ourselves in all the Scriptures. If we start to rationalize things as persons in our culture do when, for example, they want to engage in immoral sexual behavior, then we need texts outside us that remind us we are fallen and that in our fallenness our minds are also corrupted and err. We need the biblical rebukes as constant cautions against trusting our earthly desires, against overlooking our fallen tendencies. We are forgiven sinners (we learn in other acts of the play), but sinners nonetheless (this act reminds us) who will never—until the end of time—be free from the lurking craving to be our own gods.

Act 3: The story of Israel

The great advantage of Wright's idea for interpreting the Scriptures over conservative slapdash application and liberal discounting is that it frees us to value more of the Bible than only the rules for the formation of our lives. We can be immersed in all the story of Israel—its stories, love poetry, the Psalms, the proverbs, the antiwisdom movement represented in Ecclesiastes and Job. All these accounts show us both what it is like to follow God and what the consequences are when we reject the Lord and violate the Revelation. The poetry and prophecy immerse us in imaginative thinking about God.

Liberals tend to abstract generalized principles from the Hebrew literature, but Romans 9–11 teaches us that we Gentiles are grafted onto the roots of Judaica, so these are our stories, parts of our heritage—and, even as each of us is formed by the traditions and stories of our ancestors, so the First Testament in its entirety is our lineage.

Act 5: The early Church

Temporarily I skipped Act 4, because Act 5 is much like Act 3—our bloodline. The New Testament book of Acts and the epistles all tell us what it was like to follow Jesus after the Ascension. If we immerse ourselves in all the instructions given in these books, we are formed, for example, to be women who do not usurp authority or teach gnostic heresies (1 Tim. 2:11–15) and men who mutually submit to everyone in the Church (Eph. 5:21). The whole narrative forms us as a people in union with Christ.

The difference between Acts 3 and 5, of course, is that saints in the former precede Jesus and long for him and in the latter come after and learn from Him. Both, however, are narratives of people who yearn for the fulfillment of God's reign as they continue to improvise the faith life between the Creation and Fall of Acts 1 and 2 and the culmination of the play in Act 7.

Act 4: The high point of the metanarrative—Jesus

When I was an English teacher while working on my first graduate degree, I asked students to find in short stories the turning point after which the story could end no other way. That is a helpful skill for reading the Bible—for in light of the Fall, the only turning point could be some event that changes its results, so that God's original purposes in creation can be fulfilled. Act 4 gives the entire account of this turning point: the birth, life, teachings, ministry, sufferings, death, resurrection, and ascension[20] of Jesus of Nazareth.

The incarnation of God, the "tabernacling" of the Word, the fulfillment of all the First Testament promises, the foundation for all the life of the Church—this One's story *is* the high point of our metanarrative. And the crown of the pivotal narrative is the resurrection.

The resurrection of Christ changes everything! After it, the story could end in no other way, for in the resurrection the last enemy, death, is defeated; the principalities and powers are exposed, disarmed, triumphed over. Now the only way the metanarrative could end is with the ultimate victory of God and the reconciliation of the cosmos.

Before leaving this act, however, let me underscore the plurality of the word *sufferings* above. When we say the Apostles' Creed in worship here in the United States, we put an essential comma in the wrong place. We say, "I believe in Jesus Christ . . . who suffered under Pontius Pilate, was crucified, died, and was buried." We should confess "who suffered, under Pontius Pilate was crucified . . . " The latter proclaims the truth that throughout His life, Jesus suffered—not only under Pilate, but at the hands of the disciples and Jewish leaders and Roman soldiers, and at our hands! He suffered from the day He was born and was laid in a stinking, scratchy manger as the child of poor parents who had no place to stay. If we realized this more, perhaps we would not so terribly overromanticize and sentimentalize Christmas. Perhaps if we talked more about suffering at Christmastime, believers would know better that our lives are determined by suffering for the sake of the Gospel and not by triumph. The will of God is accomplished through vulnerability, servanthood, suffering, weakness.[21]

I think the main reason Christianity seems to have so little impact on our culture is that we are not willing to die for our neighbors. We are not really willing to suffer for their sake. The narrative of Jesus forms our character, and He suffered all His life. He suffered obscurity, hunger, the ridiculous misunderstandings of his disciples, crowds who constantly besieged Him even when He tried to escape for some retreat. If we want to follow Jesus, it will be by taking up a cross—not a teddy bear!—and the only reason to carry a cross is to die on it.

We are willing to bear that cross, to pay the price of loving our neighbors, because we know the end of the story and because we know the resurrection—but most people jump to Easter too fast. Perhaps we should make a rule that people cannot come to Easter worship unless they have observed the forty days of Lent and grieved in the worship of Maundy Thursday and Good Friday. Perhaps people should not be allowed to come for Christmas unless they have participated in the repentance and waiting of Advent.

We jump too easily to the victory side of our story and thus fail to recognize the whole point of the incarnation. Only forty days of Jesus' entire earthly life were spent on the other side of the grave—and during those days He still had to put up with the disciples who could not comprehend what He was saying (until after Pentecost and not always then, as the book of Acts charts). Let us remember, therefore, as the whole account of Jesus forms us, that His resurrection and ascension give us hope for the end, but rarely characterize our days in the meanwhile. When asked, Mother Teresa commented that she was called to serve Jesus, not the poor. Jesus led her to the poor. Where will He lead us if we *really* follow Him?

Act 7: The End of Time

The metanarrative of faith concludes (or does it truly begin?) at the end of time, when faith becomes sight and God will do away with all sorrow and sighing and tears and suffering forever. We don't know much about the end of the story, contrary to all those who insist that the Revelation pins down a calendar of the final events. Such an interpretation causes many people to be afraid of the book—which is an excellent tactic of the devil, since the Revelation is the only biblical book that includes a promise at both its beginning and its end to those who read and heed it.

Revelation was, rather, written to comfort those who struggled to live as Christians in a time of bitter persecution.[22] Since this is also a time of great suffering—as our postmodern, consumerist society makes it increasingly difficult to live as a Christian—the Revelation is great encouragement for us too. And it does tell us one essential thing about the end of time: that God will triumph and do away with all evil forever!

Act 6: You and I

Here, in the midst of this grand metanarrative about all of history and history's only true God, we have a place. Formed by the entire account, we improvise our parts. Every day, depending on who our audience is and where we are in our segment of the story, we live the Gospel. Because we know the high point and the freedom our salvation brings, and because we know the end of the story and the triumph of God, we can live now in great hope—even though we live in a fallen world and have to suffer to love its inhabitants. But our spirituality is this improvisation. We study the metanarrative so that our character is formed on straight doctrinal bones, and in the enfleshment of our lives we practice spiritual habits that enable us to ask the right ethical questions. And thus all is brought together in the obedience of living the Gospel.

VIGILANCE IN OUR SPIRITUALITY

Preaching on Mark 9:38–50 recently caused me to wonder how much of what we do should earn us a millstone, since Jesus warns that "if anyone causes one of these little ones who believe in me to sin, it would be better for him/her to be thrown into the sea with a large millstone tied around his/her neck." Reread the entire passage and think about whether you would have any hands, feet, or eyes left if you took Jesus seriously.

Do we consider how harmful some of our daily activities are to our spirituality? Remember that I am defining spirituality in union with doctrine and ethics as a holistic way of life inherent in salvation by grace. Do we recognize, for example, that how much and what we watch on television is a spiritual matter? How much we surf the Web is also a significant factor in our spirituality.

What does television form us and our children to be—greedy, sexually immoral, passive, violent?[23] Research shows that children who watch television at length have smaller brains because that passive activity does not lead to proliferating the dendrites or bridging the hemispheres between input and output.[24] Furthermore, it changes how they think.[25]

We talk quite a bit about spirituality, but do we think enough about what hinders it, blocks it, obstructs it, distorts it, makes it filthy, pollutes our minds or our habits? At a Christian conference talent show this past summer, before an audience of several hundred, a young girl sang an embarrassingly sexually overt song. What did her mother think in letting her sing it? Did they both *notice* the unbiblical slant of the song's content? She sang well, she was cute— but it was vulgar.

Do we realize how much the culture in which we live is a garbage dump morally? Do we recognize the extent of the moral pollution? Is it any wonder, then, that our kids—if they are immersed in it—don't seem to care much about Christianity?

How much time do we spend in families and churches on *Christian* formation of our children? Let's be idealistic and tally an hour for worship, an hour for Sunday school, and fifteen minutes each day for family devotions. That's still only about four hours a week total, while television forms them four and one-half hours each day. Or perhaps the Internet does.

Will our churches wake up to the immense task that it must be for us truly to form children in faith?[26] We must be constantly asking how what we do affects the growth of the spiritual life in ourselves and other members, especially the children, of our churches. And let us stand vigilantly against the many destructive elements that come into our children's spirituality.

ETHICAL CONCERNS—CRUCIAL ELEMENTS OF OUR SPIRITUALITY

One core element of our daily life that I believe is essential for our spirituality is the celebrative practice of giving away money. This is fundamental because Mammon is one of the leading gods in our culture. And Mammon tempts us all.[27]

Jacques Ellul's *Money and Power* alerted me to my own idolatry. I did not think money was much of a god in my life. I do not have too much of it, so I don't hoard it; I don't have too little, so that I would covet it. But Ellul suggests that some people have just the right amount and are such good stewards of it that they are not generous. Caught me! I would suppose that every reader of this book has allowed money to become Mammon at some point in your lives.

Ellul teaches instead to deliberately desacralize our money, de-divinize it so that it does not gain a hold on us.[28] Can we in our families create a monthly party to give away half our income—or whatever percentage we can distribute? For most families to talk about tithing is silly. Look how rich we are compared to the rest of the world. Do we really need all we have when so many have next to nothing?

The biblical tithe is a starting point, the amount we can give to our congregations for their mission, but then there are many other needs to which we can contribute. Remember Act 1, for example, and its creation accounts—God desires that all would be fed!

Another major element of our spirituality must be peacemaking. Even as Jesus praised the merciful, he also said that peacemakers are blessed (Matt. 5:1–12), and Paul reports that we have been given the ministry of reconciliation (2 Cor. 5:14–21). How can we become more conscious of being agents of reconciliation? How could our congregations be models of peacemaking instead of centers of conflict?

One example concerns how we decide issues in our churches. When we use majority vote, does it often split the congregation into winners and losers instead of helping us all be able to say, "It seemed good to the Holy Spirit and to us" (Acts 15:28)?

The high point of our metanarrative tells of a Savior who at the cross broke down all barriers between God's people (Ephesians 2). Do we break down all the barriers in our churches, so that black and white worship together, so that there are no divisions according to age, length of membership, social classes, musical tastes? Could it become a goal in our spirituality that we develop the process of reconciling opponents as a personal and corporate way of life?

Mainline churches have, in the past, been stronger in working for social justice than evangelicals. Why is that? Why has it happened that those who claim to know most clearly who Jesus is do not seem to be the ones leading the way in fulfilling His instructions for caring for others and building jubilee justice?

This is why we have to build such a solid cohesion of doctrine, spirituality, and ethics, so that our theology of Jesus as the cosmic reconciler is lived out in our daily peacemaking. Jesus is the one who eschewed Mammon, who exposed it when the thirty pieces of silver were thrown back. Is Jesus truly my Lord, or would I betray him, too, for silver—or to win an argument? Sometimes our churches—and we—do. Pastors have told me, "I couldn't preach that text [any text that challenges our consumption]. Our highest givers would leave the congregation."

Do we support our pastors so they are not under this pressure? Do we thank them for rebuking us (one of the tasks in their job description in 1 Thess. 5:12)? Do we rebuke each other in the community for the sake of the spirituality of the whole (1 Thess. 5:14)?

Generosity and peacemaking are just two examples of many we could cite here to link our spirituality with outreach to the world around us. Based on solid doctrinal bones, spirituality must issue in ethical commitments. Theology/doctrine, spirituality, and ethics are all one thing—living the Gospel because Jesus Christ lives in us and brings us into active relationship with His Father by the power of their Spirit.

BIBLIOGRAPHY FOR SPIRITUAL FORMATION

Arnold, Johann Christoph. *Seeking Peace: Notes and Conversations along the Way*. Farmington, Pa.: Plough Publishing House, 1998.

Bass, Dorothy C., ed. *Practicing Our Faith: A Way of Life for a Searching People*. San Francisco: Jossey-Bass, 1997.

Blomberg, Craig L. *Neither Poverty nor Riches: A Biblical Theology of Material Possessions*. New Studies in Biblical Theology. D. A. Carson, series editor. Grand Rapids: Wm. B. Eerdmans Publishing Co., 1999.

Butigan, Ken, and Patricia Bruno, O.P. *From Violence to Wholeness*. Las Vegas: Pace e Bene Franciscan Nonviolence Center, 1999.

Clapp, Rodney. *A Peculiar People: The Church as Culture in a Post-Christian Society*. Downers Grove, Ill.: Inter-Varsity Press, 1996.

———, ed. *The Consuming Passion: Christianity and the Consumer Culture*. Downers Grove, Ill.: Inter-Varsity Press, 1998.

Dawn, Marva J. *Is It a Lost Cause? Having the Heart of God for the Church's Children*. Grand Rapids: Wm. B. Eerdmans Publishing Co., 1997.

———. *Joy in Our Weakness: A Gift of Hope from the Book of Revelation*. St. Louis: Concordia Publishing House, 1994. Rev. ed., Grand Rapids: Wm. B. Eerdmans Publishing Co., forthcoming.

———. *Keeping the Sabbath Wholly: Ceasing, Resting, Embracing, Feasting*. Grand Rapids: Wm. B. Eerdmans Publishing Co., 1997.

———. *Powers, Weakness, and the Tabernacling of God*. Grand Rapids: Wm. B. Eerdmans Publishing Co., 2001.

———. *Reaching Out without Dumbing Down: A Theology of Worship for the Turn-of-the-Century Culture*. Grand Rapids: Wm. B. Eerdmans Publishing Co., 1999.

———. *A Royal "Waste" of Time: The Splendor of Worshiping God and Being Church for the World*. Grand Rapids: Wm. B. Eerdmans Publishing Co., 1999.

———. *Sexual Character: Beyond Technique to Intimacy*. Grand Rapids: Wm. B. Eerdmans Publishing Co., 1997.

———. *Truly the Community: Romans 12 and How to Be the Church*. Grand Rapids: Wm. B. Eerdmans Publishing Co., 1992, reissued 1997.

———. *Unfettered Hope: A Call to Faithful Living in an Affluent Society*. Louisville, Ky.: Westminster John Knox Press, 2003.

———, trans. and ed., *Sources and Trajectories: Eight Early Articles by Jacques Ellul That Set the Stage*. Grand Rapids: Wm. B. Eerdmans Publishing Co., 1997.

Dawn, Marva J., and Eugene Peterson. *The Unnecessary Pastor: Rediscovering the Call*. Grand Rapids: Wm. B. Eerdmans Publishing Co., 1999.

Dean, Kenda Creasy, ed. *Growing Up Postmodern: Imitating Christ in the Age of "Whatever."* Princeton, N.J.: Institute for Youth Ministry, 1999.

Ellul, Jacques. *The Ethics of Freedom*. Translated by Geoffrey W. Bromiley. Grand Rapids: Wm. B. Eerdmans Publishing Co., 1976.

————. *False Presence of the Kingdom*. Translated by C. Edward Hopkin. New York: Seabury Press, 1972.

————. *The Humiliation of the Word*. Translated by Joyce Main Hanks. Grand Rapids: Wm. B. Eerdmans Publishing Co., 1985.

————. *Money and Power*. Translated by LaVonne Neff. Downers Grove, Ill.: Inter-Varsity Press, 1984.

————. *The New Demons*. Translated by C. Edward Hopkin. New York: Seabury Press, 1975.

————. *Prayer and Modern Man*. Translated by C. Edward Hopkin. New York: Seabury Press, 1970.

————. *The Presence of the Kingdom*. Translated by Olive Wyon. New York: Seabury Press, 1967.

————. *The Subversion of Christianity*. Translated by Geoffrey W. Bromiley. Grand Rapids: Wm. B. Eerdmans Publishing Co., 1986.

Foster, Richard J. *The Challenge of the Disciplined Life: Christian Reflection on Money, Sex and Power*. San Francisco: Harper & Row, 1989.

Gushee, David P., ed. *Toward a Just and Caring Society: Christian Responses to Poverty in America*. Grand Rapids: Baker Book House, 1999.

Harris, Mark. *Companions for Your Spiritual Journey: Discovering the Disciplines of the Saints*. Downers Grove, Ill.: Inter-Varsity Press, 1999.

Hauerwas, Stanley. *A Community of Character: Toward a Constructive Christian Social Ethic*. Notre Dame, Ind.: University of Notre Dame Press, 1981.

Hauerwas, Stanley, and William H. Willimon. *Resident Aliens*. Nashville: Abingdon Press, 1989.

Hays, Richard B. *The Moral Vision of the New Testament: A Contemporary Introduction to New Testament Ethics*. San Francisco: HarperSanFrancisco, 1996.

Hunsberger, George R., and Craig Van Gelder, eds. *The Church between Gospel and Culture: The Emerging Mission in North America*. Grand Rapids: Wm. B. Eerdmans Publishing Co., 1996.

Kadlecek, Jo. *Feast of Life: Spiritual Food for Balanced Living*. Grand Rapids: Baker Book House, 1999.

Kenneson, Philip. *Life on the Vine: Cultivating the Fruit of the Spirit in Christian Community*. Downers Grove, Ill.: Inter-Varsity Press, 1999.

Lawrence, Brother. *The Practice of the Presence of God*. Translated by Donald Attwater. Springfield: Templegate Publishers, 1981.

Ortberg, John. *The Life You've Always Wanted: Spiritual Disciplines for Ordinary People*. Grand Rapids: Zondervan, 1997.

Pohl, Christine D. *Making Room: Recovering Hospitality as a Christian Tradition*. Grand Rapids: Wm. B. Eerdmans Publishing Co., 1999.

Van Gelder, Craig, ed. *Confident Witness—Changing World*. Grand Rapids: Wm. B. Eerdmans Publishing Co., 2000.

Vanier, Jean. *The Heart of L'Arche: A Spirituality for Every Day*. New York: Crossroad, 1995.

Wuthnow, Robert. *After Heaven: Spirituality in America since the 1950s*. Berkeley: University of California Press, 1998.

Yoder, John Howard. *The Politics of Jesus*. Rev. ed. Grand Rapids: Wm. B. Eerdmans Publishing Co., 1994.

10

The Evangelical Spirituality of Creation Care and the Kingdom of God

Robbie Castleman

Robbie F. Castleman is assistant professor of Biblical Studies and Theology at John Brown University. She holds degrees from Loyola University (B.A.), Florida State University (M.A.), and the University of Dubuque Theological Seminary (D.Min.). A popular speaker with student groups, she served for many years as national coordinator for the Religious and Theological Studies Fellowship of InterVarsity Christian Fellowship. Her writings include *True Love in a World of False Hope, A Theology of Human Sexuality* (1996), *Faith on the Edge* (1999), and *Parenting in the Pew* (2002).

In this chapter, Castleman draws on her own experience in the environmental movement as she calls on evangelicals to become engaged with a proper care of the earth as an expression of faithful stewardship. Environmental activism and evangelical spirituality are disparate concepts for most people. However, Castleman shows how concern for creation care grows out of, and indeed is mandated by, a true evangelical understanding of the lordship of Christ and a Christian hope for the future. At the heart of this concern are the great biblical themes of incarnation and eschatology.

❧❧❧ ❧❧❧ ❧❧❧

As he approached Bethphage and Bethany at the hill called the Mount of Olives, he sent two of his disciples, saying to them, "Go to the village ahead of you, and as you enter it, you will find a colt tied there, *which no one has ever ridden.* Untie it and bring it here. If anyone asks you, 'Why are you untying it?' tell him, 'The Lord needs it.'"

Those who were sent ahead went and found it just as he had told them. As they were untying the colt, its owners asked them, "Why are you untying the colt?"

They replied, "The Lord needs it."
They brought it to Jesus, threw their cloaks on the colt and put Jesus on it. As he went along, people spread their cloaks on the road.
When he came near the place where the road goes down from the Mount of Olives, the whole crowd of disciples began joyfully to praise God in loud voices for all the miracles they had seen:
"Blessed is the king who comes in the name of the Lord!
Peace in heaven and glory in the highest!"
Some of the Pharisees in the crowd said to Jesus, "Teacher, rebuke your disciples!"
"I tell you," he replied, "if they keep quiet, the stones will cry out."

Luke 19: 29–40
(emphasis mine)

In the fall of 1969, I attended a conference on the environment in Reston, Virginia, as a representative of the National Student Nurses Association. As I recall, there were between fifty and seventy-five college-aged students and a dozen or so mentors, teachers, and environmentalists who attended. We had gathered together to learn about environmental concerns, brainstorm ways to bring these concerns into the mainstream, and plan the first Earth Day.

Rachel Carson's book *Silent Spring* had alerted many to the need for earth care. We approached the issue from a variety of angles. The medical community I represented was concerned about biomedical waste disposal and the effects of pollutants as a health issue. All sorts of people were there to inspire our participation and inform our efforts. I remember having a brief conversation with a young Carl Sagan. Senator Mark Hatfield of Oregon was there, but I didn't know he was a committed Christian brother at the time. Eddie Albert, the actor, was there. He seemed eager to promote environmentally responsible living, but I remember a student criticizing him for being the advertising spokesperson for some detergent full of phosphates. He pleaded ignorance and promised to break his contract with the company.

Some significant things happened as a result of that conference and others like it in the years that followed. My big contribution to the first Earth Day, held April 1, 1970, was manning the "Use White Toilet Paper Only" booth at the sparsely attended event we planned for our local event in Salt Lake City. As a Christian, my commitment to honor the Lord through efforts in creation care has been sustained. Even with the inconsistencies of a middle-class North American lifestyle, my interest in environmental stewardship has not lagged through the years. I used cloth diapers for my children and recycled as much as possible before curbside pickup existed. I have a compost pile and sign petitions to save the Everglades and the like. I was amazed that it took twenty years for "Reduce, Reuse, Recycle" to find any kind of broad promotion and support. But I also drive a car when I really could ride my bike if I managed my time better, and I have attained "frequent flyer" award status using fossil fuels I know can never be replaced. Still, I keep trying and making the effort to do what I can. I routinely use a washable plate and utensils at the "Family Night Suppers" at our church to avoid Styrofoam and other disposables. I take a ceramic mug with me for beverages when I travel.

At Florida State University, I have given a lecture titled "St. Francis, Gaia and the Good News." Sponsored as an InterVarsity event, the lecture was designed to attract the activists in the environmental community of the university. I had three purposes for that engagement. First, I wanted those attending to hear the gospel. This is the good news of the Creator, who still speaks. The centerpiece of the gospel is Jesus, the incarnate Son of God, who lived in real flesh and died for the redemption of the cosmos. Jesus is the one for whom we wait with "eager longing" to come again as the redeemer of the world. Jesus has everything to do with creation care.

Second, I wanted "outsiders" to find out that Christians actually have something to contribute to "their" cause. Because God so loved the cosmos, Christians actually have something to offer that is substantive, compelling, and far-reaching in strategy, scope, and reason. Christians, who will one day reign with Christ Jesus in the new creation, find Scripture to be the definitive text on the subject.

And third, as God gave grace, creating "ears to hear," I wanted all those present to discover that environmental issues and creation care are, in fact, God's concern. Creation care is actually one of his top two priorities, set forth when he spoke creation, time and space, into being. I knew university students, Christian or not, have no trouble seeing the need for functional human relationships, and most are open to the idea that a relationship with God can help. God's concern for the care of his joyous six days of creative work is far less captivating, especially, it seems, for Christians.

I suspect there are more than a few readers who picked up this book, scanned the table of contents, and wondered what an "Evangelical Spirituality of Creation Care" was and if it could really have anything to do with the kingdom of God. I have found that evangelical Christians for the most part are unconvinced that caring for God's good creation is at all important to our witness, to the world itself, or even to God. Many evangelicals would agree that it is important to expose the heresy of Gaia because correcting muddled New Age thinking is part of the apologetic enterprise, but to connect evangelical spirituality to creation care might be a new and even suspect idea. Christians appreciate a beautiful church camp, seaside retreat center, or mountain getaway for congregational special events and youth group experiences but rarely reflect biblically on what that may have to do with theology. Nature, the environment, aesthetics, and art are viewed as matters of taste and issues of preference. We seldom reflect on these things theologically, but when someone does, it can prove challenging. An evangelical writer in *Mars Hill Review* asks,

> How would we fare if alien intelligence removed us suddenly from the earth, and with eyes wide in wonder begged us to tell it all we knew about the world God had created? Sheepishly, we might be able to recall some eighth grade science and introductory college biology, but what account could we give of the earth and its cycles, its teeming life, its intricate interconnectedness? Suddenly we'd recognize, with embarrassment, that our knowledge of popular culture, which we have consumed in earnest, is quite extensive in contrast. We could probably sing the tunes to dozens of different TV shows, recall an overwhelming amount of information on the life histories of celebrities, and discuss at length the pros and cons of a variety of consumer products, from clothes labels to cars. We would be like the random people stopped by a late-night talk show host on the streets of Hollywood, who unwittingly answer lighthearted questions that ridicule their own ignorance:
> Leno: "Can you name what elements are in the atmosphere?"
> Interviewee: "Uh . . . "
> Leno: "Can you name what characters are in the Rice Crispy Commercial?"
> Interviewee: "Snap, Crackle, Pop!"
> . . . [W]e know more about what people have created—brand names and sport franchises and media icons—than about the very basics—water, soil and biodiversity—on which all of created life depends.[1]

My contribution as a practical theologian to this anthology, *For All the Saints*, is to make a biblical case for the importance of an evangelical spirituality of creation care and its relevance in relation to the kingdom of God. Fully grounded in the Scriptures, evangelicals must be reminded God's Word has much to say about how God still loves the cosmos. God's Word must be studied, highlighted, underscored, remembered, and obeyed. We need to be reminded that creation care has a teleological purpose in the kingdom of our God. There is a final chapter that brings everything in focus, a final word that makes sense of all the characters, all the action, and all the effort we might put into caring for God's handiwork. There is an ultimate point to what we do in creation care. And we often forget it in the aches and pains and frustrations of the quasi obedience we exercise.

God has a *new* "earth day" planned, and even heaven gets included! This will be a day not of "reduce, reuse, recycle" but of redemption. The promised reality of a new heaven and a new earth is the final outcome that matters ultimately to God. There is a uniquely Christian eschatological dimension to creation care, and in the context of evangelical spirituality, it is important for several reasons.

First, as evangelicals, we need to remember that those outside the family of God, with whom we often share this work, lack the hope that God's promised "new earth day" offers. People need the hope that we find only in Christ Jesus. Christians have made "John 3:16" a TV advertisement framed by goalposts. The truth behind this biblical reference needs to remind us that environmentalists, as well as the environment, are part of the cosmos God so loves.

Second, God's final interests can serve as a safeguard against our persistent and sinfully insidious selfishness. We sense this even in our best intentions. The parallels to this in the theology of spirituality are striking. For instance, regarding worship, God's final interests can serve as a safeguard against the commodification of worship as self-pleasure where the issue of style is driven by "the market," not the Master's pleasure. Keeping God's pleasure central in earth care can have a corrective influence on our motivation for worship. It is worth asking how much the commodification of our worship experience blinds us to the ultimate "chief end" of it all: to glorify God and enjoy him forever. How much does our identification as consumers, and not caregivers, blind us to the glory of God in the world?

Third, a healthy eschatological hope takes away the common complaint, often voiced with flagging zeal, that "doing what we can will still never be enough." This is often followed by the question "So, why bother?" The comment above can be an initial exercise in good biblical theology that recognizes the penultimate nature of our growth in righteousness and our longing for the fullness of God's kingdom. The question asked has a good biblical answer: bothering with what matters to God brings him glory. Christians have good reasons to quit wasting limited energy by complaining when we are tempted to grow weary in well-doing. We can learn to enjoy and appreciate the penultimate contributions we can make without delusions of grandeur and with greater confidence that, in the final ending, it all matters to God.

Fourth, the influence of this eschatological focus, practiced with patience and persistence in creation care, can provide a pattern for discipleship that is often missing in the North American church. What is needed is a pattern of faithfulness without regard for recognition, reward, or evidence of lasting change. Patterns practiced in caring for creation can parallel spiritual disciplines in Christian discipleship. Picking up the same trash every week along a stretch of highway or a neighborhood block can remind us of the need for the habitual confession of sin within the community of faith. Our life's litter impacts other people. The discipline of time management that is efficient enough for bicycle commuting also lends itself to quiet times in the Scripture and prayer every morning. The habits of "reduce, reuse, recycle" can free funds for increasing benevolent giving and service to the poor. Spending time in nature can enhance the retreat and re-creation of the spiritual discipline of Sabbath-keeping. A weekly day of rest that regularly includes time spent out of doors enjoying, noticing, and appreciating nature should mark our spiritual life and help us find God's rhythm for walking by faith.

Last, an eschatological focus on something that transcends mere human interest is bound to be good for us. Putting God's preferences before our own is an exercise of faith and obedience. Living for God's delight, choosing God's will over our own momentary desires, is a practice of Christlike humility. And this is dependent on "having this same mind which was in Christ Jesus." When learning how to be delightful to the Lord, it is wise to begin and end with Jesus. He is the only beloved Son with whom the Father is well pleased. In the life of Jesus, we are given hints and glimpses of how "very good" creation once was and how it all will be made new. In the final messianic kingdom, the curse of Eden is undone. In Jesus' life, we can begin to envision the new earth as well as the new heaven.

Jesus was born in a barn, slept in a feed trough, and thus refused any distance from the world he came to redeem. The groans of creation in Mary's pain were stilled by his birth. Jesus, on the Sea of Galilee, in speaking a word to calm the waves, reminds us of a world where weather is no longer a threat. The Ruler of all nature subdued its futility and wildness. Jesus, at the wedding in Cana, with a powerful and transforming will, turned water into wine. It is a signpost of the new heaven and new earth where nature is overwhelmed by miracle. Jesus, when feeding the multitudes with a sack lunch, shows us the promise of sustenance as it was meant to be. In undoing for a moment the curse of the earth in Genesis 3 that made productivity uncertain and inadequate, the Maker of heaven and earth provided abundant food for all. And it was provided with thanksgiving, not toil. This work was perfect joy again. Jesus, the healer, unraveled the consequence of the banishment from Eden. Jesus, as the great physician, in healing sickness and disease, celebrated bodily wholeness as a part of what was and is to come. Jesus in Bethany reversed for a time the wages of sin in the person of Lazarus. Jesus, "the Lord, the Giver of Life," turned death into a shadow. Jesus weeping over Jerusalem was longing himself for the day when every eye is dried, when mourning, crying, and pain are passed away. The eternal architect ached for the final restoration of all he had spoken into being.

And Jesus, from our first text of this chapter, on the first Palm Sunday entered Jerusalem riding a donkey. This donkey, Mark and Luke tell us, had *never been ridden before.* The Scriptures even say the animal was procured from its owner because "the Lord needs it." Why so specific? Not just so some prophecy could be fulfilled to prove who he was. No, the prophecy was important for its own sake, a fact almost lost in our quest for apologetic evidence.

Jesus, as the *new Adam*, displayed the originally intended exercise of sovereign and benevolent dominion over all creation by easily riding this unbroken, untamed beast. It is a picture of what God declares in Isaiah 65:17–19.

> Behold, I will create
>   new heavens and a new earth.
> The former things will not be remembered,
>   nor will they come to mind.
> But be glad and rejoice forever
>   in what I will create,
> for I will create Jerusalem to be a delight
>   and its people a joy.
> I will rejoice over Jerusalem
>   and take delight in my people;
> the sound of weeping and of crying
>   will be heard in it no more.

Jesus, riding this donkey, is hinting at what will be part of his ultimate triumph.

> The wolf will live with the lamb,
>   the leopard will lie down with the goat,
> the calf and the lion and the yearling together;
>   and a little child will lead them.
> The cow will feed with the bear,
>   their young will lie down together,
>   and the lion will eat straw like the ox.
> The infant will play near the hole of the cobra,
>   and the young child put his hand into the viper's nest.
> They will neither harm nor destroy
>   on all my holy mountain,
> for the earth will be full of the knowledge of the LORD
>   as the waters cover the sea.
>   (Isa. 11:6–9)

Jesus' pointed Palm Sunday prophetic parade fulfilled the promise of Zechariah 9:9.

> Rejoice greatly, O Daughter of Zion!
>   Shout, Daughter of Jerusalem!
> See, your king comes to you,

> righteous and having salvation,
> gentle and riding on a donkey,
> on a colt, the foal of a donkey.

This prophecy could have been given and fulfilled in a myriad of ways, but it was not. It was not "Lo, your king comes to you, humble and wearing a multicolored, seamless garment, walking shoeless, with a tattoo of the star of David on his upper right arm, and singing Psalm 85 to the tune of 'Edelweiss.'" No! It was *this* prophecy, this subduing of nature's futility and bondage, wildness and brokenness, that was the choice of the sovereign God. The Creator was delighted to remind us in Jesus on the first Palm Sunday that the kingdom of the Messiah is a kingdom for all creation. He announced again that redemption accomplished would be for more than just the human being.

The new Adam rode into Jerusalem on a suddenly subdued donkey to remind us that, in the final installment of the messianic kingdom, all creation is to be released from its bondage and will willingly and joyfully serve those given responsibility for its care. *All creation* will cease groaning and enjoy the Sabbath rest of God.

Paul reminds us of this in Romans 8:19–23:

> The creation waits in eager expectation for the sons of God to be revealed. For the creation was subjected to frustration, not by its own choice, but by the will of the one who subjected it, in hope that the creation itself will be liberated from its bondage to decay and brought into the glorious freedom of the children of God.
> We know that the whole creation has been groaning as in the pains of childbirth right up to the present time. Not only so, but we ourselves, who have the firstfruits of the Spirit, groan inwardly as we wait eagerly for our adoption as sons, the redemption of our bodies.

From the beginning, before creation was subjected to futility and the bondage of decay, all that God made was "very good." It was so delightful, in fact, that he made the seventh day holy just to enjoy it. God literally had a holiday, a holy day, to celebrate for his own joy all that he had spoken into being.

It is no surprise that Paul writes that all creation "waits in eager expectation" to be set free from its futility and bondage, to cease its groaning, to be made right again, to be the perfect delight of the Creator. Jesus even hints in the Palm Sunday passage that the celebration may not be limited to animate creation. In the middle of the parade, "[s]ome of the Pharisees in the crowd said to Jesus, 'Teacher, rebuke your disciples!' 'I tell you,' he replied, 'if they keep quiet, the stones will cry out!' This is how G. K. Chesterton interpreted these words:

Christ prophesied the whole of Gothic architecture in that hour when nervous and respectable people objected to the shouting gutter-snipes of Jerusalem. . . . Under the impulse of His Spirit arose, like a clamorous chorus the facades of the medieval cathedrals . . . the very stones cry out![2]

All creation is intended to glorify the Creator. Psalm 96:11–13a says, "Let the heavens rejoice, let the earth be glad; let the sea resound, and all that is in it; let the fields be jubilant, and everything in them. Then all the trees of the forest will sing for joy; they will sing before the Lord, for he comes!" Whatever it means to include the possibility of inanimate nature contributing to the praise of God, one thing is crystal clear: God will be praised! God will be delighted with what God has made. God, in the restoration of creation to its rightful and ultimate purpose, will see to his own pleasure, his own joy and delight. The Lord will enjoy all of creation forever, as we "glorify God and enjoy him forever."

Considering Palm Sunday's riotous scene in the New Testament, and given the presence of a talking donkey in the Hebrew Scriptures, it is not surprising that C. S. Lewis and other believers with unfettered imaginations and a gift for joy have captured a possible picture of the new earth and heavens, the messianic kingdom. In *The Magician's Nephew*, Lewis writes:

Narnia, Narnia, Narnia, awake. Love. Think. Speak. Be walking trees. Be talking beasts. Be divine waters. . . . Creatures, I give you yourselves . . . and I give you myself. . . . Laugh and fear not, creatures. Now that you are no longer dumb and witless, you need not always be grave. For jokes as well as justice come in with speech.[3]

Surely, the whole world longs for the day of jokes and justice. All creation waits with "eager longing" for our redemption. For now, God's people watch and wait, work and witness. But we do so as those who "have the firstfruits of the Spirit." We live in hope of the final redemption with the Holy Spirit's presence as the down payment toward our full redemption. Creation has to wait eagerly for our final adoption, the redemption of our bodies. But our redemption has begun. We do not have to wait to give God joy. We can give God great pleasure in worship, in witness, in work, in relationships, and in how we care for all that God loves. We have a job to do, and doing it gives God pleasure until the final chapter begins.

Until that day, our care for creation (the very least we can do while the earth waits in bondage and is subject to frustration) pleases our Creator. Until the final trumpet sounds, we live to give God joy, to be his delight, to worship, learn, serve, and love. The ultimate point of evangelical spirituality is to remind us and the world that this is not all there is. There is more to the world and to ourselves than we can see. There is an ending, a final chapter, and it is very, very good.

On that new earth day, all will be changed in a moment. Paul anticipates it this way:

> Listen, I tell you a mystery: We will not all sleep, but we will all be changed—in a flash, in the twinkling of an eye, at the last trumpet. For the trumpet will sound, the dead will be raised imperishable, and we will be changed. For the perishable must clothe itself with the imperishable, and the mortal with immortality. When the perishable has been clothed with the imperishable, and the mortal with immortality, then the saying that is written will come true: "Death has been swallowed up in victory." (1 Cor. 15:51–54)

Creation *will* be set free. God's new heaven and new earth, along with the bride of Christ, the church, the new Jerusalem, *will* give God joy. It is good to remember that Paul ends his affirmation of God's promise in this foundational passage with these words: "Therefore, my dear brothers, stand firm. Let nothing move you. Always give yourselves fully to the work of the Lord, because you know that your labor in the Lord is not in vain" (v. 58).

Indeed, our work is not in vain. No matter how meager our labor may look; no matter how uncooperative government, industry, congregations, or others may be; no matter how inconvenient it can get; no matter how few join in the effort; no matter how much politics distracts; no matter if others in God's family do not understand, we do not labor in vain because it matters to God. It is a work God will finish. The ending is sure.

The evangelical spirituality of creation care is a kingdom practice of being faithful, steadfast, immovable. As thankful recipients of the firstfruits of the Spirit, it is one way God's people can practice grace, showing the world we take seriously the goodness of what was by being careful with what is, looking forward with eager longing to what will be.

11

The Spiritual Wisdom of the African American Tradition

Robert Smith Jr.

Robert Smith Jr. is professor of Christian Preaching at Beeson Divinity School of Samford University. He holds degrees from Cincinnati Bible College (B.S.) and Southern Baptist Theological Seminary (M.Div., Ph.D.). Smith's study of the African American tradition has been shaped by his extensive ministry in evangelism, pastoral work, and the teaching of homiletics. His sermons have appeared in many publications including the *Library of Distinctive Sermons*, the *Minister's Manual*, *Preaching* magazine, and the *Abingdon Preaching Manual*. He was a contributing editor for *Preparing for Christian Ministry* (1996) and coeditor (with Timothy George) of *A Mighty Long Journey: Reflections on Racial Reconciliation* (2000).

In this chapter, Smith draws on the literature of African American preaching and spirituality to examine themes of liberation, social protest, and freedom in the slave narratives and sorrow songs of the black church. Using the exilic motif of Psalm 137, he presents a mosaic of African American spirituality. Shaped by unique history and rooted in a more holistic sense of community, the spirituality of the African American tradition has much to teach other evangelical traditions about the integration of theological conviction and a lived faith.

◈◈◈ ◈◈◈ ◈◈◈

By the rivers of Babylon we sat and wept
   when we remembered Zion.
There on the poplars
   we hung our harps,
for there our captors asked us for songs,

> our tormentors demanded songs of joy;
> they said, "Sing us one of the songs of Zion!"
> How can we sing songs of the LORD
> while in a foreign land?
>
> Psalm 137:1–4

The exilic motif that defines the existence of the people of God is that we are in the world but not of the world. We are holders of a dual citizenship. We are pilgrims and strangers.

> This world is not my home, I'm just a passin' through
> My hopes and all of my treasures lay somewhere in the blue
> The angels are beckoning me from heaven's open doors
> and I just can't feel at home in this world anymore.[1]

The exilic motif that defined the existence of Jewish slaves in Babylon is that they were in Babylon but not of Babylon. In seventy years, there would be a homecoming in Jerusalem! The exilic motif that defined the existence of African slaves in America is that they were in America but not of America. Perhaps William Edward Burghardt DuBois, in his classic book *The Souls of Black Folk*, most aptly depicts this ambivalence, this dilemma, this tug of war that he calls "double consciousness." He says, "One ever feels his twoness—an American, a Negro; two souls, two thoughts, two unreconciled strivings; two warring ideals in one dark body, whose dogged strength alone keeps him from being pulled asunder."[2] And yet, in the midst of this ambivalence, the African slave was able to demonstrate and to manifest a depth of spiritual wisdom that is a testimony to the glory and the power of God. As an African American, I have been fascinated at the depth of wisdom in this tradition. Slaves who had nothing were able to leave behind them a legacy that thrived for generations.

Where did they get this kind of wisdom? In 1831, Nat Turner led an insurrection. Shortly after that riot, all the slave states, with the exception of Tennessee, reduced the teaching of slaves to oral instruction. By 1855, nine out of fifteen slave states outlawed the distribution of Bibles to slaves. If slaves could not read, write, or even own a Bible, where did they get wisdom, particularly spiritual wisdom? They got it from what I call the "sitting at the feet" phenomenon. The youth would listen to the elders talk about the customs and laws of the land, the Bible, and maturing as adults. They sat at the feet of their elders, and there they were imbued, filled, and saturated with information.

Where did they get this kind of wisdom? They got it from the oral transmission of information. They turned their ears into tape recorders. What they heard and recorded in their ears they wrote on the tablets of their minds. What they wrote on the tablets of their minds they transferred to their eyes and turned them into camcorders. What they photographed with their eyes they transmitted to their mouths and turned them into megaphones. Thus, what they saw, they talked about. They could say what they saw so graphically that people who heard them could see what they said.

Where did they get this kind of wisdom? They got it from the "grapevine telegraph." It is amazing. In a time of no education, no mass media, no fax machines, no e-mail, no telephones, in a single night through the grapevine telegraph they were able to communicate what was happening in the community to people down the road for miles. In a week's time, news would travel over hundreds of miles, relating who succeeded in making it to Canada through the Underground Railroad, what was taking place in the Civil War, what was taking place on the political scene, and what were the new agricultural inventions.

It was not just wisdom. It was spiritual wisdom. Henry and Ella Mitchell define spirituality as "sensitivity or attachment to religious values involving a belief system about God and creation that controls ethical choices and behavior and supports calmness of spirit in times of distress."[3] Slaves were able to deal with the inhumanities and the atrocities because they had a core of beliefs about God and creation that enabled them to keep sanity at a time of great human degradation. Their spirituality allowed them to respond to the questions:

Why should I feel discouraged,
Why should the shadows come,
Why should my heart be lonely
And long for heaven and home,
When Jesus is my portion?
My constant Friend is He:
His eye is on the sparrow,
And I know He watches me;
I sing because I'm happy.
I sing because I'm free.
For His eye is on the sparrow,
And I know He watches me.[4]

This belief system enabled them to keep equilibrium when they were going through rough footing.

Robert Franklin of the Interdenominational Theological Center in Atlanta has developed a topology of African American spirituality. It is important because it debunks the myth that all African Americans are the same. There are at least six traditions of African American spirituality: first, the Afrocentric tradition of African American spirituality, which concentrates on a retrieval of African American cultural distinctions, particularly a recovery of liturgics, drums, guitars, tambourines, and African dress; second, the charismatic tradition of African American spirituality, which emphasizes the impartation of the

Holy Spirit in the life of the believer; third, the contemplative tradition of African American spirituality, which focuses on intimacy with God; fourth, the evangelical tradition of African American spirituality, which concentrates on the proclamation of faith and the teaching of the Word; fifth, the holiness tradition of African American spirituality, which points toward purity of life and thought; and sixth, the social justice tradition of African American spirituality, which focuses on the transformation of the soul, the liberation of the oppressed, and the reformation of society.[5]

Consider the Hebrew slaves of Psalm 137, at least two generations removed from Jerusalem. By the rivers of Babylon they sit down. They weep. They have a nostalgic fit. They remember Jerusalem. They hang their harps on the poplar trees because their captors have required of them a song. Those who have taken them into captivity required of them mirth and entertainment. The request from their enemies is "Sing us one of the songs of Zion." We know you can do it. You are famous for it. In fact, your most famous king, David, was the sweet singer of Israel. We have heard of your singing. Sing us one of your songs. Make your choice—selection number 23: "The Lord is my shepherd, I shall lack nothing"; selection number 24: "The earth is the Lord's, and everything in it"; selection number 27: "The Lord is my light and salvation—whom shall I fear?"; selection number 46: "God is our refuge and strength, an ever present help in trouble"; selection number 121: "I lift my eyes up to the hills—where does my help come from? My help comes from the Lord, the Maker of heaven and earth"; selection number 122: "I rejoiced with those who said to me, 'Let us go to the house of the Lord'"; selection 127: "Unless the Lord build the house, its builders labor in vain"; selection number 150: "Praise the Lord. Praise God in his sanctuary; praise him in his mighty heavens. . . . Let everything that has breath praise the Lord." Any of those selections. Render us a concert, because we know you can do it. But they respond, "How can we sing songs of the Lord while in a foreign land?" Now, why did they not sing? The text does not tell us.

James Sanders, who taught canonical hermeneutics at Union Theological Seminary in New York City for many years, has said that biblical characters do not primarily serve us as models of morality but rather as mirrors of identity. The reason they did not sing is perhaps the reason we would not have sung. Maybe they did not sing because they were still hung up about their hang-ups. The Temple was demolished. Their society was ruined. Their ancestral city was plundered. Yes, the Temple of God had been destroyed, wrecked, and pulverized, but the God of the Temple was still alive. As long as the God of the Temple is alive, you can sing when the Temple of God is down. Israel was not a territorial jurisdiction for God, because God did not just reign in Jerusalem, God reigned all over the world. God was not defined by geography. God had the whole world in his hands. Why did they not sing? Maybe because of holy indignation. Perhaps the Babylonians were insensitive and they did not care how heartbroken the Hebrews were. Surely they did not appreciate the songs and struggles of the Hebrews. In a response of holy indignation, maybe the Hebrews were saying, "You don't know our God and you don't know the songs we sing to our God. And we're indignant that you would ask us to sing for your entertainment. We don't sing for that reason." Maybe they were too demoralized and despondent to sing. African slaves have done what these Jewish slaves refused to do. They have sung the Lord's song in a strange land. They sang in the fields, they sang in the slave quarters, they sang in the big house, but, most important, they sang in the church.

Elsewhere in *The Souls of Black Folk*, DuBois writes that a Negro church had three components: preaching, singing, and frenzy—the shout. After a week of being tattered, torn, and told they were three-fifths human, and that they had tails and no souls, they put on their Sunday-go-to-meeting clothes because they were going to meet the Lord. There was freedom to express themselves, freedom to cry, freedom to shout, freedom to get happy. It was the one time during the week when they could let it all out and give God glory. Preaching, singing, and shouting—three components of the Negro church.

My mentor, Dr. James Cox of the Southern Baptist Theological Seminary, once shared this analogy with me: doctrines are to preaching what steel rods are to concrete—meaning, without solid, meaningful doctrine, our preaching weakens and ultimately collapses. The rods of doctrine hold our foundation firm. Likewise, there are three steel rods that hold the concrete of African American spirituality together. The first steel rod is singing.

> Lord, I want to be a Christian in my heart.
> Ain't no grave gonna hold my body down.
> Nobody knows the trouble I've seen, nobody knows but Jesus.
> Every time I feel the Spirit moving in my heart, I will pray.
> Somebody's knockin' at your door, oh, sinner, why don't you answer.
> Wade in the water, God's gonna trouble the water.[6]

Singing in the African American church is what breathing is to life, what blood is to the body. Spirituals were born out of great sorrow. After the Nat Turner rebellion of 1831, slaves were prohibited from gathering without their white overseers. To worship freely then, slaves were forced to go down to the "hush harbors," hidden gathering places along the river banks. Here the sounds of flowing water hid the sounds of secret singing. The church during this period became known as the invisible institution. They would sing and pray and praise God. Spirituals were drawn from various sources. Sometimes they would sing about the auction block, where families would be separated forever. Sometimes they would sing about the creeping of old age. Sometimes they would sing about dying. Everything became a topic for the spirituals.

There was an eschatological dimension in their singing. They sang about the other side. Their singing was not an opiate for the masses, as Karl Marx suggested. They were not afraid of death. There were things more fearful than death. One of the spirituals asserts, "Oh, freedom! Oh, freedom all over me! . . . / An' be-fo' I'd be a slave, I'll be buried in my grave, / An' go home to my Lord an' be free."[7] Hope had been feeding on hope for such an indeterminable period of time that hope had dissipated. Hope unborn had died— it was aborted. There was nothing left; no sign of freedom, no sign of getting through this world. They talked about a better place. They would say, "Got a Savior in de Kingdom, ain't dat good news? / I'm agoin' to lay down dis world, Goin' to shoulder up mah cross, Goin' to take it home to my Jesus, ain't dat good news?"[8] "There's a bright side somewhere / Keep on searchin' til you find it / There's a bright side somewhere."[9] Exilic eschatology enabled the slaves to keep their sanity in the midst of dehumanizing circumstances, believing that God's tomorrow would be better than their today.

African Americans sang because they were confident that God was not finished with them, nor with their world. They hid their messages in cryptic coding and transmitted them on a dual trajectory so that the insider received the intended message and the outsider did not. They would sing, "Swing low, sweet chariot, coming for to carry me home: / I looked over Jordan and what did I see, / a band of angels com after me."[10] The slave master would think about heaven. The slave would think about escape. To the insider, Jordan represented Canada, and the chariot, the conductors of the Underground Railroad. The insiders looked for freedom while the outsiders looked for glory. Slaves were talking about a terrestrial and not a celestial residence.

Sometimes they would say, "I'm goin home on the mornin' train, the evenin' train may be too late, I'm goin home on the mornin' train."[11] The Underground Railroad is stopping by this morning. Don't wait until this evening. It may be too late. The insider got the message, but the outsider did not. What an ingenious way of exemplifying wisdom. As Jesus said, those who really want to hear will have their ears open to the message, and those who do not want to hear will close their ears and miss the message.

Spirituals amplified a social protest emphasis. These were called sorrow songs. Slaves would talk about the slave master and he would not even know it. They would sing, "I'm gonna tell God how you treat me, one of these days."[12] The slave master would hear but not understand. Spirituals protested about inequity and injustice in a land where God had made all people equal, had made every individual in God's own image, and had written his signature in the fabric of the souls of all people.

In the preface of Dietrich Bonhoeffer's *Life Together*, the translator wrote about a time when Bonhoeffer came to the United States in 1930 to study and eventually to teach at the Union Theological Seminary in New York. Bonhoeffer visited the Abyssinian Baptist Church, which was established in 1808. The choir would sing the spirituals and the congregation would hear the dynamic preaching of Adam Clayton Powell Sr. Bonhoeffer was touched by the spirituals. He saw a mirroring effect between the African Americans' struggles and those of the Christians in the illegal Confessing Church in Germany. When he returned to Germany, he taught the Negro spirituals to his students in his underground seminary.[13] His friend Eberhard Bethge said that twenty years before "Swing Low, Sweet Chariot" and other spirituals were sung in concert halls and over radios, they were sung in the seminary halls by Bonhoeffer and his students.[14]

Negro spirituals are kind of theo-musicology. In his dual compendium *Deep River and The Negro Spiritual Speaks to Life*, Howard Thurman exegetes the Negro spirituals "Heaven" and "Balm in Gilead."

> I got shoes. You got shoes.
> All God's children got shoes.
> And when we get to heaven, we're gonna put on our shoes
> we're gonna shout all over God's heaven.[15]

Slaves struggled with the idea of one God and two heavens. They wondered if there must be two heavens, because the slave master and his family did not want to be with them on earth, much less in heaven. Yet both the slave masters and the slaves believed they were going to heaven. Were there two heavens? They concluded that there could not be two heavens, for there is only one God. Thus, they reasoned that if there is one God and one heaven, then the slave masters enjoy heaven on earth and suffer eternity in hell. Conversely, the slaves suffer hell on earth but anticipate the delights of eternity in heaven. They would sing, "I got shoes, you got shoes / all God's children got shoes / and when we get to heaven we're gonna put on our shoes / and we're gonna shout all over God's heaven." When they got close to the front door of the "big house," they would sing "everybody's talking 'bout heaven ain't goin' there / heaven, heaven; we're goin' to walk all over God's heaven." It was a way of articulating the eschatological destinies of the oppressed righteous and their wicked oppressors.[16]

"There Is a Balm in Gilead." Jeremiah 8:22 asks, "Is there no balm in Gilead? Is there no physician there?" Thurman said that this is not a question that is asked to God, nor is it a question that is asked to Israel. It is a question that is asked to the entire ministry of Jeremiah. Jeremiah, you have been preaching and prophesying: Is there no balm in Gilead? Is there no physician there? The Negro slave did an ingenious thing. Thurman said the Negro spiritual took the question mark of Jeremiah and straightened it out into an exclamation point, saying,

> There is a balm in Gilead, to make the wounded whole,
> There is a balm in Gilead, to heal the sin-sick soul,
> Sometimes I feel discouraged, And think my work's in vain,
> But then the Holy Spirit Revives my soul again
> There is a balm in Gilead, to make the wounded whole,
> There is a balm in Gilead, to heal the sin-sick soul.[17]

If there was going to be a meeting down on the hush harbor, a boy would go through the cotton fields delivering water to the slaves. The boy would deliver the message in song: "Steal away, steal away, / steal away to Jesus! / Steal away, steal away home, / I ain't got long to stay here!"[18] In the evening, slaves would gather on the hush harbor. They would pray and sing. When they returned to their slave quarters, the house slaves would sing as they walked by the big house, "I couldn't hear nobody pray / Oh, Way down yonder by myself, / And I couldn't hear nobody pray."[19] This was a way of informing the participants in the hush harbor meetings that the white master was oblivious of their secret meeting.[20]

The second steel rod that holds African American spirituality together is that of theology. It is the core belief system of the Christian religion. Africans believed in God. They understood God as one who was transcendent above us. They did not believe in an abstract God. They believed God was omnipotent, although they did not use the word *omnipotent*. They expressed omnipotence in figurative speech: "He's got the whole world in his hands." They believed God was omnipresent, although they did not use the word *omnipresent*. When they wanted to talk about the omnipresent nature of God, they exclaimed, "He's so high you can't get over him / He's so wide, you can't get around him / He is so low that you can't get under him / You must come in at the door."[21] In the Negro slaves' mind, God was so immense that God filled the universe, and when God decided to move, he had to bump into himself.

Slaves did not use abstract words like *omniscient*. They would say, "He sits high and looks low, and sees everything that we do and hears everything that we say." This was not an abstract God. They believed that God was eternal. In God they found something that was immortal and they saw someone who was eternal. They would talk about God as if time—past, present, and future—collapsed into immediate consciousness in him. God *is*. God is not an abstract God but a concrete, relatable, relational, and experiential God. They believed in Jesus Christ, the Son. They began to understand the incarnation. Africans believed in the most high god. When they came to America, they were able to relate to Jesus Christ as the Son of the Most High God. They believed in the Christ of faith and the Jesus of Nazareth. They were not concerned with Albert Schweitzer's quest for the historical Jesus. They were not concerned with all the theories about Jesus. He was just Massa Jesus, high enough to sit on his throne but small enough to be tucked away in our little bitty souls. There was no separation between Jesus and God in their Christology. They saw Jesus as God and God as Jesus. They believed in God, they believed in Jesus, and they believed in the Holy Spirit. They believed in the Trinity. Yes, there were spirits: bad spirits—demons—and good spirits—angels. In their thinking, the Africans converted the good spirit who lived within to the Holy Spirit, who was sent by the Father and promised by the Son.

The third steel rod that holds the concrete of African American spirituality together is preaching. The slave preacher preached their theology. To the African Americans, theology that is not preachable is really no theology at all. It must be preachable. The slaves preached about the immediacy of the presence and work of God. They talked as if they had just spoken with the biblical authors and characters: "I saw John on the Isle of Patmos and he told me to tell you not to be nervous about it because the kingdoms of this world shall become the kingdoms of our Christ." "I was talking to Paul the other day and Paul wanted me to remind those of you who are concerned about your destination after you die that once you are absent from the body you are present with the Lord." It was as if the slave preacher had a box seat and God was reminding him of how God created the world, standing on nothing because there was nothing to stand on, taking nothing and making something. Genesis 1:1 simply says, "In the beginning, God created the heavens and the earth."

The slave preacher transformed these words into pictures the people could cling to. God is pictured as placing the sky and flinging the stars from flaming fingertips, causing the black velvet of the night to be a background for them. God is pictured as making floating, fluffy, fleecy, white clouds and putting the sun in the middle. The earth and the moon and the other planets participate in a merry-go-round system, and there has not been a collision since the day of creation. God painted the sky blue without a stepladder or paintbrush. God wrote music for the robins, a song to sing.

The slave preacher turned theological ink into blood. It was incarnational preaching. They believed in preaching God as the deliverer of the oppressed. The slave preacher pictured Moses primarily as the liberator and David primarily as the shepherd boy who killed Goliath and jumped for joy. Did not the Lord deliver Daniel? Surely he will deliver me. Black congregations know that when the black preachers picture Jesus dying at Calvary on Good Friday, they never leave him in the grave. They declare that on

Sunday morning, he arose. Slave preachers preached the core belief system of the Christian religion.

Bonhoeffer struggled with what it meant to be a citizen of Germany and a Christian in a demonic state. In a German cell, struggling with conflict between flesh and spirit, seeking to understand his true identity, he penned a poignant and moving poem titled, "Who Am I?" In spite of the external trials and internal doubts that plagued him, Bonhoeffer confidently concludes, "Whoever I am, Thou knowest, oh, God, I am thine."[22]

The question ultimately is not, "Who am I?" but "Whose am I?" *I am thine, oh Lord, I have heard thy voice and it told thy love to me. But I long to rise in the arms of faith and be closer drawn to thee. Draw me nearer, nearer, nearer blessed Lord to the cross where thou hast died, draw me nearer, nearer, nearer, blessed Lord to thy precious bleeding side.* I am thine.[23]

PART 5

Disciplines

12

C. S. Lewis: Spiritual Disciplines for Mere Christians

Wallace A. C. Williams

Wallace A. C. Williams is associate dean for Community Life at Beeson Divinity School. A native of Kentucky, he holds degrees from the Georgetown College (B.A.), University of Kentucky (M.A.), and Southern Baptist Theological Seminary (M.Div., Ph.D.). Before coming to Beeson, Williams served as a pastor and mission strategist in New York and Pennsylvania. He offers a popular course at Beeson on C. S. Lewis and also coordinates a curricular program in spiritual formation.

Although C. S. Lewis was not a typical evangelical, his writings have had a major influence in shaping popular evangelical understandings of the Christian faith. This chapter examines the spiritual basis of Lewis's appeal and draws together his reflections on the spiritual disciplines—meditation, prayer, fasting, simplicity, solitude, submission, and service. While Lewis is often thought of as a tough-minded apologist for the Christian faith, which he certainly was, this study emphasizes his role as one of the primary shapers of contemporary evangelical practice.

✺✺✺ ✺✺✺ ✺✺✺

INTRODUCTION

The weekly television program on PBS *Religion and Ethics Newsweek* named C. S. Lewis one of the top twenty-five most important religious figures in the twentieth century.[1] One author has called him "[t]he greatest lay champion of basic Christianity" in the twentieth century.[2] He even made the cover of *Time* magazine in 1947 because his brilliant but persuasive writing about the Christian religion contrasted so sharply with the postwar cynicism of Oxford University. Such was the extraordinary recognition by the secular world of Clive Staples ("Jack") Lewis (1898–1963), who spent most of his life among the stately spires of Oxford and the quiet quadrangles of Cambridge as a fellow, tutor, and professor of Medieval and Renaissance Literature.

Born in Belfast, Northern Ireland, and living a life of happy "monotony" as a bachelor-scholar, this apologist for orthodox Christianity left a legacy of sixty-two works (thirty-seven published during his lifetime). The subject matter ranged from literary criticism to children's books to popular presentations of Christian doctrine. Today, all his writings are still in print (in twenty-four languages), and total copies in circulation range higher than 100 million.[3]

Lewis converted to the Anglican faith when he was thirty-three years old. His struggles with skepticism, doubt, and atheism were used by God to enable his literary gifts to shine with understanding and cogency. Even his short, tragic marriage to Joy Davidman (1956–60) became the stimulus for a book and a movie that helped the faithful struggle with loss and grief.

Lewis's literary legacy seems secure, both in scholarly circles and among popular Christian audiences. But the thrust of this essay is to demonstrate how carefully Jack Lewis chose to live a Christian life. His writings focus on the necessity to live in obedience to the truth. This was expected by Socrates and clearly taught by Jesus (Matt. 7:21). Jack Lewis was an intentional practitioner of a holistic, mature Christian life. The importance of becoming Christlike, in his mind, far exceeded the highest goals in literature: "The Christian knows from the outset that the salvation of a single soul is more important than the production or preservation of all the epics and tragedies in the world."[4]

A MATURE MERE CHRISTIAN

Richard Foster has written a book on spiritual disciplines that has been widely read by Christians of all stripes. It has served as a wake-up call for modern believers once again to discover and practice the spiritual disciplines. Like Christians of old, we too can find ways to integrate our inner and outer lives, writes Foster. These can become instruments of joy that lead us into mature Christian spirituality. The book is *Celebration of Discipline: The Path to Spiritual Growth*, now in its third edition with over one million copies sold.

Foster proposes a taxonomy around three divisions, each with four disciplines: the inward disciplines—meditation, prayer, fasting, and study; the outward disciplines—simplicity, solitude, submission, service; the corporate disciplines—confession, worship, guidance, celebration. Foster's approach is original, comprehensive, and honest. He identifies superficiality as the curse of our age.[5] The search for instant spiritual satisfaction is a cancerous illness in the churches. There is radical need not for a greater number of intelligent people but for deeper people. The above "classical" disciplines can help move practitioners beyond superficiality into the depths with Christ.[6]

It is this writer's view that Foster is correct in his diagnosis and holistic in his approach. His framework seems to connect head and heart, orthodoxy and imagination, Scripture and common sense, in such ways as to echo C. S. Lewis. The remainder of this chapter attempts to demonstrate how C. S. Lewis incarnated in his life these very disciplines, and how he thereby embodied for us that most appealing combination of Geoffrey Chaucer's parson: "First he wrought, then he taught."

THE INWARD DISCIPLINES

Meditation

Meditation in Christian terms is basically the ability to hear God's words and to obey God's commands.[7] Popular views of this practice would seem to evoke mysterious methods, secret mantras, and mental gymnastics. This was not the psalmist's approach. He knew well this practice and described it as basically listening to God's words, reflecting on them, and rehearsing God's deeds. Repentance, obedience, and changed behavior are essential facets of Christian meditation. Lewis added that in the act of meditation one must participate from within the relationship with God, not from mere objective analysis from without.

Lewis was quite aware of the bane of busy-ness. We live in a world starved for meditation and solitude, he said.[8] In his autobiography Lewis said, "To know God is to know our obedience is due to Him. In his nature His sovereignty *de jure* is revealed."[9] Later, in *Reflections on the Psalms*, Lewis wrote that the psalmist probably felt about the law as he did about his poetry—"both involved exact and loving conformity to a very intricate pattern."[10]

Prayer

Both Foster and Lewis believed prayer to be central to the Christian life, because it brings us into communion with the Father. True prayer is "life creating and life changing."[11] The entire community of the Trinity calls us to pray:

the Father creates us with the capacity to commune with Him and initiates in us the desire to do so; Jesus the Son taught us to pray, gave us the authority for access to God through His shed blood, and embodied a life of prayerful obedience for us to follow; the Holy Spirit "helps us in our weakness" and "intercedes for us with groans that words cannot express" (Rom. 8:26).

Accordingly, Lewis wrote about prayer but quickly disclaimed any expertise, or even adequacy.[12] He refused to critique the prayer practices of others but warned against prayers at evening, when sleepiness would prevail and demoralize. With refreshing honesty Lewis wrote:

> Prayer is either sheer illusion or a personal contact between embryonic, incomplete persons (ourselves) and the utterly concrete Person. Prayer in the sense of petition, asking for things, is a small part of it; confession and penitence are its threshold, adoration its sanctuary, the presence and vision and enjoyment of God its bread and wine. In it God shows Himself to us. That He answers prayers is a corollary— not necessarily the most important one—from that revelation. What He does is learned from what He is.[13]

Self-honesty is foundational to prayer, wrote Lewis:

> The prayer preceding all prayers is "May it be the real I who speaks. May it be the real Thou that I speak to." Infinitely various are the levels from which we pray. Emotional intensity is in itself no proof of spiritual depth. If we pray in terror we shall pray earnestly; it only proves that terror is an earnest emotion. Only God Himself can let the bucket down to the depths in us. And on the other side, He must constantly work as the iconoclast. Every idea of Him we form, He must in mercy shatter. The most blessed result of prayer would be to rise thinking, "But I never knew before. I never dreamed. . . . " I suppose it was at such a moment that Thomas Aquinas said of all his own Theology, "It reminds me of straw."[14]

Douglas Gresham wrote that his stepfather developed a regular routine for prayer:

> I remember that he spent much time in prayer. He had his own regular prayer times, both morning and evening, but was often to be found in prayer at anytime during the day. I think that when a question or issue turned up that required prayer . . . Jack wasted no time but turned at once to the Lord.[15]

Lewis also prayed for healings and the salvation of others and found it helpful to keep prayer lists. This was such serious business that he was reluctant to remove any names.[16]

Dramatic answers to prayer occurred sometimes. Joy's remission from her cancer, Sheldon Vanauken's conversion, and the testimony of Jack's barber are prime examples. In summary, one can observe that Jack Lewis learned the truth of St. Paul: "but in everything, by prayer and petition, with thanksgiving, present your requests to God" (Phil. 4:6).

Fasting

Lewis thought that fasting at its core was the assertion of will against the appetite: the reward could be self-mastery but the eminent danger might be pride.[17] Foster creatively applied this discipline to such activities as watching television or reading popular magazines, as well as eating. The issue for the Christian is self-denial. Ascetic practices strengthen the will but are useful only as a means of preparation for offering the whole man to God. What a travesty if, when subduing the animal self, one exchanges it for the diabolical self. Yet Jack brought balance with his wit to this discipline in *Letters to an American Lady:*

> Perhaps if we had done more voluntary fasting before God would not now have put us on these darn diets! Well the theologians say that an imposed mortification can have all the merit of a voluntary one if it is taken in the right spirit.[18]

By contrast, Jack did not tolerate the intolerance of those who were so zealous and sanctimonious about teetotalism with alcoholic beverages:

> I do however strongly object to the tyrannic and unscriptural insolence of anything that calls itself a church and makes teetotalism a condition of membership. Apart from the more serious objection (that our Lord Himself turned water into wine and made wine the medium of the only rite He imposed on all His followers) it is so provincial (what I believe you people call "small town").[19]

Study

The Christian discipline of study is the renewing of the mind by applying it to those things that will transform it. As the apostle Paul wrote:

> Finally, brothers, whatever is true, whatever is noble, whatever is right, whatever is pure, whatever is lovely, whatever is admirable— if anything is excellent or praiseworthy—think about such things. (Phil. 4:8)

"To think about such things" is strengthened by the discipline of study. Study is the central vehicle God uses to change us. Jesus made it abundantly clear that the knowledge of the truth liberates: "Then you will know the truth, and the truth will set you free" (John 8:32). Conversely, ignorance or false teaching enslaves.

Richard Foster reminds the reader that study is "a specific kind of experience in which through careful attention to reality the mind is enabled to move in a certain direction . . . [for] the mind will always take on an order conforming to the order upon which it concentrates."[20] Foster wisely adds to the study of books the study of nature, the study of relationships between people, the study of ourselves and the things that control us. By all counts, Jack Lewis was a model student.

Lewis was constantly reading books. His autobiography, *Surprised by Joy*, is a literary road map of his journey back to God. His letters are filled with references of what he is reading and rereading. Always he is immersed in studying books. In one essay, he admonished readers to dip deeply into old books:

> Naturally, since I myself am a writer, I do not wish the ordinary reader to read no modern books. But if he must read only the new or only the old, I would advise him to read the old. And I would give him the advice precisely because he is an amateur and therefore much less protected than the expert against the dangers of an exclusive contemporary diet. A new book is still on trial. . . . It has to be tested against the great body of Christian thought down through the ages, and all its hidden implications have to be brought to light.[21]

Furthermore, Lewis gave himself to careful, arduous study when trying to master a subject. When asked by the delegates of Oxford University Press to write the volume *English Literature in the Sixteenth Century, Excluding Drama* in their series Oxford History of English Literature, Jack was deeply honored but felt inadequate. Nevertheless, he gave himself to the task from 1935 to 1954 in reading, research, and writing. It reached its embryonic state as the Clark Lectures given in Cambridge in 1944. However, much more work was poured into it, for he was a prodigious reader.

When Francis Warner (one of Lewis's last pupils) asked Lewis how he went about writing that volume on sixteenth-century authors, Lewis responded "that he tried to read every book in that century. . . . Every time he read an author he wrote himself an essay on the subject, dated it, put it away in a drawer for a year and a day. He would then take it out and mark it. Any essay falling below a clear alpha was sent back to be done again."[22]

Lewis spent every spare minute in the Duke Humfreys Library of the Bodelian in Oxford. It is reported he read the entire works of about two hundred authors, including such literary lights as Shakespeare, Spenser, and Sidney. In addition, for the section "Religious Controversy and Translation,"

Lewis read the entire works of Thomas More, Martin Luther, John Calvin, and William Tyndale.[23] The obligatory "ploughing through back numbers of learned periodicals" was performed. Lewis said this weary task was not done in the hope of fresh knowledge but mostly from the fear of missing something. Dame Helen Gardner, a colleague on the English faculty at Magdalen, Oxford, wrote: "The merits of this book are very great indeed. . . . The book is also brilliantly written, compulsively readable, and constantly illuminated by sentences that are as true as they are witty."[24] Many think this is Lewis's greatest work.

Jack Lewis studied not only books but also nature and people. These disciplines were most often practiced on his famous long walks. With two or three chosen companions, Lewis would sometimes travel by foot through the English or Northern Irish countryside for up to fifty miles. The interests of the walking group were architecture, archaeology, flora, fauna, and most of all the people they met. Always there were the pubs for lunch or overnight. Good conversation about books, recent interesting people, or private worries always accompanied the pints of beer. Jack talked often and listened carefully. "He was in all respects the perfect walking companion."[25]

THE OUTWARD DISCIPLINES

Simplicity

Simplicity is the discipline that liberates; its antithesis is duplicity. Simplicity produces joy and balance. The author of Ecclesiastes observed that "God made man simple; man's complex problems are his own devising" (Eccles. 7:30, JB). This discipline strengthens the inward reality that becomes manifest. Simplicity is made possible only when a person has been grasped by what Søren Kierkegaard emphasized in his devotional book *Purity of Heart Is to Will One Thing*. When the core of a person is centered in Christ, then that soul is free to let go of the unimportant circumference issues.

Foster believed that the Christian who strives for simplicity must reckon with the clear teaching of the Bible about riches. The psalmist warns, "[T]hough your riches increase, do not set your heart on them" (Ps. 62:10). Jesus said, "No servant can serve two masters. Either he will hate the one and love the other, or he will be devoted to the one and despise the other. You cannot serve both God and Money" (Luke 16:13).

From his early student days until the award of the Magdalen fellowship, Jack lived in poverty. That period marked him for life, as he always found it very difficult to spend more than a minimum on himself.

He seems never to have owned a watch or a good fountain pen. What he gained from those years was a complete freedom from the snobbery that is based on possessions, and sympathy with and understanding of poor people. The many thousands of pounds he was to give away in the years ahead were nearly always bestowed on those short of money.[26]

So baffled was Lewis about money and budgets that he asked Owen Barfield, a friend and family lawyer, to set up a charitable trust—the Agape Fund—in 1942. Thereafter, until 1958 and his marriage to Joy, Jack had two-thirds of all his royalties paid into the trust in order to supply anonymous gifts to various needy people.[27] What was the divine center that freed Lewis to give away so much and to live so simply? Jack gave the answer in a printed sermon:

He cannot bless us unless he has us. When we try to keep within us an area that is our own, we try to keep an area of death. Therefore, in love, He claims us all. There's no bargaining with Him.[28]

Again Lewis, the mentor, had written a letter to a new convert named Sheldon Vanauken:

Seek ye first the Kingdom . . . and all these other things shall be added unto you. Infinite comfort in the second part. Inexorable demand in the first. Hopeless if it were to be done by your own endeavors at some particular moment. But "God must do it." Your part is what you are already doing: "Take me—no conditions."[29]

With a man so squarely settled on the rock of the kingdom of God, it is little wonder that Lewis had the strength and wisdom to refuse to receive the honorary title Commander of the British Empire. In his letter to Prime Minister Winston Churchill, Lewis declined on the basis that some might infer from his award that his Christian writings were "all covert, anti-leftist propaganda."[30] The kingdom work was not for sale, for money or the acclaim of man.

Jack craved predictable daily routine allowing him to worship, read, write, and talk. Plenty of variety and surprise could and did occur within the familiar boundaries of his ordinary pursuits. Christ was the center of his life. As Thomas Kelly said, "The fruit of holy obedience is the simplicity of the trusting child, the simplicity of the children of God."[31] And so it was with Lewis. He knew his very days were sacred time, holy hours through which one comes to God. A simple life was not a boring life but a life of freedom to focus on God.

How little people know who think that holiness is dull. When one meets the real thing . . . it is irresistible. If even ten percent of the world's population had it, would not the whole world be converted and happy before a year's end?[32]

Solitude

Solitude is the antithesis of loneliness. Solitude is the result when one cultivates practicing the presence of God. The world needs this discipline practiced widely. Busy-ness and noisiness have effectively crowded out God from our lives. Look again and listen again, writes Lewis: "We may ignore, but we can nowhere evade, the presence of God. The world is crowded with Him. He walks everywhere *incognito*. . . . The real labor is to remember, to attend. In fact, to come awake. Still more to remain awake."[33]

Jack preferred long walks in nature to strenuous visits to London, which jaded and deafened one's sensibilities. His holidays of choice were to walk the hills of his native Donegal, Ireland, or the farms and trails around Oxford. Perhaps that view explains why Lewis said he craved monotony instead of the overstimulation of the hurried life:

> I love the monotonies of life—getting up and going to bed—looking out at the same view and meeting the same people at the same time everyday. I never "want things to happen." They're always happening; and I'd rather they happen in the right order than in the wrong order. I don't like interferences in the normal order of events; and to me the most disagreeable experience would be the one that suspended normality.[34]

Why? Because there is "a dignity and poignancy in the bare fact that a thing exists." The purpose of solitude and silence is to enable one to have eyes that see and ears that hear, to develop attentiveness to the actual particulars of what George MacDonald called "the holy present." "Where, except in the present, can the eternal be met?" asked Lewis.[35] People must go cultivate the gardens of their soul, or they miss the whole point of life. The scene of Lewis's conversion captured in his autobiography is quite riveting. His solitude is crowded with the presence of God:

> You must picture me alone in that room in Magdalen, night after night, feeling, wherever my mind lifted, even for a second from my work, the steady unrelenting approach of Him whom I so earnestly desired not to meet. That which I greatly feared had at last come upon me. In the Trinity Term of 1929 I gave in, and admitted that God was God, and knelt and prayed: perhaps that night, the most dejected and reluctant convert in all England. I did not see then what is now the most shining and obvious thing; the Divine humility which will accept

a convert even on such terms. . . . The hardness of God is kinder than the softness of men, and His compulsion is our liberation.[36]

Submission

The biblical discipline of submission helps us focus on how we view other people. We are freed from the need to have our way all the time. We are enabled to value other people and their dreams and plans.[37] Jesus taught and modeled a radical servanthood and a revolutionary subordination (Matt. 20:26). Martin Luther captured this paradox in his observation "A Christian is a perfectly free lord of all, subject to none. A Christian is a perfectly dutiful servant of all, subject to all."[38]

Jack Lewis's practice of this discipline is best demonstrated in his support of Janie K. A. Moore (1872–1951). Mother of Jack's cadet battalion friend "Paddy" Moore, they first met in Oxford right before Jack and Paddy were shipped out to the front in France in 1917. After Paddy's death and Jack's wounds, the two met again during Jack's convalescence. Their mutual grief over Paddy's death and Jack's vow to take care of Paddy's mother, if he should be killed, brought them together again.

In the late summer of 1920, Janie Moore rented a house in Headington (suburb of Oxford), and Jack made his home with her and her thirteen-year-old daughter, Maureen. Jack contributed his paternal allowance (unbeknownst to his father). When Jack and his brother, Warren, purchased the Kilns in 1931, Janie and Maureen Moore moved in also. Maureen left in 1940 when she married, but Janie Moore remained until her death in January 1951. Jack referred to Mrs. Moore as "his mother" or "Minto" (after her favorite candy).[39]

Moore was hospitable enough to guests, but her propensity to mother, dominate, and control others became an increasing problem. She called Warren and Jack "bar boys" when she needed them to help in some trivial domestic task.

Warren ("Warnie") wrote of how Jack for three decades lived "under the autocracy of Mrs. Moore—an autocracy that developed into stifling tyranny, as I experienced myself during the years of my inclusion."[40] Every day she produced crises and chaos—especially among the maids. The emotional burden for arbitrating such problems "had then to be placed squarely on the uncomplaining shoulders of Jack." Meal times were totally unpredictable. Moore once observed that having Jack was as good as having an extra maid. She apparently had no real sense of the importance of Jack's work, often interrupted him, read very little, resented Jack and Warnie's conversion to Christianity, and, when committed to a nursing home, was incoherent, senile, grumpy, and blasphemous. Evidence seems to indicate that, though the daughter of a vicar, she did not welcome Christianity herself. Jack visited her almost every day in the nursing home and prayed for her regularly.[41] Her follies, demands, and lies produced an enormous burden on Jack, but he told Warren he had made a commitment to her and he would stick by it.[42]

Service

The cross is the sign of submission, and the towel (used by Jesus to wash the feet of his disciples) is the sign of service. The two disciplines are linked—Jesus lived out his servanthood and then challenged his disciples to do the same: "Now that I, your Lord and Teacher, have washed your feet, you also should wash one another's feet" (John 13:14). Daily courtesies, the practice of hospitality, small kind acts—these are the stuff of service. The biographies of Lewis often highlight such deeds.

Two examples in Lewis's life serve to illustrate the practice of this discipline. First, Jack opened up the Kilns to participate in hosting children sent from London to escape wartime bombing by the Germans. Even though it was extra work and their house staff had dwindled, Jack still enjoyed the children. Heretofore he had been ignorant of children, but now he acquired knowledge and even affection for them. He wrote to Warnie:

> Our school girls have arrived and all seem to me—and what's more important, to Minto—to be very nice, unaffected creatures and all most falteringly delighted with their new surroundings. They're fond of animals (which is a good thing for them as well as us).[43]

Among his extra duties was chopping wood for the fireplace, tutoring the children, and taking them for strolls around Shelley's Pond. Probably their presence gave him the knowledge that made it possible for him to write the Narnia books. Additional houseguests needing special teaching and attention in 1943 were Margaret and the retarded child sent in October. Lewis took special pains to attempt to teach them how to read and write.

Another longtime and demanding service that Lewis offered was his ministry of counseling through his correspondence. His letters have been published in six separate volumes. In a day prior to a good telephone system (and certainly e-mail), one would expect active correspondence from a literate person. However, the letters written to children and to the American lady (Mary Shelburne, whom he had never met face to face) stand as striking examples of a type of Christian service to the marginalized and unimportant "least of these." In the introduction to *Letters to Children*, the editors illustrate Lewis's attitude toward children:

> The child reader is neither to be patronized nor idolized: We talk to him as man to man. . . . We must of course try to do [children] no harm: we may, under the Omnipotence, sometimes dare to hope that we may do them good. But only such good as involves treating them with respect.[44]

When writing to the children, Lewis always tried to write on their level and to address their particular needs. He knew the kingdom of Heaven belonged to such children as he addressed.

> If you continue to love Jesus, nothing can go wrong with you, and I hope you may always do so. I'm so thankful that you realized the "hidden story" in the Narnian books. It is odd, children nearly always do, grownups hardly ever.[45]

Lewis's role as Christian counselor is best seen in his correspondence to Mary Shelburne, a widow and minor author who wrote him regularly from Washington, D.C., for thirteen years. She wrote C. S. Lewis for the first time in 1950, praising his writing and confiding some of her current troubles. He responded by pointing out evidence in her life of God's grace to help free her from bitterness. Except when he was in his exams, on Christmas holidays, or in the depths of Joy Davidman's cancer, Lewis wrote Mary monthly (132 letters in the book) until his own health forbade it. Even though this was Lewis's greatest period of literary production, he hardly mentions his own works but takes time to critique the poetry and reviews Mary submits. In 1954, Lewis was elected unanimously to a full professorship of a new chair in Magdalen, Cambridge, but he was attentive to Mary's fears and illnesses. His anticipation and anxieties about married life with Joy are mentioned, but he constantly assures Mary she is in his prayers.

The remarkable thing about this spate of letters to this one far distant person is that Lewis loathed letter writing. In *Surprised by Joy*, he describes the good life as one in which no letters come.[46] With no typewriter and increasing arthritic pain, with heavy burdens as a writer, speaker, and scholar, Lewis could easily justify throwing all those letters into the trash can. Why did he then persist and write hundreds of letters to people he hardly knew and had not the slightest chance to meet? Some of the answer lies in a letter to Arthur Greeves:

> My correspondence involves a great number of theological letters already, which *can't* be neglected because they are answers to people in great need of help and often great misery.[47]

One can only conclude that Lewis's impulse to continue this costly service was because the love of Christ constrained him to do so.

THE CORPORATE DISCIPLINES

Richard Foster's last quartet of disciplines for the Christian—confession, worship, guidance, and celebration—are classified as corporate ones, practices that help unite the body. In *Life Together*, Dietrich Bonhoeffer spoke of how our very shared life in Christ joins us together by faith. We are united and combined into one body through Jesus Christ and in Jesus Christ. "No Christian community is more or less than this."[48]

Confession

Confession is a private matter between the individual and God and also a corporate discipline. In biblical teaching, believers accept the paradox that "there is one God and one mediator between God and men, the man Christ Jesus" (1 Tim. 2:5), and that we must also follow the dictum "Therefore confess your sins to each other and pray for each other" (Jas. 5:16). This discipline seems especially difficult because Christians want to view the believing community as a fellowship of saints rather than a fellowship of sinners.

C. S. Lewis wrote to Sister Penelope Lawson (of the Anglican Community of St. Mary the Virgin at Wantage) on October 24, 1940:

> I am going to make my first confession next week which will seem odd to you, but I wasn't brought up on that kind of thing. It's an odd experience. The decision to do so was one of the hardest I have ever made: but now that I am committed (by dint of posting the letter before I had time to change my mind), I began to be afraid of the opposite extremes—afraid that I am merely indulging in an orgy of egoism.[49]

Earlier in his life, Lewis had detested confession and rejected it whether practiced by traveling evangelists (notably, Dr. E. G. Frank Buchman) who persuaded undergraduates to confess their sins to one another or by Roman Catholics who spoke their sins to a priest in a confessional booth.[50] However, a few days after his first confession, Lewis wrote to Sister Penelope of a successful experience of confession:

> Well—we have come through the wall of fire and find ourselves (somewhat to our surprise) still alive and even well. The suggestion about an orgy of egoism turns out, like all the Enemy propaganda, to have just a grain of truth in it, but I have no doubt that the proper method of dealing with that is to continue the practice, as I intend to do.[51]

In a letter to Mrs. Arnold (April 6–7, 1953), Lewis wrote of Christian vocation, personal evangelistic witnessing, and confession. He rather liked that the

Book of Common Prayer makes confession permissible but not compulsory. However, the chief advantage of a first confession is that it helps one really to believe in forgiveness:

> Also, there is gain in self-knowledge: most of us have never really faced the facts about ourselves until we uttered them aloud in plain words, calling a spade a spade. I certainly feel I have profited enormously by the practice.[52]

Worship

Richard Foster appropriately quotes for an epigraph Archbishop William Temple's definition of worship:

> To worship is to quicken the conscience by the holiness of God, to purge the imagination by the beauty of God, to open the heart to the love of God, to devote the will to the purpose of God.[53]

Jesus declared that God actively seeks worshipers (John 4:23). Worship is in a way the human response to the divine initiative. God alone is to be worshiped (Matt. 4:10). If our Lord is truly first in our lives, then the worship of God with all facets of our being will be the highest priority.

Jack Lewis knew this truth. On Christmas Day 1931 he received communion for the first time at Holy Trinity Church in Headington outside Oxford. His conversion had been a slow process from 1926 to 1931. He had not taken communion since his boyhood days in Belfast and Malvern. In his early years as a Christian, he took the sacrament only on Christmas or Easter. Later the pattern was monthly. During the last fifteen years of his life, Jack normally took communion each week. He especially seemed to enjoy private communions he shared with his new wife, Joy, and the priest.[54]

Though Jack seemed to enjoy and anticipate Holy Communion increasingly, the rest of public worship and "church business matters" were irksome. Lewis favored liturgy and read prayers over spontaneous ones. He was cautious of innovations and feared them as intrusions that stole attention from God. As a conservative in his own theological traditions, Lewis disliked the apparent liberal theology of the Anglican clergy of his time. He challenged them to quit serving "Christianity and water" and to return to the undiluted spiritual wine offered by Christ and the apostles. The most difficult part of church participation was hymns, which Lewis described as "fifth-rate poems set to sixth-rate music."[55] Finally, in a typical magnanimous observation, Lewis wrote in a letter (December 7, 1951):

> If people like you and me find much that we don't naturally like in the public and corporate side of Christianity all the better for us; it will

teach us humility and charity towards simple low-brow people who may be better Christians than ourselves. I naturally *loathe* nearly all hymns; the face and life of the charwoman in the next pew who revels in them, teach me that good taste in poetry or music are *not* necessary to salvation.[56]

Guidance

This discipline is historically associated with monastic life but today seems to enjoy reappearance in broader Christian circles. In this discipline a "soul friend" stands alongside another and attempts to help the other discern the activity of God in that person's life. Spiritual direction (another name for guidance) takes up the concrete daily experiences of our lives and gives them sacred significance. The spiritual director is likewise on the inward journey toward God and willing to share his or her own struggles and doubts. All activity is bathed in prayer and pursued with humility and holiness.

Lewis himself prayerfully sought a spiritual director and found him in Father Walter Adams, a priest in the Society of Saint John the Evangelist in Cowley. "If I ever met a holy man, he is one," Lewis wrote to Mary Neylan (April 30, 1941).[57]

In a state of depression, Mary Neylan (a former student) had written Lewis as though he were a spiritual director. (Indeed, much of Lewis's correspondence—sometimes one hundred letters in a week—manifests that very Christian discipline.) An earlier letter had welcomed her conversion and started her on a regimen of prayer and reading. Lewis, too, knew the despair of attempts to overcome chronic temptations. But he had the wisdom and the light from Father Adams to know that impatience and anger were from Satan, not God. When closest to God's light is when we notice our filthiness:

> No amount of falls will really undo us if we keep on picking ourselves up each time. We shall, of course, be very muddy and tattered children by the time we reach home. But the bathrooms are ready, the towels put out, and the clean clothes in the airing cupboard, the only fatal thing is to lose one's temper and give it up.[58]

Celebration

Celebration and praise are at the center of the Christian walk. The joy of obedience is real and radical for the believer. The apostle Paul tells us to "rejoice in the Lord always" (Phil. 4:4). Therefore, Foster lists singing, laughter, creative gifts of imagination, and thanksgiving for family events as representative of this discipline. In fact, "All the disciplines freely exercised bring forth the doxology of *celebration*," wrote Foster.[59]

Pursuant to that theme, George Sayer portrayed Lewis from 1934 to 1961 as rarely unhappy or depressed. "He was a walking celebration of life. He was usually great fun, witty and amusing, often boisterously so."[60] It was no accident that Jack chose for the title of his autobiography *Surprised by Joy*. Even in his last months, while struggling with his own pains and illnesses, Jack managed to write an encouraging letter to Mary Shelburne in America:

> Pain is terrible, but surely you need not have fear as well? Can you not see death as the friend and deliverer? It means stripping off that body which is tormenting you: like taking off a hairshirt or getting out of a dungeon. What is there to be afraid of? You have long attempted (and none of us does more) a Christian life. Your sins are confessed and absolved. Has this world been so kind to you that you should leave it with regret? There are better things ahead than any we leave behind.
> . . . Of course this may not be the end. Then make it a good rehearsal.[61]

Only a man who thought and wrote so much about heaven could speak with such assurance. Because of his faith in Christ, Lewis wrote with great conviction that earth was but the shadowlands; real life is that which begins at what we call death. We are all made for eternity.

Regardless of the problems Jack faced—a dictatorial "stepmother," an alcoholic brother, prostate and heart diseases, the ostracism and abuse of professional colleagues at Oxford because of his public Christian witness—all this he counted dross. He knew the main business of life: "The glory of God, and, as our only means to glorifying Him, the salvation of human souls, is the real business of life."[62] However, if one is truly to praise God in this life as the psalmist demands, if one is to know and appreciate the great Creator, then one must be attentive and grateful:

> We—or last I—shall not be able to adore God on the highest occasions if we have learned no habit of doing so on the lowest. At best, our faith and reason will tell us that He is adorable, but we shall not have found Him so, not have "tasted and seen." Any patch of sunlight in a wood will show you something about the sun which you could never get from reading books on astronomy. These pure and spontaneous pleasures are "patches of Godlight: in the woods of our experience."[63]

In a brilliant essay on the Psalms, Lewis describes praising as "inner health made audible." People spontaneously praise whatever they value. When the psalmists tell everyone to praise God, they are doing what all persons do when they speak of what they care about. The worthier the object, the more intense the delight.[64] When God commands us to glorify him, God is really inviting us to enjoy him.[65] Lewis knew that "the Lord is good and his love endures forever" (Ps. 100:5). That is true celebration.

CONCLUSION

Jack Lewis read with great attentiveness the words of Jesus: "Not everyone who says to me, 'Lord, Lord,' will enter the kingdom of heaven, but only he who does the will of my Father who is in heaven" (Matt. 7:21). He understood that "by their fruit you will recognize them" (Matt. 7:16). Lewis wrote boldly and often about "Joy" as the "serious business of heaven." But the serious business here on earth might well contain some sandpapering for the soul. Among the things that Lewis practiced frequently were the inward spiritual disciplines (meditation, prayer, fasting, and study), the outward disciplines (simplicity, solitude, submission, and service), and the corporate disciplines (confession, worship, guidance, and celebration).

Inwardly, Christ was at the center. He was the Truth, and Truth must be acknowledged and obeyed. It was Clyde Kilby of Wheaton College who wrote shortly after Lewis died that Lewis was "a man who had won, inside and deep, a battle against pose, evasion, expedience, and the ever-so-little lie and who wished with all his heart to honor truth in every idea passing through his mind."[66]

Lewis was guided by two presuppositions. First, there are no *ordinary* people. We have never talked to a mere mortal. We should conduct ourselves with deep respect for one another. "Next to the Blessed Sacrament itself, your neighbour is the holiest object presented to your senses."[67] Second, he described his vocation in the preface to *Mere Christianity* as an "ordinary layman of the Church of England" who "thought that the best, perhaps the only, service I could do for my unbelieving neighbours was to explain and defend the belief that has been common to nearly all Christians at all times."[68] The only trustworthy way to do this was to have "a standard of plain central Christianity" ("mere Christianity," as Richard Baxter called it) that put the current controversies in their proper perspective. He considered it his duty to submit to truth and to serve his neighbors by explaining and defending this standard.

Finally, C. S. Lewis knew that it was the amazing grace of God that instigated this call in his life. He had been "decided upon." He himself had experienced a fresh encounter with God and it was life-changing.[69]

With his eyes fixed on heaven Lewis, in one of the most sublime, sermonic passages ever penned, speaks of what the end will be like when the believer faces God:

In the end that Face which is the delight or the terror of the universe must be turned upon each of us either with one expression or with the other, either conferring glory inexpressible or inflicting shame that can never be cured or disguised. I read in a periodical the other day that the fundamental thing is how we think of God. By God Himself, it is not! How God thinks of us is not only more important, but infinitely more important. Indeed, how we think of Him is of no importance except insofar as it is related to how He thinks of us. It is written that we shall "stand before" Him, shall appear, shall be inspected. The promise of glory is the promise, almost incredible and only possible by the work of Christ, that some of us, that any of us who really chooses, shall actually survive that examination, shall find approval, shall please God. To please God . . . to be a real ingredient in the Divine happiness . . . to be loved by God, not merely pitied, but delighted in as an artist delights in his work or a father in a son—it seems impossible, a weight or burden of glory which our thoughts can hardly sustain. But so it is.[70]

"But so it is" with this layman who had the gift to turn thought into feeling and feeling into thought. Eventually Lewis came to see that worldly success is a secondary matter. The real story is not the change in a man's career but the deep changes in the man's soul. Lewis had that rare ability to combine goodness with greatness. He was shaped by God to blend brilliance of mind with singleness of heart. Walter Hooper concluded about Jack, "He was the most thoroughly converted man I ever met."[71] For these reasons, C. S. Lewis is not only an inspiring writer but also a meaningful mentor for those who seek maturity as "mere Christians" in this life.

13

The Depths of God

Calvin Miller

Calvin Miller is professor of Preaching and Pastoral Ministry at Beeson Divinity School of Samford University. A native of Oklahoma, he
holds degrees from Oklahoma Baptist University (B.S.) and Midwest-
ern Baptist Theological Seminary (M.Div., D.Min.). A popular
preacher and lecturer, he has written more than thirty books, including *The Singer Trilogy* (1975), *The Table of Inwardness* (1984), *Spirit,
Word, and Story* (1996), *Into the Depths of God* (2000), and *The Sermon
Maker* (2002).

In this chapter, Miller offers a meditation on 1 Corinthians 2:1–10,
especially the verse "The Spirit searches all things, even the deep
things of God." Miller appeals for Christians to move beyond the plastic spirituality of a consumerist culture into the mysterious depths of
an encounter with the true God. Such a transformation, he says, will
bring with it a renewed sense of wonder, awe, and centered stillness,
as well as exuberant praise.

⁓❧⁓ ⁓❧⁓ ⁓❧⁓

When I came to you, brothers, I did not come with eloquence or
superior wisdom as I proclaimed to you the testimony about God.
For I resolved to know nothing while I was with you except Jesus
Christ and him crucified. I came to you in weakness and fear, and
with much trembling. My message and my preaching were not
with wise and persuasive words, but with a demonstration of the
Spirit's power, so that your faith might not rest on men's wisdom,
but on God's power.

We do, however, speak a message of wisdom among the mature,
but not the wisdom of this age or of the rulers of this age, who are

coming to nothing. No, we speak of God's secret wisdom, a wisdom that has been hidden and that God destined for our glory before time began. None of the rulers of this age understood it, for if they had, they would not have crucified the Lord of glory. However, as it is written:

"No eye has seen,
            no ear has heard,
      no mind has conceived
            what God has prepared for those who love him"—
but God has revealed it to us by his Spirit.

                                                      1 Corinthians 2:1–10

INTRODUCTION

"When I came to you, brothers, I didn't come to you with eloquence or superior wisdom as I proclaimed to you the testimony about God." So begins 1 Corinthians 2:1. Ambrosiaster said that the phrase "the testimony about God" is really speaking about the incarnate Word, Jesus.[1] I would like to expand Ambrosiaster's smaller definition into talking about your whole growing, ongoing affair with Jesus. Let us then turn our neediness to a sharp focus on this incarnate Word. Let us consider in joy how we first got mixed up with him.

Ambrosiaster also commented fully on a lot of good things about verse 9 in the same chapter: "No eye has seen, no ear has heard, no mind has conceived what God has prepared for those who love him." We know that Paul is talking about heaven. But it does no violence to the text to let this transcendence lower its vision to speak of things here and now. Even here, in this small world of ours, the best things in life our eyes cannot see, our ears cannot hear, and our minds cannot conceive. The Latin word *limen* means "threshold." The threshold in this verse refers to the *limen* between our hard, fast here and now and our richer world of mystery. It is a blessed *limen* between things as they are and as they should be. When we do the very best we can to talk about how we really feel about Jesus, we are still trapped in the hard, fast here and now. We just cannot quite cross this wonderful threshold of mystery. No eye can do this. No ear can do this. No mind can do this.

Let us finally consider the tenth verse: "God has revealed it to us by his Spirit. The Spirit searches all things, even the deep things of God." The "deep things" of God are the substance of our indefinable wealth. We are made rich with a treasure chest not yet unlocked.

Marva Dawn has warned us of the danger that we as a culture are dumbing down. It is a term most accessible to me. I was raised in a pretty dumbed-down place. "I was born again" fifty-five years ago in the dumbed-down world of rural Oklahoma. "I was saved," as we used to say. Those are terms that I would really like not to use because they do not seem theologically suave, but Jesus used one of them and Paul the other, so it looks like we will forever be stuck with them. When I was a child of nine in 1945, a neighborhood chum named Francis James and I were walking home from school. They were putting up a tent down at the corner of Seventh and Ash in Enid, Oklahoma. We thought it was going to be a circus and were very excited. Naturally we were disappointed when, on the next day, they put up a "revival" sign in front of it. Even at this age I still agree with Tom Sawyer that "church ain't shucks to a circus." Francis came over that day to tell me that his folks insisted that he go to that revival.

He was a mean boy with a lot of emotional problems. He enjoyed torturing any little thing that had a nervous system. So in some ways I was sorry his folks were making him go to the revival; but in other ways it seemed a giant step for grade-school morality in northern Oklahoma. I thought if anyone really needed to go to the revival, it was he. And go he did! Later that night he came home and then came directly to my house.

"Guess what happened?" he asked.

"I don't know," I said.

"I have been saved," he said.

"Who saved you?" I said.

"God."

"Why did God save you when your folks have been trying to drown you for nine years?" I said.

"Why don't you come tomorrow night and see?"

So I did.

There, the following night, I first met some wonderful Pentecostals, two huge guys named Salermo or Palermo; both played John Deere accordions and produced some wonderful music. The kingdom of God was all excitement. Best of all was the sermon of this mesmerizing preacher. I found myself caught in the web of an athletic and warm homily preached by a man in a buckskin jacket dripping with rawhide fringe.

He looked like an angel in the candlelight. He moved like air awash with color. He preached.

I came to know Christ.

I have never gotten over the joy of that evening. Joy was both my mood and my teacher. My suspicion is that the inwardness Paul is talking about in the Corinthians passage is not something we ever really aim at. It is more a by-product of our obedience to God. When you obey, inwardness happens.

At any rate, I went home that night clothed in sunshine. A lighter-than-air feeling, a lightness of being, suffused my soul. I came home that night to report to my mother that, like Francis James, I had been saved. I have never gotten over it.

In 1966, I moved to Omaha, Nebraska, to start a church. I began to witness door to door. I know that, too, was not very sophisticated, but I went door to door to "tell people about Jesus." I wanted to share the gospel everywhere. Over the next twenty-five years, twenty-eight hundred people would come to faith in Jesus Christ. They were baptized in the church. To none of those who came to Jesus did I ever have to say, "Let's all buy a study book and try to get inward."

When people are finding Christ and obedience is being served, inwardness is just a natural corollary. It is the ongoing gift of those who find the love of God compelling. Our evangel is simple, and yet we sometimes make it harder than it needs to be. I agree with Ann Graham-Lotz, who said, in words like these, "Maybe we have overdefined postmodernism. Maybe we ought to say, just give me Jesus." I think she is on target. Maybe the recipe for inwardness is simpler than what we have made it. Kierkegaard suggested that the central neurosis of our time is the absence of inwardness.

As I was running into Midlands Hospital in Omaha one day, I ran by the X-ray room. Plastered on the door of that room, I noticed, was a quotation from Shakespeare. The quotation was taken from that scene in *Hamlet* where the grieving prince shoves his mother down in a chair and says to her, "Come, come, and sit you down, you shall not budge. You go not till I set up a glass where you may see the inmost part of you."[2] It is a good sign for an X-ray room.

My suspicion is that there is something highly introspective about passages like this. People who want to read the depths of God have to be quite readable by God. Paul says that it is in such a way that we proclaim the testimony. Our testimony, whether we speak only of Jesus or of our affair with him, is hidden in a glorious mystery

Good thing!

We have had our fill of things we can understand. Indeed, all we can understand are things that fail really to minister to us.

Nothing excites us like coming in contact with forces we do not understand. How rich it makes us. I can understand why Findley Edge argues that people can accept anything in religion except the absence of vitality.[3] This vitality comes wrapped in God's saving mystery. When we touch the stuff of God's hiddenness, we touch high-voltage stuff that we can never understand.

So what is our answer to the plastic world around us? My daughter called me not too long ago and said, "Dad, it's time we take the boys to Disney World," which means "Can you afford it?" "What about the Southern Baptist interdict against Disney?" I asked. "It's time to take the boys to Disney World," she again said.

I said, "Okay, just give me time to mortgage the house and car."

We went.

During the drab days of Disney in which I was spending all our money, I began to realize I wasn't really having all that much fun. I got this feeling that I was being smothered in plastic. Consider, for instance, the ride "It's a Small World After All." Fifty people at a time embark in charming little boats and are whisked through little blue canals where a million rubber pixies sing in the unknown tongue, "It's a small world after all." Does all this brilliant enchantment endure? Hardly. Watch them get off the boat. Their faces are hard as Baptists after a business meeting.

This is why we need the mystery of Godness. The only time I really ever enjoyed Disney World was when my son was little and he had chicken pox and he was all scabbed over. We never had to wait in line very long!

We need less plastic and more mystery in life. Somehow, Paul says, this mystery is embedded in the testimony of God. So let us leave Ambrosiaster's former definition and talk about our testimony—our own delightful stories about how we first got mixed up with God.

One of the most powerful organizations in the world, Alcoholics Anonymous (AA), thrives on testimony. Think of the healing in such simple statements as "Hi. I'm Joe. I'm an alcoholic." AA has no budget, no honorariums, no buildings or endowment. They live and thrive on the basis of sharing one thing: their life experiences. The work becomes real, and maybe this is the last, best key to this inner thing that Paul is talking about, *into the depths of God.*

Frederick Buechner tells of his own need for sermonic deep inwardness. One morning his teenage daughter came downstairs and had herself a glass of water and a carrot stick. He saw nothing very unusual about it, but three years later they had a feeding tube in her stomach just to keep her alive. In those dark days of her anorexia, he said he woke every morning aware that he was about to lose the dearest, most precious thing in his life. In desperation he went to church.[4] What he needed was the mystery that absorbs our need—something so powerful it overwhelmed him with the reality that absorbs our desperation. What he got in so many churches was merely three-point sermons and word studies.

Our sermons can degenerate into a kind of systematic deadness.

In reading the Sermon on the Mount, I am always amazed. In just three chapters—seventeen minutes of talking—Jesus says nothing about casseroles. Yet this seems to have become the central doctrine of so many churches.

We are absorbed in the deadness of our hyperorganization.

I love that story about the carpenter who was building a house and hit his thumb with a hammer. It hurt ever so bad. Somebody suggested, "Zeke, if you go down to the clinic on Third Street, they'll fix that broken thumb." So he took off for the clinic on Third Street. When he got there, he walked into the clinic holding his poor broken thumb out ahead of him. He walked in the door of the anteroom of the clinic and found no one. There was just a desk and chair, a picture on the wall, and a couple of doors. One door said "illness" and one said "injury." He took the door that said "injury" and went into the next room of the clinic. Once again this second room held nobody. There was just a desk and chair, and picture on the wall, and two doors, one of which said "internal" and the other of which said "external." He took the door that said "external" and got into the third room of the clinic to find nobody. Once more there was a desk and chair, a picture on the wall, and two doors, one that said "major" and one that said "minor."

It felt "major," but he took the door that said "minor" and got into the fourth room. Nobody! Picture! Chair! Desk! Two doors! One of these doors said "cash" and the other "credit." He didn't have any money, so he took the door that said "credit" and found himself back out on the street.

When he got back to work they said, "Your thumb is still hurt? Didn't they help you at the Third Street clinic?"

"No," he replied. "They really didn't do me much good, but they were the most organized people I ever saw."

Too bad organization will not do it. If it did, all Southern Baptist churches would be healing places. We are all aware that there is something more to the mystery of God we cannot quite explain. We have an affair for which we can only scrape the surface. We cannot take our inward testimony and make it outward. We evangelicals try. We try all kinds of things to make our inward testimony outward. Why? Well, we're good at outward stuff. We so prize the outer testimony. I have always wanted a dynamic, famous-sounding testimony. I've always wanted to wrangle with God like C. S. Lewis. I once had a friend who accepted Christ leaning against one of the smokestacks of one of the crematoriums at Belsen. He had one of those historical, wonderful conversions.

I, by contrast, found Christ between four big Pentecostal ladies in flower-print dresses. Nobody pays to hear my testimony, but all it brings to my life is equally authentic. Further, I have come to know that the best part of my affair with God cannot be made outward. There is something so rich about the Spirit who bears witness that we are the children of God, that we cannot say it to each other. It's undisclosable in its finest moment.

I was once invited to speak at "Super Summer Week" down in Missouri. I always tell my preaching students, "Know your limitations. There are people you should never try to speak to. They are not your group." One group I should never try to speak to is the high schoolers. It's not who I am. But when they told me the honorarium was to be good, I agreed to "pray about it" and at last snapped at the lure.

There were thirty-five hundred of them.

When I walked out on the platform that night, I was deafened by the roar of gum chewing. I was the third person to speak. The first one to speak was Elvis Presley's little brother. He had been on drugs before he was born again and so had a most interesting testimony. Once he got saved, his testimony became flat and uninteresting. The next person that night was the Southern Baptists' leading prostitute. She was incredibly exciting. She knew what former prostitutes did and how they did it. I was all agape. Then she got saved and the love storm was past. Finally . . . it was my turn. I had nothing of interest to confess. My wretchedness was so ordinary.

The man beside me leaned over and he said, "Have you ever been on drugs?"

"No sir," I said. "I'm ashamed that I never have been."

He went on, "Have you ever been a prostitute?"

"No," I said.

"Well, what are you doing here anyway?"

"I'm here," I said, "because somehow I believe that God has a redeeming mystery set for each life. If he can get it early enough and live it long enough, the world would be better because of this inwardness we possess."

A couple years ago, my wife, my son, and I were at the Great Barrier Reef in Australia. I think I understand what Paul means when he uses the word *deep* there in verse 10. The Greek word for this is *bathos*. From this word we derive the word *bathysphere*. A bathysphere is a steel-walled diving bell that can be lowered into the ocean depths. The water cannot crush you in this steel-walled bell, because you are armed against the pressures of the deep.

A bathysphere serves a wonderful purpose, because on the surface of the ocean there is flotsam and jetsam and trash, but silence is the gift of the depths. Down, down, down it gets quiet.

At the Great Barrier Reef, ninety miles out to sea, you can stand ankle deep in the ocean and not see land. You appear tall standing "on" the ocean.

My wife and I are beyond the scuba years and so we went out to the depths to snorkel. My son, however, was young, and he went to scuba dive. I remember watching all those skinny young people pull on their black spandex suits. I looked at my cellulite and pale skin and wished I, too, had a black suit that would cover my varicose veins.

Soon all the spandexed divers fell over into the water dramatically. Then my wife and I put on our rubber masks and went snorkeling around on top of the water.

What we all saw—both the snorkelers and the scuba divers—through the rubber masks was pretty much the same. The difference was a matter of depth. Psychologist Abraham Maslow explained that most people never leave adolescence. Most of us never reach the real peak where we are self-actualized. Most in life become only "nonpeakers" talking to "nonpeakers" about "peak" experiences.

I have read and seen a lot of books on the inner life. Many of these books lead us to say, "I'm really going to get deep this week." But true inwardness is never a product. It is always a by-product that comes with our obedience. It is more than an attempt to read a "deeper life book" and submerge our souls. The difference is a matter of depth. I came to the conclusion, while we were sunburning our backs on the top of the water, that much of our talk about depth in the spiritual life is but a lot of snorkelers talking to other snorkelers about scuba experiences.

Paul says the deep things of God should be our hunger. This is what our dreams ought to be. We are to care about, to love and pursue Jesus. Then our zeal for inwardness will take care of itself.

In 1976, I was reading from Philippians and later sat down to write a sonnet to my own brain. Philippians 2:5 says, "Your attitude should be the same as that of Christ Jesus." The sonnet declares all:

> The Brain
> Gray-wrinkled, three-pound thing, I clearly see
> I cannot trap you with an EEG.
> You nervy organ you! Skull-cased but free—
> A brazen challenge to psychiatry.
> Soft mass, I can not help resenting you
> Each time they search and probe for my IQ.
> Half of Einstein's lobe was twice of you,
> You joyless, megavolt, computer shoe.
> Be careful, Judas organ, or you'll find
> God cauterizes every rebel mind.
> You small gray lump, you always seethe and grind,
> Spend small electric currents thinking blind.
> Yet you're the only shabby place I see
> That His great mind may come to dwell in me.[5]

I am a real lover of the spiritual classics. I am particularly intrigued with Francis de Sales. After Francis de Sales was ordained into the priesthood in Geneva in 1593, he went to Chegle to reconvert Catholics who had become Calvinists. This was no easy job. For four years he worked at it—ever trying to get Calvinists back into the Catholic Church. In him was born the agony of a man who was cast out onto the streets, where he lived without much human support. He had few friends, but he learned that the most powerful thing he could know was the pleasure of obedience. Caught up in his appetite for God, he wrote:

> He has put us like a statue in its niche. When there is added to this simple staying some feeling that we belong completely to God, and as he is our all, we must indeed give thanks for His goodness. If the statue that had been placed in some niche in some room could speak, and was asked, "Why are you there?" it would say, "Because my Master has put me here."
>
> "Why don't you move?"
>
> "Because He wants me to remain immovable."
>
> "What use are you there; what do you gain by doing so?"
>
> "It is not for my profit I am here; it is to serve and obey the will of my Master."
>
> "But you do not see him."
>
> "No, but he sees me, and takes pleasure in seeing me where he has put me."
>
> "Would you not like to have movement so that you could go nearer to Him?"
>
> "Certainly not, except that he might command me."
>
> "Don't you want anything else, then?"
>
> "No, for I am where my Master has placed me, and his good pleasure is the unique contentment of my being."[6]

This is the credo of all who hunger for inwardness. It is the covenant of all who treasure the wealth of the depths.

Conclusion

Alister McGrath

As this volume makes clear, "spirituality"—both as a term and as a concept—has now found wide acceptance within the evangelical community. Many who in the past have complained of the lack of attention paid to spirituality in evangelicalism are now finding themselves embarrassed by the rich stream of material pouring forth from evangelical writers.[1] This is a most welcome development, which the writers assembled in this volume will applaud. Much work still remains to be done on how understandings of spirituality may be developed that are faithful to the evangelical heritage. Nevertheless, it is clear that the movement has tackled this issue with commendable vigor and enthusiasm.

This book has set out to stimulate its readers to explore new terrain in their personal encounter with the living God and the risen Christ. The contributors are convinced of the need to offer a compelling vision of the Christian life, which addresses the specifics of Christian existence in a given time and place. It affirms the coinherence of the evangelical intellect and piety, melding head and heart to yield a formidable amalgam of living faith that will sustain them throughout the pilgrimage of faith, offering them nourishment and encouragement as they travel. The essays presented here represent a resource that will enable many to set out on a rich journey of Bible-focused and Christ-centered reflection, which can only lead to an enrichment of the quality of their faith and personal devotion.

The contributors to this collection have sought to remain faithful to the great evangelical tradition in fostering a deepened appreciation and awareness of "living to God" (William Ames), based on attentiveness to Scripture.[2] At times, this has meant being critical of specific approaches to spirituality. At others, it has meant uncovering approaches that evangelicals once knew and loved but have since forgotten, or challenging them to critically appropriate what is good and true in other approaches to spirituality, following Paul's mandate to "test everything" and "hold on to the good" (1 Thess. 5:21).

As will be clear, this involves important and occasionally delicate negotiations concerning the involvement of heart and head, of understanding, imagination, and emotions, in ensuring that we appreciate the riches of Christ to their full capacity. There are important debates underlying the pages of this volume over the merits and value of "techniques" in spirituality and of the legitimacy of the entire project of attempting to foster an enhanced engagement with the living God, as we encounter and know God through Christ and in Scripture. Yet these discussions can and must continue. We trust that the issues may be explored graciously and carefully, noting that they often entail the evaluation of individuals as much as ideas.

Yet underlying the divergent approaches to evangelical spirituality that may be found in this volume is a profound and unshakeable unity. The approaches here represented all bear witness to the immense richness of the Christian gospel and its superabundant adequacy to meet the needs and aspirations of fallen and redeemed humanity, in all its glorious diversity. The same gospel is appreciated in different manners, and for different reasons, by those who have experienced its healing touch. Precisely because of the diversity of those who know Christ, a diversity of spiritualities is inevitable. A "one size fits all" approach to evangelical spirituality is simply not going to work and is without theoretical justification.

Aesthetic, psychological, and sociological factors affect the type of spirituality that is most appropriate to the individual. For example, there is widespread disagreement over what constitutes "beauty" in art, architecture, music, and the spoken or written word. Many Christians believe passionately that the most appropriate response to the beauty of God is to worship and praise God using the most beautiful language, music, and architecture possible. Yet there is no agreement as to exactly what these forms should be. Thus some find that spirituality is assisted by Baroque architecture and church music; others prefer the simplicity of open-air worship and simple folk tunes. Issues of personal taste play a major role in spirituality and cannot be predetermined by theological considerations.

Furthermore, some individuals are very "verbal" in their thinking and find it relatively easy to think of God conceptually. Others (possibly the majority) find that they need images or mental pictures to help them in both their thinking and their devotion. For the former, spirituality might be best assisted by good sermons and helpful books that set out the interconnectedness of

Christian ideas and make a powerful appeal to the believing mind. For the latter, however, images are of central importance to spirituality, appealing to
what C. S. Lewis styled "the baptized imagination." For example, the use of
illuminated images in *Books of Hours* or works of religious art in churches—
such as the wonderful imagery that adorns the chapel of Beeson Divinity
School itself—does not simply reflect an interest in beautification. It represents a response to the recognition that many people require images or "visual
aids" for the purposes of devotion and reflection. Once more, an issue that is
more psychological than theological can be seen to have a major potential
impact on the area of spirituality.

Alongside these aesthetic considerations must be set the great issues of gender, class, and race. It must be pointed out that these factors interconnect,
making it extremely problematic to isolate them as determinative individually.
Thus, issues of gender are of considerable importance to spirituality, even
though there continues to be debate over the nature and extent of the differences between the genders. At one level, this is reflected in the language used
to conceive and refer to God: for example, Julian of Norwich (ca. 1342–1416)
makes extensive use of language of motherhood when speaking of Christ. At
another, it is reflected in differing conceptions of sin, which are held to reflect
gender differences: for example, the often-encountered suggestion that the
predominantly male sin is that of pride, whereas its female equivalent is that
of low self-esteem.[3]

Issues of race must also be noted, particularly in multicultural contexts
(such as North America) in which race and cultural identity are often closely
linked. Traditions of spirituality that have emerged in black holiness churches
are often quite distinct from those found elsewhere in Protestant Christianity.
Similarly, Asian Christians (particularly those with origins in China or Korea)
often incorporate elements deriving from their native culture into their
approaches to spirituality. The great spiritual tradition that has emerged from
the African American community, represented in this volume, may well have
an appeal that extends far beyond its original audience; nevertheless, it res-
onates superbly with the needs, aspirations, and situations of that community,
which continues to find it a rich source of inspiration and consolation.

Issues of class must also be noted, not least in that class is often linked with
matters of taste and the issue of literacy. Forms of spirituality that are strongly
populist often adopt the cultural standards of the groups to which they are
directed. These are reflected in the music and literature used to sustain contemplation, as well as the forms of art used to encourage meditation and reflection. Thus, nineteenth-century American revivalism made extensive use of
techniques normally associated with the popular theater in its worship, to the
horror of those who regarded themselves as more sophisticated culturally.

Recognizing these issues, this volume has sought to set out and explore a wide range of approaches, all of which are faithfully grounded in the same gospel yet which recognize the need to address the situations of specific individuals or communities. The universality of the gospel is not in the least compromised by the recognition of the particularities of those whom it has touched and transformed. We believe that readers will benefit from knowing all the approaches here explored and commended, while recognizing that some will touch our readers more passionately and deeply than others.

Timothy George and I hope this book will encourage a process of reflective growth. The crucial question concerns how this process can be *sustained*. It is one thing to begin a journey; it is quite another to be able to continue it. How many of us have resolved to learn new skills (such as a foreign language) or to become a better person (cultivating a habit of personal civility or more faithful Bible reading) only to find that it turns out to be much harder than we imagined? Discouraged, we are sometimes tempted to give up the journey that we began in such hope.

Yet let us remember that through God's good grace, there are others who have made this journey before us. They have traveled through the wastelands of this world and have shed tears in times of loneliness. They can be our companions on the journey to the heavenly city. Every step of the long kingdom road has been graced by the presence of others before us and moistened with their tears of joy and sorrow. We may learn from what they have already experienced, just as we may find reassurance in the knowledge that they have been through the wildernesses of this world before us. We may also take comfort from the presence of others who even now are making that journey alongside us, and from the approaches they developed to help them arrive safely at their destination.

Perhaps this may be the most helpful aspect of this volume—to encourage its readers to realize that they are not alone as they make the journey of faith. Both the contributors and those whom they cite can help and encourage us as we travel, keeping our hope alive and our hearts on fire as we journey. As the great Scottish preacher and hymn writer Horatius Bonar (1808–89) knew so well, the hope of heaven allows us to carry on through the vale of suffering and cope with the hardship of exile while knowing that its days are numbered. One day, we shall return home. Let the final words of comfort go to Bonar:

> We are but as wayfaring men, wandering in the lonely night, who see dimly upon the distant mountain peak the reflection of a sun that never rises here, but which shall never set in the "new heavens" thereafter. And this is enough. It comforts and cheers us on our dark and rugged way.[4]

Notes

Introduction

1. William Ames, *The Marrow of Theology*, translated from the 3d Latin ed. (1629), ed. John D. Eusden (Boston: Pilgrim Press, 1968), p. 77.
2. David Bebbington, *Evangelicalism in Modern Britain* (Grand Rapids: Baker Books, 1989), pp. 1–19.
3. James I. Packer, *Knowing God*, 20 anniv. ed. (Downers Grove, Ill.: Inter-Varsity Press, 1993).
4. Francis A. Schaeffer, *The God Who Is There* (Downers Grove, Ill.: Inter-Varsity Press, 1968).
5. John H. Sammis, "Trust and Obey," in *The Worshiping Church: A Hymnal* (Carol Stream, Ill.: Hope Publishing, 1990).
6. C. H. Spurgeon, "The Inexhaustible Barrel," *The New Park Street Pulpit*, vol. 6 (London: Banner of Truth, 1964): 37.

Chapter 1: Loving God with Heart and Mind

1. For my reflections on the inadequacies of my spiritual life and some lessons I learned in consequence, see Alister McGrath, *The Journey: A Pilgrim in the Lands of the Spirit* (New York: Doubleday, 2000), and *Knowing Christ* (New York: Doubleday, 2002).
2. See the important material in Walter L. Liefield and Linda M. Cannell, "Spiritual Formation and Theological Education," in J. I. Packer and L. Wilkinson, eds., *Alive to God: Studies in Spirituality* (Downers Grove, Ill.: Inter-Varsity Press, 1992), pp. 239–52.
3. For a survey of the issues and potential solutions, see Alister E. McGrath, *Christian Spirituality: An Introduction* (Oxford: Blackwell Publishing, 1999).
4. For important corrections to this historical ignorance, see Gordon James, *Evangelical Spirituality* (London: SPCK, 1991); and Dewey D. Wallace, *The Spirituality of the Later English Puritans* (Macon, Ga.: Mercer University Press, 1987).

5. See Andrew Fox, "The Intellectual Consequences of the Sixteenth-Century Religious Upheaval and the Coming of a Rational World View," *Sixteenth Century Journal* 18 (1987): 63–80.
6. Thomas à Kempis, *De imitatione Christi* 1.1–2, in *De imitatione Christi libri quatuor*, ed. T. Lupo (Vatican City: Libreria Editrice Vaticana, 1982), pp. 4–8.
7. James I. Packer, *A Quest for Godliness* (Wheaton, Ill.: Crossway, 1990), pp. 13–15.
8. Ibid.
9. Ibid.
10. For the background to this work, see Alister McGrath, *J. I. Packer: A Biography* (Grand Rapids: Baker Book House, 1997), pp. 186–95.
11. James I. Packer, "An Introduction to Systematic Spirituality," *Crux* 26, 1 (March 1990): 2–8; quote at p. 3.
12. This series of works began to appear in 1749. For details of Wesley's appreciative use of Puritan writings, see John A. Newton, *Methodism and the Puritans* (London: Dr. William's Trust, 1964).
13. Gerard of Zutphen, *The Spiritual Ascent* (London: Burns & Oates, 1908), p. 26. Translation slightly altered.
14. For this and other relevant citations from Spurgeon, see Lewis A. Drummond, "Charles Haddon Spurgeon," in T. George and D. S. Dockery, eds., *Baptist Theologians* (Nashville: Broadman, 1990), pp. 267–88.
15. Leonardo Boff, *Trinity and Society* (London: Burns & Oates, 1988), p. 159.
16. Isaac Watts, *The Improvement of the Mind* with corrections, questions, and supplement by Joseph Emerson (Boston: Brewer and Tileston, 1833).
17. Isaac Watts, "When I Survey the Wondrous Cross," in *The Psalms and Hymns of Isaac Watts* (Morgan, Pa.: Soli Deo Gloria, 1997), p. 525.
18. J. Randall Nichols, *The Restoring Word: Preaching as Pastoral Communication* (San Francisco: Harper & Row, 1987), p. 199.
19. See, for example, Erik Routley, *The Church and Music: An Enquiry into the History, Nature, and Scope of Christian Judgement on Music* (London: Duckworth, 1978); Friedrich Blume, *Protestant Church Music: A History* (London: Victor Gollancz, 1975).
20. Jonathan Edwards, "The Christian Pilgrim," in *Basic Writings* (New York: New American Library, 1966), pp. 136–37.
21. John Stott, "The Biblical Basis for Declaring God's Glory," in D. M. Howard, ed., *Declare His Glory among the Nations* (Downers Grove, Ill.: Inter-Varsity Press, 1977), p. 90.

Chapter 2: Christian Spirituality

1. Friedrich Nietzsche, *The Gay Science*, trans. Walter Kaufmann (New York: Random House Books, 1974), p. 338.
2. Harold Bloom, *The Western Canon: The Books and School of the Ages* (New York: Riverhead Books, 1994).
3. Louis Dupré, *Passage to Modernity: An Essay in the Hermeneutics of Nature and Culture* (New Haven, Conn.: Yale University Press, 1993).
4. F. R. Leavis, *Lectures in America* (London: Chatto & Windus, 1969), p. 51.
5. David Cooper, ed., *The Dialectics of Liberation* (Harmondsworth: Penguin Books, 1968); and R. D. Laing, *The Divided Self* (Harmondsworth: Penguin Books, 1965).
6. Antonio R. Damasio, *Descartes' Error: Emotion, Reason and the Human Brain* (New York: Grosset/Putnam, 1994).

7. Daniel Goleman, *Emotional Intelligence: Why It Can Matter More than IQ* (New York: Bantam, 1995).

8. Robert Langs has written several works, including *Unconscious Communication in Everyday Life* (New York: Jason Aronson, 1983) and *Decoding Your Dreams* (New York: Henry Holt and Co., 1989).

9. This is the subtitle of Andrew G. Hodges, *The Deeper Intelligence* (Nashville: Thomas Nelson, 1994).

10. Danah Zohar and Ian Marshall, *Spiritual Intelligence: The Ultimate Intelligence* (London: Bloomsbury Publishing, 2000), pp. 91–112.

11. Michael Polanyi, *Personal Knowledge: Towards a Post-Critical Philosophy* (London: Routledge and Kegan Paul, 1958), pp. 69–248.

12. Thomas F. Torrance, ed., *Belief in Science and in Christian Life: The Relevance of Michael Polanyi's Thought for Christian Faith and Life* (Edinburgh: Handsel Press, 1980).

13. Paul L. Holmer, *The Grammar of Faith* (San Francisco: Harper & Row, 1978).

14. Richard H. Bell, ed., *The Grammar of the Heart: Thinking with Kierkegaard and Wittgenstein* (San Francisco: Harper & Row, 1988).

15. Donald Evans, *Spirituality and Human Nature* (Albany: State University of New York Press, 1993), pp. 1–14.

16. G. K. Chesterton, *Autobiography*, vol. 16, *The Collected Works of G. K. Chesterton* (San Francisco: Ignatius Press, 1988), p. 212.

17. Ibid., p. 43.

18. See Tad Dunne, *Lonergan and Spirituality: Towards a Spiritual Integration* (Chicago: Loyola University Press, 1985).

19. Lawrence S. Cunningham and Keith J. Egan, *Christian Spirituality* (Mahwah, N.J.: Paulist Press, 1996), p. 5.

20. Michel de Certeau, *The Mystic Fable* (Chicago: University of Chicago Press, 1992), p. 94.

21. See John H. Whittaker, "Christianity Is Not a Doctrine," in *The Grammar of the Heart*, ed. R. H. Bell, pp. 54–74.

22. Gustavo Gutierrez, *We Drink from Our Own Wells* (Maryknoll, N.Y.: Orbis Books, 1983), pp. 52–53.

23. Dietrich Bonhoeffer, *The Cost of Discipleship* (New York: Macmillan, 1963), pp. 63–64.

24. Micah 3:8; 6:8.

25. John H. Plumb, *The Death of the Past* (New York: Columbia University Press, 1968).

26. Gordon Wakefield, ed., *A Dictionary of Christian Spirituality* (London: SCM Press, 1983), p. 362.

27. Philip Sheldrake, *Spirituality and History* (New York: Crossroad, 1992), p. 35.

28. M. T. Clanchy, *Abelard: A Medieval Life* (Oxford: Blackwell Publishing, 1999).

29. Colloque de Lyon-Citeaux-Dijon, *Bernard de Clairvaux: Histoire, Mentalities, Spiritualité* (Paris: Editions du Cerf, 1992).

30. A Society of Gentlemen in Scotland, *Encyclopaedia Britannica* (Edinburgh, 1771), 3:622.

31. Pierre Pourrat, *Christian Spirituality*, trans. W. H. Mitchell and S. P. Jacques (London: Burns Oates and Washburne, 1922–27) 1:v.

32. Louis Bouyer, *A History of Christian Spirituality*, 3 vols., trans. Mary P. Ryan (New York: Seabury Press, 1963).

33. Hans urs von Balthasar, "Theology and Sanctity," in *Word and Redemption: Essays in Theology* (New York: Herder & Herder, 1965), p. 57.

34. Philip Sheldrake, *Spirituality and Theology: Christian Living and the Doctrine of God* (London: Darton, Longman and Todd, 1998), p. 83.
35. Philip Sheldrake, *Spirituality and History: Questions of Interpretation and Method* (New York: Crossroad, 1992), pp. 214–17.

Chapter 3: Spiritual Formation in Christ
Is for the Whole Life and the Whole Person

1. Erich Przywara, ed., *An Augustine Synthesis* (Gloucester, Mass.: Peter Smith, 1970), p. 89.

Chapter 4: Humility and Prayer

1. Seneca, *Epistle* 16.3.
2. Ibid.
3. This study includes material that was written prior to the first century but was familiar to first-century readers. It also includes works that were written after Luke that are relevant because they continue to reflect the deep-seated cultural assumptions of the first century regarding expectations for ideal leaders.
4. The nature of this chapter lends itself to the study of ancient biographies, since it is the lives of ideal heroes who are under consideration. This study also explores moral treatises reflecting the cultural assumptions of the first century that discuss the ideals of spirituality for society's heroes.
5. Plutarch, *Lives* Numa 3.6.
6. Ibid., 14.1.
7. Xenophon, *Oeconomicus* 5.20.
8. Xenophon, *Memorabilia* 1.1.2.
9. Xenophon, *Oeconomicus* 5.19.
10. Plato, *Timaeus* 27c.
11. Xenophon, *Memorabilia* 1.1.2.
12. Xenophon, *Cyropaedia* 1.6.3.
13. Xenophon, *Oeconomicus* 5.19.
14. Xenophon, *Cyropaedia* 1.6.46.
15. Ibid., 2.4.18; 3.3.20, 21, 34.
16. Ibid., 8.7.3.
17. Plutarch, *Lives* Numa 6.2.
18. Ibid.
19. Ibid., 6.3.
20. Plutarch, *Lives* Lycurgus 5.3.
21. Plutarch, *Lives* Numa 7.3.
22. Ibid., 6.2.
23. Plato, *Laws* 4.712b.
24. Plato, *Phaedrus* 257a.
25. Ibid., 278b.
26. Ideal kings often do such before significant events in their lives.
27. Xenophon, *Cyropaedia* 1.6.2.
28. Plutarch, *Lives* Camillus 6.2.
29. Virgil, *Aeneid* 5.85.
30. Ibid., 6.190.
31. Ibid., 7.140.
32. Plutarch, *Lives* Numa 7.1.
33. Ibid., 7.1.
34. Ibid., 3.6.

35. Ibid., 4.1.
36. Ibid., 5.4.
37. Ibid., 14.2.
38. Ibid., 15.1.
39. Ibid., 20.6–7.
40. Aristotle, *Nicomachean Ethics* 4.3.3.
41. Epictetus, *Discourses* 3.23.8.
42. Epictetus, *Encheiridion* 48.2.
43. Plutarch, *Flatterer* 55f.
44. Plutarch, *Praising* 543d.
45. Ibid., 545f.
46. Aristotle, *Nicomachean Ethics* 4.3.36.
47. Epictetus, *Encheiridion* 33.9.
48. Plutarch, *Flatterer* 65f.
49. Plutarch, *On the Control of Anger* 463e.
50. Epictetus, *Discourses* 4.8.34–36.
51. Epictetus, *Encheiridion* 23.
52. Plutarch, *Progress* 81c–d.
53. Epictetus, *Encheiridion* 46.2.
54. Epictetus, *Discourses* 4.8.26.
55. Plutarch, *Progress* 80b.
56. Plutarch, *Praising* 539d.
57. Ibid., 547b.
58. Epictetus, *Discourses* 3.23.25.
59. This refers to Socrates' practice of introducing people to renowned philoso-
    phers, rather than being insulted that he was not taken for a famous philoso-
    pher.
60. Epictetus, *Discourses* 3.23.22–23.
61. Plutarch, *Lives* Agis and Cleomenes 13.1–2.

Chapter 5: What Evangelicals Have to Do with Athens and Jerusalem

1. For a fuller discussion of what follows see Werner Jaeger, *Early Christianity and
   Greek Paideia* (Cambridge, Mass.: Harvard University Press, 1961); M. L.
   Laistner, *Christianity and Pagan Culture in the Later Roman Empire* (Ithaca, N.Y.:
   Cornell University Press, 1951); and Henry Chadwick, *Early Christian Thought
   and the Classical Tradition* (New York: Oxford University Press, 1966).
2. *Didascalia apostolorum* 12; quoted in Laistner, *Christianity and Pagan Culture*,
   p. 50.
3. Jaeger, *Early Christianity*, p. 35.
4. *De praescriptione haereticorum* 7, 9–13; also see *Apology* 46, 18; quoted in Marcel
   Simon, "Early Christianity amid Pagan Thought: Confluences and Conflicts,"
   Religious Studies (December 1973): 385.
5. *First Apology* 59.1–5; in R. A. Norris, *God and World in Early Christian Theology*
   (New York: Seabury Press, 1965), p. 49.
6. *Second Apology* 13.3–6; in Norris, *God and World*, p. 49.
7. *Stromata* 1:5.
8. See Jaeger, *Early Christianity*, p. 57.
9. Laistner, *Christianity and Pagan Culture*, p. 61.
10. Chadwick, *Early Christian Thought*, p. 259 n.21.
11. Especially see Jaeger, *Early Christianity*, pp. 60–69.
12. Ibid., pp. 75–81 and 138.

13. Ibid., p. 51.
14. Laistner, *Christianity and Pagan Culture*, p. 61.
15. Jaeger, *Early Christianity*, p. 89.
16. Domenico Comparetti gives a thorough survey of the role Virgil played in education in *Vergil in the Middle Ages*, trans. E. F. M. Benecke (Hamden, Conn.: Archon Books, 1966).
17. For the definitive treatment of Augustine and how he uses his classical heritage see Harald Hagendahl, *Augustine and the Latin Classics* (Göteborg: Stockholm Universitetet, 1967). I am greatly indebted to his work for the following discussion of Augustine and Virgil.
18. Ibid., p. 424.
19. *De divinatione daemonum* 7.11; see Hagendahl, *Augustine*, p. 456.
20. Hagendahl, *Augustine*, pp. 454–57.
21. Ibid., pp. 393–418.
22. Ibid., p. 728.
23. Ibid., p. 458.
24. Ibid., p. 459.
25. Albert C. Outler, "Augustine and the Transvaluation of the Classical Tradition," *Classical Journal* 54 (1959): 215.

Chapter 6: Outward Faith, Inward Piety

1. C. S. Lewis, *Perelandra* (New York: Macmillan Co., 1965), p. 91. Emphasis added.
2. Art Ross and Martha Stevenson, *Romans*, Interpretation Bible Studies (Louisville, Ky.: Geneva Press, 1999), pp. 30–31.
3. Declan Marmion, *A Spirituality of Everyday Faith* (Louvain: Peeters, 1998), pp. 10–16.
4. Jacques Leclercq, *The Love of Learning and the Desire for God* (New York: Fordham University Press, 1982), pp. 2–4.
5. Alven M. Neiman, "Self-Examination, Philosophical Education, and Spirituality," *Journal of Philosophy of Education* 34, 4 (2000): 580.
6. For a fine philosophical account of this revolutionary development, see Charles M. Taylor, *Sources of the Self: The Making of the Modern Identity* (Cambridge, Mass.: Harvard University Press, 1989).
7. Karl Barth, *Protestant Thought: From Rousseau to Ritschl* (New York: Simon & Schuster, 1969), pp. 52–54.
8. *The J. I. Packer Collection*, selected and introduced by Alister McGrath (Downers Grove, Ill.: Inter-Varsity Press, 1999), p. 198.
9. Diogenes Allen, "Academic Theology and Christian Spirituality," *inSpire* (winter 2002): 11. Asked how contemporary spirituality might answer the Taliban's terrorist destruction of American lives on September 11, 2001, Allen cites Sir Robert Shirley's response to the Puritans' terrorist destruction of English churches during the civil war: he built a beautiful church in Staunton Harold, Leicester, above whose entrance are carved the words "In the year 1653 when all things Sacred were throughout the nation Either demolisht or profaned Sir Robert Shirley, Barronet, Founded this church; Whose singular praise it is, to have done the best of things in the worst of times, and hoped them in the most callamitous. The righteous shall be in everlasting remembrance."
10. Quoted in David Lyle Jeffrey, ed., *English Spirituality in the Age of Wesley* (Grand Rapids: Wm. B. Eerdmans Publishing Co., 1994), pp. 383–84. George

Herbert, a seventeenth-century Anglican poet, reveals how profoundly suggestive is the metaphor of "putting on Christ" in his poem titled "Aaron."

11. Robert C. Fuller, *Spiritual, but Not Religious: Understanding Unchurched America* (New York: Oxford University Press, 2001). This same exaltation of the spiritual over the religious is thoroughly documented in the excellent study by Conrad Cherry, Betty A. DeBerg, and Amanda Porterfield, *Religion on Campus* (Chapel Hill: University of North Carolina Press, 2001).

12. See John David Dawson's excellent critique of Fuller in "Table for One," *Christian Century*, March 13–20, 2002, pp. 30–34.

13. Quoted by Robert Wuthnow in *After Heaven: Spirituality in America Since the 1950s* (Berkeley: University of California Press, 1998), p. 158.

14. Ibid., p. 162.

15. Quoted in Ramie Targoff, *Common Prayer: The Language of Public Devotion in Early Modern England* (Chicago: University of Chicago Press, 2001), p. 88.

16. Stanley M. Hauerwas and William H. Willimon, *The Truth about God: The Ten Commandments in Christian Life* (Nashville: Abingdon Press, 1999), p. 89.

17. C. S. Lewis, *Letters to Malcolm: Chiefly on Prayer* (London: Geoffrey Bles, 1964), p. 12.

18. Gerard Manley Hopkins, "Thou art indeed just," in *Poems of Gerard Manley Hopkins*, ed. Robert Bridges (London: Oxford, The Oxford Bookshelf, 1937), p. 68.

19. Kallistos Ware, *The Orthodox Way* (Crestwood, N.Y.: St. Vladimir's Seminary Press, 1995), p. 113.

20. Barth wittily observed that whenever the musical angels play their harps before the throne of God, they resort to Bach. But when they're off to themselves, it's always Mozart.

21. Karl Barth, *Church Dogmatics*, vol. 4, *The Doctrine of Reconciliation* (Edinburgh: T. & T. Clark, 1958), part 2, p. 552.

22. Richard Heyduck propounds this thesis in *The Recovery of Doctrine: An Essay in Philosophical Ecclesiology* (Waco, Tex.: Baylor University Press, 2002).

23. Leclercq, *Love of Learning*, p. 261.

24. Robert W. Burtner and Robert E. Chiles, eds., *John Wesley's Theology* (Nashville: Abingdon Press, 1982), p. 26.

25. Ibid., p. 36.

26. Charles Wesley, "Soldiers of Christ, Arise," in *The Worshiping Church: A Hymnal* (Carol Stream, Ill.: Hope Publishing, 1990), p. 756.

27. Charles Wesley, "Jesus, Lover of My Soul," *The Worshiping Church*, p. 461.

28. Burtner and Chiles, *John Wesley's Theology*, pp. 248–49.

29. Frederick C. Gill, ed., *Selected Letters of John Wesley* (London: Epworth, 1956), p. 237.

30. John Bunyan emphasizes precisely this point when he has Christian and Hopeful confront one of the early Protestant spiritualizers, a Quaker-like figure named Ignorance. Ignorance is scandalized at the antinomian risk inherent in total reliance on Christ's objective, all-efficacious atonement: "What! Would you have us trust to what Christ in his own person has done *without us*? This conceit would loosen the reines of our lust, and tollerate us to live as we list: For what matter how we live if we may be Justified by Christs personal righteousness from all, when we believe it?" (*The Pilgrim's Progress*, ed. N. H. Keeble [Oxford: Oxford University Press, 1984], p. 121, emphasis added).

31. Thomas Howard, "The Power of Wise Custom," *Touchstone* 13, 10 (December 2000): 11.

32. The late Moelwyn Merchant made this case in a lecture at the University of Chicago Divinity School in the mid-1960s.
33. Isaac Watts, "When I Survey the Wondrous Cross," *The Psalms and Hymns of Isaac Watts* (Morgan, Pa.: Soli Deo Gloria, 1997), p. 525.

Chapter 8: Growing in the Grace and Knowledge of Our Lord and Savior Jesus Christ

1. This paragraph and the next repeat some of my points in "Starting from Scripture," in Robert C. Roberts and Mark R. Talbot, eds., *Limning the Psyche: Explorations in Christian Psychology* (Grand Rapids: Wm. B. Eerdmans Publishing Co., 1997), p. 110.
2. Charles Taylor, *Sources of the Self: The Making of the Modern Identity* (Cambridge, Mass.: Harvard University Press, 1989), p. 27. My talk about "evaluative space" adapts Taylor's talk about "moral space." See also my "Starting from Scripture," pp. 110–13.
3. Robert C. Roberts, *The Strengths of a Christian* (Philadelphia: Westminster Press, 1984), pp. 17–18. The second set of emphases is mine.
4. James M. Houston, in Walter A. Elwell, ed., *Evangelical Dictionary of Theology* (Grand Rapids: Baker Book House, 1984), s.v. "Spirituality," p. 1046.
5. See, for instance, John Hick's "Religious Pluralism," in Philip L. Quinn and Charles Taliaferro, eds., *A Companion to Philosophy of Religion* (Cambridge, Mass., and Oxford: Blackwell Publishers, 1997).
6. Boris Pasternak, *Doctor Zhivago* (New York: New American Library/Signet Books, 1958), p. 40.
7. See F. F. Bruce, *The Defence of the Gospel in the New Testament* (Grand Rapids: Wm. B. Eerdmans Publishing Co., 1959), chap. 2.
8. Gordon S. Wakefield, in Alan Richardson and John Bowden, eds., *The Westminster Dictionary of Christian Theology* (Philadelphia: Westminster Press, 1983), s.v. "Spirituality," p. 549.
9. Houston, "Spirituality," p. 1046. The next two quotations are also from this page.
10. Wakefield, "Spirituality," pp. 549–50.
11. Jonathan Edwards, *Religious Affections* (New Haven, Conn.: Yale University Press, 1959), p. 198 (Part III. First Sign, *ab initio*). All the remaining quotations in this paragraph are from the same page. Ephesians 6:12 suggests that Edwards has slightly overstated his case about the invariable origin and meaning of "spiritual." Yet he is basically right, as Gordon Fee corroborates:

    Unfortunately, [the meaning of πνευματικός] in Paul tends to be obscured by one of the rare impoverishments of the English language, in that our translations of this word are limited almost exclusively to the small case "spiritual." The net result is one of those "slippery" words that tends to mean whatever its user wants it to mean (and who often could not define it, if required to do so). But such users seldom stray close to Pauline usage, where the word functions primarily as an adjective for the Spirit, referring to *that which belongs to, or pertains to, the Spirit*. (Gordon D. Fee, *God's Empowering Presence: The Holy Spirit in the Letters of Paul* [Peabody, Mass.: Hendrickson Publishers, 1994], p. 29.)

12. "And it must be here observed, that although it is with relation to the Spirit of God and his influences that persons and things are called spiritual; yet not all those persons who are subject to any kind of influence of the Spirit of God, are ordinarily called spiritual in the New Testament. They who have only the

common influences of God's Spirit, are not so called, . . . but only those, who have the special, gracious and saving influences of God's Spirit. . . . And though the extraordinary gifts of the Spirit, which natural [i.e., unsaved] men might have, are sometimes called spiritual, because they are from the Spirit; yet natural men, whatever gifts of the Spirit they had, were not, in the usual language of the New Testament, called spiritual persons. For it was not by men's having the gifts of the Spirit, but by their having the virtues [i.e., fruits] of the Spirit, that they were called spiritual" (Edwards, *Religious Affections*, p. 199).

13. See Deut. 4:5, 14; 18:15, 18–19, etc., for Moses' identification of his teaching—and the teaching of later true prophets—with God's teaching. See 4:10; 11:18–21; 17:18–20; 32:44–47; etc., for Moses' affirmation of the importance of these divinely inspired words.

14. For more on this, see my "Starting from Scripture."

15. See Robert C. Roberts, "Parameters of a Christian Psychology," in *Limning the Psyche*, p. 81, along with my "Starting from Scripture."

16. J. I. Packer, *Hot Tub Religion: Christian Living in a Materialistic World* (Wheaton, Ill.: Tyndale House Publishers, 1993). All unidentified quotations in the next three paragraphs are from pp. 1–4 of this book.

17. See chaps. 2 and 3 of J. N. D. Kelly's *Early Christian Doctrines*, rev. ed. (San Francisco: Harper & Row, 1978).

18. The term *evangelical* became popular only at the time of the Reformation, when it was applied to the fledgling Protestant movement by its detractors as a term of abuse. This was because Luther claimed to have rediscovered the core of the biblical gospel, the *euangelion*, or evangel. The Reformation, then, is where historical evangelicalism starts. And historical evangelicalism is then to be characterized in terms of the two great rallying cries of the Reformation, namely, *Sola scriptura*—"Scripture alone!"—and *Sola fide*—"Faith alone!"

19. Westminster Larger Catechism, the answer to question 3. The next quotation is from the Westminster Confession, chap. 1, sec. X.

20. This is not to say that Christians cannot learn important things about Scripture from non-Christians. But it is to affirm that one of the reasons God's Spirit indwells us is that the Spirit may guide us into all of Scripture's truth (see John 16:13; 1 Cor. 2:6–16).

21. "Certainty," as Herman Bavinck said, "is the normal and natural condition of the spirit as health is of the body" (*The Certainty of Faith* [St. Catharines, Ontario: Paideia Press, 1980], p. 20). Indeed, the Bible views proper Christian certainty as a major component in spiritual health (see Heb. 11:1; Matt. 14:22–33; Acts 24:14–16, NASB; Rom. 6:5).

Chapter 9: Practiced Theology—Lived Spirituality

1. See George Lindbeck, *The Nature of Doctrine: Religion and Theology in a Postliberal Age* (Philadelphia: Westminster Press, 1984). See also Timothy R. Phillips and Dennis L. Okholm, eds., *The Nature of Confession: Evangelicals and Postliberals in Conversation* (Downers Grove, Ill.: Inter-Varsity Press, 1996).

2. Robert Wuthnow, *After Heaven: Spirituality in America Since the 1950s* (Berkeley: University of California Press, 1998).

3. Ibid., pp. 52–84.

4. Ibid., pp. 85–114.

5. Ibid., p. 113.

6. Ibid., p. 123.

7. Ibid., p. 138.
8. Ibid., pp. 142–67.
9. Ibid., p. 188.
10. Ibid., p. 196.
11. Robert Bellah, Richard Madsen, William M. Sullivan, Ann Swidler, and Steven M. Tipton, *Habits of the Heart: Individualism and Commitment in American Life* (Berkeley: University of California Press, 1985).
12. Martin E. Marty, "'Who Is Jesus Christ for Us Today?' as Asked by Young People," in *Growing Up Postmodern: Imitating Christ in the Age of "Whatever,"* ed. Kenda Creasy Dean (Princeton, N.J.: Institute for Youth Ministry, 1999), p. 25.
13. See especially Catherine Mowry LaCugna, *God for Us: The Trinity and Christian Life* (San Francisco: HarperSanFrancisco, 1992); and also James B. Torrance, *Worship, Community, and the Triune God of Grace* (Downers Grove, Ill.: Inter-Varsity Press, 1996).
14. I join many other scholars and pastors in calling the first three-fourths of the Bible the First Testament or the Hebrew Scriptures, to avoid our culture's negative connotations of the name *Old* Testament and to emphasize both the consistency of God's grace for all God's people and also the continuity of God's covenants in the Bible, first with Israel and then, in addition, with Christians.
15. See a translation and commentary on this article in chap. 8 of Marva J. Dawn, trans. and ed., *Sources and Trajectories: Eight Early Articles by Jacques Ellul That Set the Stage* (Grand Rapids: Wm. B. Eerdmans Publishing Co., 1997).
16. For thorough discussion of the false teaching in Ephesus and its implications for interpreting 1 Timothy 2, see Richard Clark Kroeger and Catherine Clark Kroeger, *I Suffer Not a Woman: Rethinking I Timothy 2:11–15 in Light of Ancient Evidence* (Grand Rapids: Baker Book House, 1992). See also my "Hermeneutical Considerations for Biblical Texts" and "I Timothy 2:8–15," in *Different Voices/Shared Vision: Male and Female in the Trinitarian Community*, ed. Paul Hinlicky (Delhi, N.Y.: American Lutheran Publicity Bureau, 1992).
17. N. T. Wright, *The New Testament and the People of God* (Minneapolis: Fortress Press, 1992), pp. 140–43. See others' use of this wonderful idea in J. Richard Middleton and Brian J. Walsh, *Truth Is Stranger than It Used to Be* (Downers Grove, Ill.: Inter-Varsity Press, 1995), pp. 182–84; and Rodney Clapp, *A Peculiar People: The Church as Culture in a Post-Christian Society* (Downers Grove, Ill.: Inter-Varsity, 1996), pp. 138–39.
18. Wright suggests that the play has five Acts, but I find it more helpful to modify his basic schema by dividing what he calls the fifth Act in order to emphasize the differences in our lives (my Act 6) from those of biblical characters in immediate touch with Jesus (Act 5) and at the end of time (Act 7).
19. Martin Luther, "The Small Catechism," *The Book of Concord* (Philadelphia: Fortress Press, 1959), p. 347.
20. Too often we forget the ascension as a critical formative part of the life of Jesus and of His Church. See chap. 7 of Marva J. Dawn and Eugene H. Peterson, *The Unnecessary Pastor: Rediscovering the Call* (Grand Rapids: Wm. B. Eerdmans Publishing Co., 1999); and Douglas Farrow, *Ascension and Ecclesia: On the Significance of the Doctrine of the Ascension for Ecclesiology and Christian Cosmology* (Grand Rapids: Wm. B. Eerdmans Publishing Co., 2000).
21. See Marva J. Dawn, *Powers, Weakness, and the Tabernacling of God* (Grand Rapids: Wm. B. Eerdmans Publishing Co., 2001).

22. See Marva J. Dawn, *Joy in Our Weakness: A Gift of Hope from the Book of Revelation*, rev. ed. (Grand Rapids: Wm. B Eerdmans Publishing Co., 2002).

23. See chaps. 6–7 of Marva J. Dawn, *A Royal "Waste" of Time: The Splendor of Worshiping God and Being Church for the World* (Grand Rapids: Wm. B. Eerdmans Publishing Co., 1999).

24. See the research of Jane M. Healy, *Endangered Minds: Why Our Children Don't Think* (New York: Simon and Schuster, 1990).

25. See Neil Postman, *Amusing Ourselves to Death: Public Discourse in the Age of Show Business* (New York: Viking Penguin, 1985).

26. See Marva J. Dawn, *Is It a Lost Cause? Having the Heart of God for the Church's Children* (Grand Rapids: Wm. B. Eerdmans Publishing Co., 1997). Let me suggest also that you discuss this book's study questions in small groups in your congregation, so that parents and other community members can work together for the nourishing of faith life in our church's children.

27. See Marva J. Dawn, *Unfettered Hope: A Call to Faithful Living in an Affluent Society* (Louisville, Ky.: Westminster John Knox Press, 2003).

28. See Jacques Ellul, *Money and Power*, trans. LaVonne Neff (Downers Grove, Ill.: Inter-Varsity Press, 1984); and also chap. 5 of Dawn and Peterson, *Unnecessary Pastor*; and chap. 9 of Dawn, *Is It a Lost Cause?*

Chapter 10: The Evangelical Spirituality of Creation Care and the Kingdom of God

1. Tricia O'Connor Elisara, "Spending the Currency of Our Lives," *Mars Hill Review* (winter/spring 2000): 23–29.

2. G. K. Chesterton, *Orthodoxy* (New York: Doubleday/Image Books, 1990), p. 102.

3. C. S. Lewis, *The Magician's Nephew* (New York: Collier Books, 1986), pp. 116, 118.

Chapter 11: The Spiritual Wisdom of the African American Tradition

1. Traditional African American spiritual, "This World Is Not My Home."

2. W. E. B. DuBois, *The Souls of Black Folk* (New York: Penguin, 1989), p. xv.

3. Cheryl J. Sanders, *Saints in Exile* (New York: Oxford University Press, 1996), p. 136.

4. Civilla D. Martin, "His Eye Is on the Sparrow," in *Songs of Zion* (Nashville: Abingdon Press, 1982), p. 33.

5. Sanders, *Saints in Exile*, pp. 136–37.

6. "Lord, I Want to Be a Christian," *Songs of Zion*, p. 76; Traditional African American spiritual, "Ain't Nobody Gonna Hold My Body Down"; "Nobody Knows the Trouble I See," *Songs of Zion*, p. 170; "Ev'ry Time I Feel the Spirit," *Songs of Zion*, p. 121; "Somebody's Knocking at Your Door," *Songs of Zion*, p. 154; "Wade in the Water," *Songs of Zion*, p. 129.

7. "Oh Freedom," in *Songs of Zion*, p. 102.

8. "Ain't Dat Good News," in *Songs of Zion*, p. 114.

9. Traditional African American spiritual, "Keep on Searchin.'"

10. "Swing Low, Sweet Chariot," in *Songs of Zion*, p. 104.

11. Traditional African American spiritual, "Morning Train."

12. Traditional African American spiritual, "I'm Gonna Tell God."

13. Dietrich Bonhoeffer, *The Cost of Discipleship* (New York: Macmillan, 1959).

14. Ibid., p. 71.

15. Howard Thurman, *Deep River and The Negro Spiritual Speaks to Life* (Richmond, Ind.: Friends Unite Press, 1975), pp. 43–44.
16. Ibid.
17. "Balm in Gilead," in *Songs of Zion*, p. 123.
18. "Steal Away," in *Songs of Zion*, p. 134.
19. "I Couldn't Hear Nobody Pray," in *Songs of Zion*, p. 78.
20. Thurman, pp. 43–44.
21. Traditional African American spiritual, "So High."
22. Bonhoeffer, *Cost of Discipleship*, p. 15.
23. Fanny J. Crosby, "Draw Me Nearer," in *The Worshiping Church* (Carol Stream, Ill.: Hope Publishing, 1990), p. 534.

Chapter 12: C. S. Lewis

1. "National Notes," *New England Baptist* (October 1998): 8.
2. Kathryn Lindskoug, *C. S. Lewis: Mere Christian*, 4th ed. (Chicago: Cornerstone Press, 1997), p. 15.
3. Walter Hooper, *C. S. Lewis: A Companion and Guide* (San Francisco: HarperSanFrancisco, 1996), p. 291.
4. C. S. Lewis, "Christianity and Literature," in *Christian Reflections*, ed. Walter Hooper (Grand Rapids: Wm. B. Eerdmans Publishing Co., 1967), p. 10.
5. Richard Foster, *Celebration of Discipline: The Path to Spiritual Growth*, 20th anniversary ed. (San Francisco: HarperSanFrancisco, 1998), p. 1.
6. Ibid.
7. Ibid., p. 17.
8. C. S. Lewis, "Meditation in a Toolshed," in *God in the Dock: Essays on Theology and Ethics*, ed. Walter Hooper (Grand Rapids: Wm. B. Eerdmans Publishing Co., 1970), p. 215.
9. C. S. Lewis, *Surprised by Joy: The Shape of My Early Life*, Harvest Book ed. (New York: Harcourt, Brace & Co., 1956), p. 232.
10. C. S. Lewis, *Reflections on the Psalms* (London: Geoffrey Bles, 1958), p. 59.
11. Foster, *Celebration of Discipline*, p. 33.
12. C. S. Lewis, *Letters to Malcolm: Chiefly on Prayer*, Harvest Book ed. (New York: Harcourt, Brace & World, 1964), p. 4.
13. C. S. Lewis, "The Efficacy of Prayer," in *The World's Last Night and Other Essays* (New York: Harcourt, Brace & World, 1960), p. 8.
14. Lewis, *Letters to Malcolm*, p. 82.
15. Perry Bramlett, *C. S. Lewis: Life at the Center* (Macon, Ga.: Peake Road, 1996), p. 20.
16. Lewis, *Letters to Malcolm*, p. 66.
17. C. S. Lewis, *The Problem of Pain*, a Touchstone book (New York: Macmillan Co., 1962), p. 100.
18. C. S. Lewis, 7 March 1962, in *Letters to an American Lady* (Grand Rapids: Wm. B. Eerdmans Publishing Co., 1967), p. 102.
19. C. S. Lewis, *Letters of C.S. Lewis*, ed. with a memoir by W. H. Lewis, rev. and enlarged ed., ed. Walter Hooper (Orlando, Fla.: Harcourt Brace, 1993), p. 447.
20. Foster, *Celebration of Discipline*, p. 63.
21. C. S. Lewis, "On the Reading of Old Books," in *God in the Dock*, p. 201.
22. Hooper, *C. S. Lewis*, p. 478.
23. Ibid., p. 479.

24. Ibid., p. 410.
25. George Sayer, *Jack: C. S. Lewis and His Times* (San Francisco: Harper & Row, 1988), p. 210.
26. Ibid., p. 107.
27. Hooper, *C. S. Lewis*, p. 32.
28. C. S. Lewis, "A Slip of the Tongue," in *Screwtape Proposes a Toast and Other Pieces*, special centenary ed., Fount paperback (London: Harper Collins, 1965), p. 117.
29. Sheldon Vanauken, *A Severe Mercy* (New York: Harper & Row, 1977), p. 206.
30. Hooper, ed., *Letters of C. S. Lewis*, p. 414.
31. Thomas R. Kelly, *A Testament of Devotion* (New York: Harper & Brothers, 1941), p. 73.
32. C. S. Lewis, unpublished letter (1 August 1953), in *A Mind Awake: An Anthology of C. S. Lewis*, ed. Clyde S. Kilby (London: Bles, 1968), p. 136.
33. Lewis, *Letters to Malcolm*, p. 75.
34. William Griffin, *Clive Staples Lewis: A Dramatic Life* (San Francisco: Harper & Row, 1986), p. 261.
35. C. S. Lewis, *Christian Reflections* (Grand Rapids: Wm. B. Eerdmans Publishing Co., 1964), p. 113.
36. Lewis, *Surprised by Joy*, pp. 228–229.
37. Foster, *Celebration of Discipline*, pp. 111–12.
38. Ibid., p. 110.
39. John Brenner, "Janie King Askins Moore (1872–1951)," in *The C. S. Lewis Reader's Encyclopedia*, ed. Jeffrey D. Schultz and John G. West (Grand Rapids: Zondervan, 1998), p. 285.
40. W. H. Lewis, "Memoir of C. S. Lewis," in *Letters of C. S. Lewis*, ed. Hooper, p. 42.
41. Brenner, "Janie King Askins Moore," p. 286.
42. Ibid.
43. Sayer, *Jack*, p. 161.
44. C. S. Lewis, *Letters to Children*, ed. Lyle W. Dorsett and Marjorie Lamp Mead (New York: Macmillan Publishing Co., 1985), p. 4.
45. Ibid., p. 111.
46. Lewis, *Surprised by Joy*, p. 143.
47. C. S. Lewis, *They Stand Together: The Letters of C. S. Lewis to Arthur Greeves (1914–1963)*, ed. Walter Hooper (New York: Macmillan Publishing Co., 1979), p. 520.
48. Dietrich Bonhoeffer, *Life Together*, translated from the 5th ed. (1949) by John W. Doberstein (San Francisco: Harper & Brothers, 1954), p. 21.
49. Griffin, *Clive Staples Lewis*, p. 181.
50. Hooper, ed., *Letters of C. S. Lewis*, p. 253.
51. Griffin, *Clive Staples Lewis*, p. 181.
52. Hooper, ed., *Letters of C. S. Lewis*, p. 431.
53. Quoted in Foster, *Celebration of Discipline*, p. 158.
54. Bramlett, *C. S. Lewis*, p. 79.
55. Marvin D. Hinten and Bruce L. Edwards, "Church," in *C. S. Lewis Reader's Encyclopedia*, p. 123.
56. Kilby, ed., *A Mind Awake*, p. 132.
57. Hooper, *C. S. Lewis*, p. 32.
58. Hooper, ed., *Letters of C. S. Lewis*, p. 365.
59. Foster, *Celebration of Discipline*, p. 201.

60. George S. B. Sayer, "C. S. Lewis: The Man" in *C. S. Lewis Reader's Encyclopedia*, p. 246.
61. Lewis (17 June 1963), in *Letters to American Lady*, p. 114.
62. C. S. Lewis, "Christianity and Culture," in *Christian Reflections*, p. 14.
63. Lewis, *Letters to Malcolm*, chap. 17, p. 91.
64. Lewis, *Reflections on the Psalms*, p. 95.
65. Ibid., p. 97.
66. Quoted by Lindskoug in *C. S. Lewis*, p. 15.
67. C. S. Lewis, "The Weight of Glory," in *Screwtape Proposes a Toast*, p. 162.
68. C. S. Lewis, *Mere Christianity* (New York: Macmillan, 1952), p. vi.
69. Sherwood E. Wirt, "An Interview with C. S. Lewis," *Decision* (September 1963): 3.
70. Lewis, "Weight of Glory," pp. 96–97.
71. Quoted in *C. S. Lewis at the Breakfast Table and Other Reminiscences*, ed. James T. Como (New York: Macmillan Co., 1979), p. xxvii.

Chapter 13: The Depths of God

1. *Corpus Scriptorum Ecclesiasticorum Latinorum* (Vienna: Hoelder-Pichler-Tempsley, 1888), 81.21–22.
2. *Hamlet*, 3.4.19–21.
3. Findley B. Edge, *A Quest for Vitality in Religion* (Nashville: Broadman, 1963).
4. Frederick Buechner, *Telling Secrets* (San Francisco: HarperSanFrancisco, 1991), pp. 23–27.
5. Calvin Miller, "The Brain," in *An Owner's Manual for the Unfinished Soul* (Wheaton, Ill.: Harold Shaw Publishers, 1997), p. 14. Reprinted by permission from the author.
6. Francis de Sales, *Thy Will Be Done* (1894), trans. Henry Benedict Mackey (Manchester, N.H.: Sophia Institute Press, 1955), pp. 34–35, as quoted by Calvin Miller in *Into the Depths of God* (Minneapolis: Bethany House Publishers, 2000), p. 22.

Conclusion

1. I number myself among these embarrassed critics. See Alister McGrath, *Evangelicalism and the Future of Christianity* (Downers Grove, Ill.: Inter-Varsity Press, 1995), pp. 119–37.
2. William Ames, *The Marrow of Theology*, trans. from the 3d Latin ed. (1629), ed. John D. Eusden (Boston: Pilgrim Press, 1968), p. 77.
3. Valerie Saiving, "The Human Situation: A Feminine View," in *Womanspirit Rising: A Feminist Reader in Religion*, ed. Carol P. Christ and Judith Plaskow (San Francisco: Harper & Row, 1979), pp. 25–42.
4. Horatius Bonar, *When God's Children Suffer* (New Canaan, Conn.: Keats Publishing, 1981), p. 121.

Name Index

Subject Index

Abyssinian Baptist Church, 171
activism, 36
almsgiving. *See* generosity
Apostle's Creed, The, 148
arts, the 23, 158, 205–6
   See also literature; music
asceticism, 32, 122, 181
assurance, 113–15, 192

baptism, 5
   See also sacraments
Bible, 3, 5, 144
   application of, 146–47
   authority of, 14, 98
   claims of, 124, 129, 132
   commitment to, 133
   interpretation of, 38, 58, 80, 83, 129,
      144–45, 147
   meditation upon, 19
   memorization, 48, 107
   metanarrative of, 144, 148
   and philosophy, 78–80
   reading, 19–20, 38, 139, 148, 207
   study of, 79
   sufficiency of, 14, 124

   See also revelation; Word of God
Book of Common Prayer, The, 93, 99–100,
   190
brain, 30, 156

Calvinism
   of Whitefield, 18
   See also theology: Reformed
Cappadocian Fathers, 74, 79–82, 86
Catholicism. *See* Church of Rome
celebration, 192–93
charismatic movement, 29, 47, 52, 142,
   167
charity. *See* generosity
Christ, 30, 49–50, 58, 67, 149, 196
   devotion to, 7
   equality with God, 112
   faith in, 27, 93, 102, 124, 128–29, 145
   humility of, 65–67, 72, 160
   knowledge of, 26, 133, 205
   life in, 40–42 ,44–46, 52, 95, 105,
      114, 189
   Logos, 77, 79, 82
   Lordship of, 6
   love of, 37, 188